FROM RUSSIA WITH BLOOD

**PUTIN'S RUTHLESS KILLING CAMPAIGN
AND SECRET WAR ON THE WEST**

HEIDI BLAKE

BASED ON A BUZZFEED NEWS INVESTIGATION

**WILLIAM
COLLINS**

William Collins
An imprint of HarperCollins*Publishers*
1 London Bridge Street
London SE1 9GF

WilliamCollinsBooks.com

First published in Great Britain in 2019 by William Collins
First published in the United States by Mulholland Books in 2019

2

A catalogue record for this book is
available from the British Library

ISBN 978-0-00-830005-0 (hardback)
ISBN 978-0-00-830006-7 (trade paperback)

Typeset in Janson Text
Printed and bound in Great Britain by
CPI Group (UK) Ltd, Croydon

MIX
Paper from
responsible sources
FSC™ C007454

This book is produced from independently certified FSC™ paper
to ensure responsible forest management.

For more information visit: www.harpercollins.co.uk/green

FROM
RUSSIA
WITH
BLOOD

This book is dedicated to Mark Schoofs, always a guiding light; to my investigative comrades Tom Warren, Richard Holmes, Jane Bradley, Jason Leopold, and Alex Campbell, without whom this story would have stayed buried; and to those brave members of the independent Russian media who risk their lives every day in the pursuit of truth.

CONTENTS

FOREWORD

A note on the original BuzzFeed News investigation

In December 2014, I flew to New York to meet Mark Schoofs, the legendary editor who then headed investigations at BuzzFeed News, to discuss setting up a new investigative unit at the company's office in the United Kingdom. I came carrying a newspaper clipping containing the first clues to a mystery I hoped the new team might solve. It described how a multimillionaire property tycoon had plunged to his death from the fourth-floor window of a London town house a few days earlier—becoming the latest in a group of men, including the exiled Russian oligarch Boris Berezovsky, who had all died under bizarre circumstances. I was fascinated by what lay behind this expanding web of death at the heart of London—and Mark was equally intrigued.

Soon after I joined BuzzFeed News and set about recruiting the new UK team, I got a call out of the blue summoning me to a mysterious meeting at an apartment in a smart part of London. When I arrived, I found myself face-to-face with the ex-wife of the very tycoon who had died in that fatal fall. Her ex-husband had been murdered, she said, and by coincidence she wanted my new team to investigate. More serendipitously still, she was sitting on a large trove of documents detailing the activities of her ex-husband and his associates in the years before their untimely deaths.

I was soon joined by an extraordinary group of colleagues in the quest to get to the bottom of the story. Tom Warren, Jane Bradley, and

FOREWORD

Richard Holmes came aboard the new investigations unit in London, and we teamed up with our American colleagues Jason Leopold and Alex Campbell to chase leads across the Atlantic. Over the next two years, under Mark's inspired oversight, our team connected the property mogul's fatal fall to a web of fourteen deaths in the UK—and one in the United States—all of which had glaring links to Russia. Astonishingly, not one of those cases had been deemed suspicious by the authorities. But we obtained hundreds of boxes of documents, hours of surveillance footage and audio recordings, a huge cache of digital files from forensically restored mobile phones and computers, and bags of discarded police evidence that blew a hole in the official story.

We fed all our exclusive material into a huge custom-built database, supplementing it with thousands of pages of public records, and ran advanced searches across the entire cache to piece together a sprawling international story of money, betrayal, and murder. Then we tracked down and interviewed more than two hundred people connected to the fifteen dead men, while also gathering information from more than forty current and former intelligence and law enforcement sources on both sides of the Atlantic. And we obtained readouts of multiple secret US intelligence files—including a classified report sent to Congress by America's top intelligence official detailing Vladimir Putin's campaign of targeted killing in the West.

Every single reporter was pivotal to the project. Richard personally scanned hundreds of thousands of documents by hand so we could digitize and search them, and he contributed vital law enforcement source-work. Tom set up our gargantuan evidence database and applied his forensic genius to fathoming the dizzyingly complex financial maneuvers at the heart of the story. Jane deployed her unparalleled skills at tracking people down and persuading them to talk against all the odds, and Alex wore out his shoe leather running down leads across America. Jason—the sort of rock 'n' roll reporter who'll stop to get a new tattoo in between meetings with spies—blew the story wide open by getting a multiplicity of US intelligence sources to spill details of secret files linking every single one of the deaths in Britain to Russia.

Reporting this story was, at times, a dicey ride. A man in a black car appeared every night for months outside one reporter's house, another reporter came home to find personal items had been moved around in his bedroom, and it appeared one team member was being followed. We used trackers, panic buttons, intruder alarms, encryption, and countersurveillance techniques to stay safe—and in the final phase of the project, some reporters were moved to discreet locations for their security.

Our initial investigation was published by BuzzFeed News in June 2017. The shock waves it sent are detailed in the pages that follow. Since then, we have carried on investigating and gathering fresh evidence that places the fifteen suspected assassinations we initially uncovered at the center of a much wider campaign of Kremlin-sanctioned killing around the world.

This book is based on that body of work. Details of the events described are taken from our vast repository of documentary and digital evidence, as well as interviews with people who were present, and the dialogue recounted here is based on the best recollections of those who heard it. What follows is a story that more than one government wanted to keep secret—and it would have lain buried forever without the tireless work of my incomparable colleagues at BuzzFeed News.

Heidi Blake

FROM RUSSIA WITH BLOOD

INTRODUCTION

Salisbury, England—March 4, 2018

The fog that enveloped the city overnight had cleared by lunchtime, revealing the cloud-tipped spire of Salisbury Cathedral to the smattering of Sunday diners ambling up Castle Street. The afternoon was cold and quiet, and a light rain was fizzling on the medieval rooftops as two figures emerged from a columned restaurant door. The couple—a smart, plump, snowy-haired man with a blonde some decades his junior—would have gone unnoticed among the lunch crowd at Zizzi, where they had been washing down risotto with white wine, had it not been for his outburst midway through their meal. The pair left the restaurant suddenly after he flew into a loud temper, ducking down an alley and hurrying away from the marketplace, but their pace slackened once they emerged and crossed the bridge over the swollen river. Across the Avon lies a small tree-fringed playground where children were feeding ducks in the drizzle, and the man paused to press some bread he'd saved from lunch into their hands before the pair strolled on toward the edge of the green. It was here that they came to a sudden halt. Within minutes, passersby would stop to stare at a bizarre scene.

The man and woman were slumped together on a bench—she unconscious, he making strange hand gestures and apparently transfixed by the sky. As onlookers cautiously approached, the man seemed to freeze. Then the woman began convulsing, her eyes white and mouth foaming.

3

The Sunday shoppers who rushed to help were unaware of the seismic global significance of what was unfolding before them. This was the latest salvo in a secret war being waged on the West by a hostile foreign superpower, and their peaceful Wiltshire city had become a battleground: the site of the first chemical weapons attack unleashed on European soil since the Second World War. Still more alarming, the good samaritans themselves were being exposed to a lethal poison even as they stood on the green sheltering the stricken pair under umbrellas while they waited for paramedics.

The couple on the bench were Sergei Skripal—a former Russian spy turned double agent for MI6—and his thirty-three-year-old daughter, Yulia. Skripal, then sixty-six, had arrived in the United Kingdom eight years earlier, after being freed from a Russian prison where he was serving time for high treason. The onetime senior military intelligence officer had been convicted of selling secrets to Britain and blowing the cover of some three hundred Russian agents in 2006. He was released four years later, along with three other men convicted of spying for the West, in exchange for the return to Moscow of ten Russian spies caught living under deep cover in suburban America. The agents were traded on the tarmac of the Vienna airport in the biggest East-West spy swap since the Cold War—but no sooner had the Russian returnees stepped safely onto home soil than Vladimir Putin made his intentions toward the men he had released clear.

"Traitors will kick the bucket," he announced on state television. "Trust me. These people betrayed their friends, their brothers in arms. Whatever they got in exchange for it, those thirty pieces of silver they were given, they will choke on them."

The events unfolding on the green in Salisbury proved the Russian president true to his word. Sergei and Yulia Skripal lay choking on the bench as their airways were shut down by a deadly chemical that had been smeared on the door handle of his suburban home hours before.

By the time they were admitted to the intensive care unit at Salisbury District Hospital, the Skripals were both suffering convulsions as their lungs filled with fluid and their hearts slowed to a near stop. Doctors were initially perplexed, but when police informed them that the man in their care was a Russian turncoat living under British government protection, the symptoms began to make terrible sense. The Skripals were showing all the signs of having been exposed to a nerve agent—a military-grade chemical that attacks the central nervous system and causes the collapse of all vital bodily functions. These poison gases, fluids, and vapors are so indiscriminately deadly that the world had banned their development or stockpiling some two decades before. In the unthinkable event that the pair had been attacked with a chemical weapon on the streets of Salisbury, wouldn't there be other casualties?

Those fears were compounded with the arrival of a new patient in intensive care. Detective Sergeant Nick Bailey was a decorated officer of the Wiltshire Police who had been deployed to search Sergei Skripal's home, and he had been hit with all the same symptoms as the spy and his daughter. Soon after, two more police officers were admitted with itchy eyes and respiratory difficulties. Then came the three children who had taken handfuls of bread from Sergei Skripal to feed the ducks and an off-duty doctor and nurse who had rushed to administer mouth-to-mouth to the Skripals in advance of the paramedics arriving. Before long, twenty-one people had presented with signs of nerve poisoning.

It looked abundantly clear that a deadly chemical had been used to attack the Skripals—indiscriminately endangering the lives of potentially hundreds of British citizens. The medics in Salisbury District Hospital braced themselves for an all-consuming public health crisis while counterterrorism officers from Scotland Yard swept in to take over the investigation from the local police and 180 military personnel were deployed alongside specialist investigators in white protective suits to comb the streets for traces of a nerve agent. But without identifying the exact chemical that had been used in the attack, it was impossible to know where it had come from—or how its awful effects could be treated.

To the northeast of Salisbury, encircled by barbed wire and set in seven thousand acres of open land, is a sprawling complex of windowless labs and bunkers that harbors some of Britain's most closely guarded secrets. The Skripals had been poisoned just a few miles from Porton Down, home to the British government's Defence Science and Technology Laboratory, one of the world's foremost centers for research into chemical and biological weapons. As soon as medics spotted the signs of possible nerve-agent poisoning, samples were taken from the Skripals and rushed to the top-secret laboratory for testing.

It did not take long for the government scientists to identify the poison. This was a pure strain of Novichok—a chemical weapon as deadly as it is conspicuously Russian—and researchers at Porton Down had been studying nerve agents like it for years. The toxin was developed in the 1970s and 1980s under a Soviet program code-named Foliant at the Shikhany military research base, in southwest Russia. The existence of the Novichok stockpile was exposed by two Russian state chemists in 1992, just after the collapse of the Soviet Union and just as the country was signing on to the Chemical Weapons Convention outlawing the development and retention of chemical and biological weapons—and MI6 had been gathering intelligence about its adaptation for use in targeted assassinations ever since. The discovery that the Skripals had been poleaxed by this distinctly Soviet poison was met with stark astonishment. This wasn't just a covert attempt to liquidate a traitor and settle a score: it was also a deliberately overt act of aggression. The poisoning of Sergei and Yulia Skripal was a message, and the return address was clear. The Kremlin.

The prime minister needed to be briefed. Theresa May called her intelligence chiefs to a meeting, where she heard evidence that Putin had sent state agents to exterminate the Skripals on British soil. MI6 had compelling intelligence that the Russian president had personally overseen a program to repurpose an arsenal of chemical and biological weapons, including Novichok, for use in targeted assassinations over the past decade. Specialist hit squads had been trained in the use of nerve agents to target individual enemies of the Russian state—and they had been specifically taught to smear the chemicals on door handles, where the highest concentrations of Novichok were identified in samples taken from Sergei Skripal's home. Russian spies had been showing an interest in the Skripals as far back as 2013, when the country's military intelligence unit had hacked multiple email accounts owned by Yulia. More alarmingly still, Sergei's wife and son had both died suddenly in the years since the family relocated to the UK, and there were suspicions that they, too, may have been poisoned.

The British government had no option but to act. On March 12, eight days after the Skripals collapsed, the prime minister announced on the floor of the House of Commons that it was "highly likely" that Vladimir Putin was responsible. "Either this was a direct act by the Russian state against our country, or the Russian government lost control of this potentially catastrophically damaging nerve agent," she said, demanding an explanation from the Kremlin by midnight the following day. Russian officials hit back immediately, calling the remarks a provocation and describing the prime minister's statement as a "circus show in the British parliament," but no explanation was forthcoming. Two days later, May announced the expulsion of twenty-three Russian spies operating under diplomatic cover in London. Russia quickly followed suit, ejecting twenty-three British diplomats from Moscow.

The accusation that Russia had carried out a chemical weapons attack in Britain sparked an unprecedented international reaction, leading to the expulsion of more than 150 Russian diplomats from twenty-eight Western countries. The leaders of the United States, Britain, France, and Germany issued a joint statement condemning

Russia for "the first offensive use of a nerve agent in Europe since the Second World War," describing the attack as "an assault on UK sovereignty" and a breach of international law that "threatens the security of us all." The fallout plunged relations between Russia and the West to the kind of subzero temperatures not seen since the end of the Cold War. For a Britain increasingly isolated by its decision to leave the European Union, the attack on the Skripals had occasioned a heartening show of international solidarity. And, at least ostensibly, it enabled a prime minister beleaguered by bruising failures in the Brexit negotiations to reposition herself as a redoubtable global stateswoman. But back in Moscow, Putin was looking on with scarcely disguised glee.

The West's response to the attempted assassination of the Skripals could not have been more of a gift to the man in the Kremlin. The Russian presidential elections fell on March 18—a fortnight after the attack—and Putin needed to mobilize his electorate. True, he did not have much competition. The opposition figurehead, Alexei Navalny, had been repeatedly attacked and imprisoned during his campaign before ultimately being banned from running, and Putin's previous leading opponent, Boris Nemtsov, had been gunned down on a bridge outside the Kremlin three years earlier. The election result was a foregone conclusion. But Putin wanted a resounding victory as he closed his grip on another six years in power, and that meant getting a strong turnout at the polls. To achieve his goal, he needed to rouse the Russian people into a state of patriotic fervor and distract them from the dire state of Russia's sanctions-stricken economy, rampant corruption, crumbling infrastructure, chronically underfunded health service, and failing education system. What better way to do that than to invoke the looming menace of Russia's enemies in the West, from whom only he could be trusted to defend the motherland?

That had been the principal objective of the state of the nation address Putin delivered three days before the attack on the Skripals, in which he announced that Russia had developed a new arsenal of nuclear missiles capable of penetrating US air defenses. Squaring up to the podium in a sharp-shouldered black suit and deep-red tie, he declared: "I would like to tell those who have been trying to escalate the arms race for the past fifteen years, to gain unilateral advantages over Russia, and to impose restrictions and sanctions…The attempt at curbing Russia has failed." Behind him, two vast screens lit up with footage of snow-covered rocket launchers blasting gigantic missiles into a glowering sky, followed by animations charting a ballistic trajectory encircling the entire globe.

Putin's warmongering state of the nation was the first turn in his well-practiced pre-election performance as a global strongman, and the attack on the Skripals made the perfect sequel. After Britain pointed a finger at the Kremlin and the countries in the United States–led NATO alliance followed suit, all the mechanisms of the Russian state went into overdrive to whip up national hysteria about the iniquity of its Western enemies. Even by the prodigious standards of the Russian propaganda machine, rarely had such a dazzling variety of alternative conspiracy theories been spewed out by the state's multiplicity of troll factories, fake-news farms, and organs of agitprop. Britain had deliberately put the Skripals into a coma and fabricated evidence to frame Russia—or to detract attention from its difficulties in the Brexit negotiations, or to smear Putin ahead of the presidential election or to destroy Russia's reputation as a "peacemaker" in Syria, or out of sour grapes over having lost the right to host the 2018 World Cup. MI6 had poisoned Skripal out of fears he would flip and start selling British secrets back to Moscow. The pro-Western government of Ukraine was behind the attack. Sweden, Slovakia, or the Czech Republic was responsible. A mafia group had taken out a contract on the Skripals. The Novichok had originated from the lab at Porton Down, or the United States had made its own version of the nerve agent or stolen it while performing chemical weapons inspections in former Soviet states. So the theories wound on and on.

Sergei Naryshkin, the director of Russia's Foreign Intelligence Service, called the poisoning a "grotesque provocation rudely staged by the British and US intelligence agencies"—and Putin himself was scornfully dismissive, describing Britain's accusations as "delirium and nonsense." But the president and his propagandists also took care to fan the flames of suspicion.

Three days after the attack on the Skripals, before Britain had publicly accused Russia of the attempted assassination, the Kremlin's Channel One TV station used the main bulletin of its flagship current affairs show to issue an unambiguous warning. Skripal was "a traitor to his country," the host said. "I don't wish death on anyone," he continued, "but for purely educational purposes, for anyone who dreams of such a career, I have a warning: being a traitor is one of the most dangerous professions in the world." Anna Chapman, the glamorous linchpin of the network of ten Russian sleeper agents caught spying on the United States in 2010, also publicly accused Skripal of treachery. And, on the cusp of the presidential election, Putin himself used a specially commissioned documentary to issue his own monition. Asked by the handpicked interviewer if he was capable of forgiveness, the president nodded. Then a glacial smile crept across his face.

"But not everything," he said. The interviewer wanted to know what it was the president could not forgive.

"Betrayal," Putin spat back.

The Russian people are used to living with this sort of cognitive dissonance. This is how a nation is hypnotized: sowing confusion with conspiracy and contradiction, distorting debate with disinformation, and muddying fact with falsehood so that the collective consciousness is clouded by a perpetual fog of ambiguity in which nothing is true and no one is accountable. Sergei Skripal betrayed the motherland by selling Russian secrets to the West—and Putin is a strongman, so traitors will kick the bucket. The West is smearing Russia with false accusations to threaten its power—and Putin is a strongman, so only he can save the nation. These were the dissonant messages that the people of Russia received—and, by and large, believed.

When election day came, Putin swept to victory with 77 percent of the vote and a turnout of more than two-thirds of the population. Almost as soon as the polls had closed on March 18, his campaign spokesman attributed the success to a single event.

"Turnout is higher than we expected, by about eight to ten percent, for which we must say thanks to Great Britain," said Andrey Kondrashov.

"Whenever Russia is accused of something indiscriminately and without any evidence, the Russian people unite around the center of power. And the center of power is certainly Putin today."

The attack on Sergei Skripal was a blatant provocation designed to give Britain—and the West—no choice but to react exactly as they did, and the gambit had paid off handsomely. But it was also part of a far bigger and more sinister picture.

The truth was that Putin had been using deadly force to wipe out his enemies from the first days of his presidency, and the West had long been looking away. Dissenting politicians, journalists, campaigners, defectors, investigators, and critics had been gunned down, poisoned, hit by cars, thrown out of windows, beaten to death, and blown up on Russian soil since his ascent to the Kremlin on the last day of 1999. Turning a blind eye to this brutality was the cost of doing business with an economically renascent nuclear power that had a stranglehold on Europe's energy supply and a superwealthy class of oligarchs pouring billions into Western economies. Successive leaders had let themselves be lulled into the belief that Putin was a man they could do business with—a man who, with the right coaxing, might finally come in from the cold and integrate the world's largest country into the warmth of the rules-based liberal world order. That had proved a catastrophic misjudgment.

Putin never really wanted to join the club. He remained what he had always been: a creature of the totalitarian Soviet security state. To his mind the collapse of the USSR, with its mass killings, censorship, political repression, and bellicose isolationism, was "the greatest geopolitical catastrophe of the twentieth century," and he blamed it on the West. The 1989 revolutions that led to the fall of the Iron Curtain, the reunification of Europe, and the accession to the EU and NATO of the former Soviet satellite states—these were outrages to be avenged. So he had risen through the ranks of the KGB and arrived at the Kremlin ready to use all the tactics in his Soviet security-service tool kit to restore Russia to its former glory. While the leaders of the United States and Europe courted him with summits and state visits, handing him the presidency of the G8 and establishing the NATO-Russia Council to foster closer military and political relations, Putin was smiling for the camera, shaking hands, and plotting a silent war on the liberal institutions and alliances upon which the stability of the West depends. The fox was in the chicken coop.

The systematic extermination of enemies, traitors, and opponents was at the core of Putin's clandestine campaign. Covert killing is a deeply Soviet form of statecraft, a prized lever of power that had rested for more than half a century in the hands of the feared USSR security service from which the new president had emerged. The KGB had led the world in the art and science of untraceable murder, with its poison factories and weapons labs churning out such deadly marvels as plague sprays, cyanide bullets, lipstick pistols, and ricin-tipped umbrellas. Those capabilities had dwindled since the USSR fell—but not on Putin's watch. While the West welcomed him to the fold, the Russian president was busy reviving the KGB's targeted killing program. He plowed public money into researching and developing chemical and biological weapons, psychotropic drugs, obscure carcinogens, and other undetectable poisons, and he armed specialist hit squads to hunt down his foes at home and abroad. He restored the fearsome power of the Soviet state security apparatus—

enriching and empowering the FSB, the KGB's successor agency, and giving its agents special worldwide powers to kill enemies of the state with impunity. Anyone who betrayed the motherland, anyone who threatened the absolute power of the Russian state, anyone who knew too much—all put themselves squarely in the Kremlin's crosshairs. And every dead body sent a signal. If you cross Vladimir Vladimirovich Putin, there is no safe place for you on earth.

The covert killing campaign was one crucial line of attack in a much wider war of subversion. As soaring oil prices swelled the state's coffers, Putin shoveled resources not only into the development of cyberweaponry capable of shutting down foreign infrastructures at the touch of a button but also hacking labs that could gather *kompromat* on his adversaries. He ramped up Russian espionage operations to Cold War levels, inserting Anna Chapman's illegal sleeper cell into the American suburbs, pouring spies into every major European capital, and developing a network of agents of influence to push the Kremlin's agenda in the corridors of Western power. He weaponized Russia's fearsome organized crime complex, enmeshing the country's powerful mafia groups ever more deeply with his government and security services and extending their tentacles around the world as an unofficial outgrowth of the Russian state. He grew a sprawling international propaganda machine to disseminate disinformation, assembled a troll army of social media warriors running millions of fake accounts to stoke conspiracy theories and sow chaos in the West, and built black-money channels to finance extremism, terror, and despotism abroad. And he doubled down on defense spending, pumping the equivalent of hundreds of billions of dollars into a sweeping military modernization program to replace crumbling Soviet weaponry with hundreds of spanking-new bombers, submarines, warships, and intercontinental missiles.

As Putin expanded his web, his use of targeted assassination beyond his own borders grew more brazen. By 2006, he was sufficiently emboldened to pass new laws explicitly giving the FSB a license to kill Russia's enemies on foreign soil. Since then, his regime's critics, opponents, and traitors have dropped dead in violent or perplexing circumstances in both the United States and Europe. But nowhere has Putin pursued his killing campaign with more vigor—or greater impunity—than in the United Kingdom.

London proved the perfect playground for superrich Russians on the run from Putin's regime. Its booming banks and skyrocketing property market gave them a safe place to stash the money they had looted during the smash-and-grab post-Communist era, while its opulent hotels, luxury department stores, and star-studded nightclubs made for appealing places to spend it. England was a land where both an ill-gotten fortune and a tarnished reputation could be laundered to look as white as a sheet in a flash. Its world-class lawyers and accountants were on hand to help siphon cash safely out of Moscow and into respectable-looking UK companies via opaque offshore structures. Its estate agents were ready to hand over the keys to the country's most prestigious addresses without asking too many questions, and its lacquered PR gurus flocked to polish away any lingering reputational taint from the mucky business of getting rich in Russia. An endowment to an Oxbridge college here, a donation to the ruling party there, a stately home, a child enrolled at Eton—it didn't take much more to make a new arrival from Moscow look presentable in the loftiest circles of British society.

Before long, billions of pounds' worth of Russian money was pouring into London's banks and properties each year. The governments of Tony Blair, Gordon Brown, and David Cameron were all anxious to preserve this new lifeline for an economy increasingly dependent on financial services to supplant its dying manufacturing industry. That was why grants of political asylum and investment visas were doled out so liberally to the wealthy new arrivals from Moscow. But it was equally important to cultivate close ties with Putin and smooth the path for British energy investments in Russia. And that was why the establishment discreetly averted its eyes when the Kremlin's enemies started dropping dead on British soil.

Boris Berezovsky was the linchpin of the community of exiled Russians who fled to Britain after Putin came to power. The brilliant Soviet mathematician had become a billionaire by looting state assets during his time as a high-ranking member of Boris Yeltsin's government, and he viewed himself as the kingmaker who had plucked Putin out of obscurity. But when his protégé lurched toward autocracy and began quashing all opposition, Berezovsky used the newspapers and TV channels he had amassed to launch blistering attacks. Enraged, Putin had warned publicly that oligarchs who stepped out of line would be crushed and began demolishing Berezovsky's business empire in Moscow. But to the president's fury, the oligarch had escaped to the green hills of England with his fortune intact.

Berezovsky found a network of British lawyers and financiers to help spirit his money out of Moscow and stash it out of the reach of the Russian authorities in a byzantine network of offshore vehicles. Then he began using his vast expatriated fortune to finance an international campaign of opposition to Putin's regime from his new home in the English countryside and to bankroll the activities of a group of dissidents, including the whistle-blowing FSB defector Alexander Litvinenko, who joined him in Britain. Within a matter of months, the man who had helped bring Putin to power had made himself the number one enemy of the Russian state.

Berezovsky and his turbulent associates thought they had found a safe haven in England. They hoped that their grants of political asylum from the government would be enough to save them from the long arm of the Kremlin. They were wrong. One by one, in the years that followed, the lawyers, fixers, dissidents, and businessmen in Berezovsky's circle would drop dead in strange or suspicious circumstances. One by one, the British authorities would close the cases with no investigation and carry on courting the Kremlin.

There was a single exception. The 2006 murder of Litvinenko with radioactive polonium in a London hotel was an act of provocation the British government could not ignore. The two assassins sent to poison the FSB defector botched their mission so badly that they left a radioactive trail all over the capital. Litvinenko died slowly in the full glare of the world's media, allowing time for images of his gaunt and hairless frame to be beamed around the globe and for him to solve his own murder by accusing the Kremlin of ordering his killing in a statement issued from his deathbed.

Britain had no option but to respond, and the authorities charged the two assassins with murder in absentia after they fled back to Russia. But even in the face of a blatant act of nuclear terrorism on the streets of the capital, the government's reaction was muted. The UK expelled a mere four Russian diplomats, and four British embassy staff were sent packing from Moscow in return. When Russia refused to extradite the two killers, foreclosing any hope of a criminal trial, the government stood in the way of efforts by the dead man's widow, Marina Litvinenko, to secure a public inquiry into her husband's murder. Theresa May personally intervened to quash the possibility during her tenure as home secretary, citing the need to protect "international relations" with Russia. It was a full decade later, after Russia's annexation of Crimea had made reparation with the Kremlin impossible, that the government finally relented to demands for the inquiry, which ultimately found that Litvinenko had likely been assassinated on Putin's orders. But back in 2006, Britain had too much at stake to pick an unwinnable fight with the Kremlin.

The cold, mercenary reality was that Anglo-Russian business was booming. The UK had become the biggest investor in Russia's energy sector by the time Litvinenko was poisoned, and the British oil giant BP signed on to a historic joint venture with the then state-owned Russian energy company Gazprom just a week after the two countries played tit for tat with their diplomatic expulsions over the murder. Russian energy firms were investing big in the UK, too, and initial public offerings by Moscow firms were by then worth tens of billions of pounds each year to the London Stock Exchange. All that was a critical prop to the British economy, and it suited Putin just fine. Inward investment in Russia, and the global expansion of homegrown business, meant more rubles to pour into his campaign of foreign subversion, cyberweaponization, and military revampment. And as much as Putin was a creature of his Soviet training, he was also a kleptocrat. He wanted to make Russia great again, and he intended to enrich himself and his inner circle in the process. The more money that flowed into Moscow, the more he could siphon off into the secret network of offshore accounts, trusts, and properties that would ultimately make him, by some estimates, the world's richest man.

But still, the diplomatic pain caused by the row over Litvinenko's murder impeded Anglo-Russian relations at a time when Britain wanted nothing more than to stay in step with the rest of the West and keep the Kremlin close. In the years that followed, when Russian émigrés and their British fixers died with ever greater frequency, the authorities were all the more steadfast in their determination to look the other way. And the more the British government showed itself willing to shut its eyes, the more emboldened Russia became.

The reasons for Britain's inaction were more than just financial. Russia's murderous organized crime and state security complex began encroaching on the West just as the September 11, 2001, attacks drew all the firepower of Anglo-American intelligence and security machinery into the war on terror. Security-service officials at MI5 and counterterrorism detectives at Scotland Yard tasked with tracking organized crime groups and monitoring the subversive activities of foreign states were yanked off the job and redeployed in the fight against jihadist extremism while foreign intelligence chiefs at MI6 downsized the Russia desk and poured the lion's share of their resources into the Middle East. When Berezovsky and his fellow exiles arrived in Britain, they brought with them extensive organized crime connections and came tailed by teams of Russian spies, turning London into a crucible of Russian secret service and mafia activity just as

Britain's security and intelligence establishment had taken its eye off the ball.

The few officials who did remain dedicated to monitoring Russian threats in Britain faced a Sisyphean challenge. Russia's criminal networks are so deeply entangled with its state security apparatus, and Berezovsky and his associates were themselves so extensively connected to organized crime, that when threats were detected it was often impossible to tell whether they emanated from the government, the mafia, or both. The FSB would frequently enlist organized crime hoodlums to carry out crude hits on its behalf, while powerful mafia groups could enlist moonlighting state assassins to conduct more refined killings if required. And when the state was involved in a murder, the sophistication of its methods was often way beyond the ken of Scotland Yard, let alone the rural police forces that often picked up the job when rich Russians dropped dead in the home counties. FSB assassins were expert at disguising murders as accidents or suicides—even using drugs and psychological tactics to drive their targets into taking their own lives—and the state's weapons labs had developed an arsenal of undetectable poisons designed to make a murder look like a natural death. Even if Britain's spy agencies had strong intelligence pointing to an assassination, it was often impossible to share classified material with a court or a coroner without blowing the cover of sources and revealing highly sensitive methods. In such instances, it was easier to pronounce a death unsuspicious than to stoke diplomatic tension and public alarm over an accusation of political assassination that would be unlikely to stand up to judicial scrutiny.

As Russia's activities in the wider world grew more blatantly hostile, the British authorities had a new consideration to add to the calculus. Fear. The government's security advisers began cautioning that the Kremlin could inflict massive harm on Britain by unleashing cyberattacks, destabilizing the economy, or mobilizing elements of Britain's large Russian population to cause disruption. Deep police funding cuts following the financial crisis of 2008 had weakened the

UK's law enforcement capabilities, and a decade of focus on jihadist terror had withered the institutional expertise on Russia within the security and intelligence services, leaving the nation exposed and vulnerable. Defense chiefs warned that Putin's modernized military far outstripped the diminished capabilities of the austerity-ravaged British armed forces, and there were concerns that Russia could be creeping toward a full-scale conflict with the West as its actions became more overtly hostile. Suddenly, the specter of general war with Russia was being discussed in the corridors of Whitehall. If it came, the mandarins agreed, it could happen very rapidly—and Britain would be unprepared. This was no longer just about business. There were genuine existential threats to consider when the government calculated its response to Russian operations on its soil.

Putin had been flexing his muscles more boldly since the murder of Litvinenko. He set his weapons modernization plans in motion within weeks of the killing, quickly followed by a wave of crippling cyberattacks on Estonia, and embarked upon his first foreign military adventure with the invasion of Georgia in 2008. Cyberattacks on Germany, France, and the United States were to come, accompanied by Russia's increasingly overt financing and support for far-right and separatist groups across Europe. But as the aggressions grew more audacious, the British government found itself stuck between its more hawkish American ally and European partners who remained heavily dependent on Russian oil and gas and who had no appetite for a fight. The invasion of eastern Ukraine was the tipping point.

Russia's annexation of Crimea in March of 2014 marked the end of any serious hope that Putin could be coaxed into the liberal fold. Russia was suspended from the G8, the NATO countries ceased all political and military cooperation with Moscow, and the United States and European Union imposed scorching sanctions that, coupled with the slump in global oil prices, threatened to cripple the Russian economy. Undeterred, Putin pressed on with his latest adventure, sending tanks and heavy weapons over the border into the turbulent Donetsk and Luhansk regions and sparking a full-blown armed conflict with the Ukrainian government. Further waves of sanctions followed. Then pro-Russian forces shot down Malaysia Airlines flight 17, en route from Amsterdam to Kuala Lumpur, over eastern Ukraine, killing all 283 passengers and fifteen crew members on board—and only then did the British government finally relent and announce a public inquiry into the death of Alexander Litvinenko.

Even after that, the UK authorities continued to suppress evidence of the full scale of Russia's killing campaign on British soil. It would take an indiscriminate chemical weapons attack on the streets of Britain to force the government to confront the menace it had long ignored.

By the time Sergei and Yulia Skripal collapsed in Salisbury, the West had finally woken up to the severity of the Russian threat. The attack came hot on the heels of a series of jaw-dropping moves by the Kremlin: brazen meddling in the US election in favor of Donald Trump; interference in democracies across Europe with state-sponsored hacking, internet trolling, and financing for extremist groups; an attempted coup in Montenegro; increasingly malignant cyberattacks on Western governments; and a military intervention in support of the Syrian regime as it unleashed wave after wave of chemical weapons attacks on its own people. Russia's activities amounted to an all-out asymmetric war of subversion, using the full spectrum of state powers to disrupt and destabilize its Western enemies.

At the same time, Britain's intelligence agencies were facing scrutiny from their US counterparts over their failure to get to grips with the escalating spate of Russian assassinations in the UK. US intelligence officials had been watching the pattern of deaths from across the Atlantic with mounting alarm, concerned that it could spread to American shores. They had for years been sharing intelligence with MI6 connecting the deaths of the men in Berezovsky's circle and others to Russia and had looked on with consternation as every case was shut down by the authorities without investigation. Fears that Britain's quiet complicity could be emboldening Putin to ramp up his killing campaign had intensified in 2015, following the strange death in Washington, DC, of Mikhail Lesin, a onetime Kremlin henchman who was preparing to start talking to the US Department of Justice. Relations between senior Russia officials at MI6 and their CIA counterparts were becoming increasingly strained.

Then in 2017, the summer before Skripal's collapse, a team of investigative journalists at BuzzFeed News published a series of stories laying bare the pattern of Russian assassinations on British soil—and exposing the government's attempts to suppress the evidence.

When Russia struck again, the prime minister no longer had any option but to take a stand. But the tough rhetoric and waves of diplomatic expulsions that followed the nerve-agent attack on the Skripals did not perturb a gleeful Putin as he careered toward reelection. Just hours after Theresa May accused Russia of a state-sponsored assassination attempt on British soil, the body of another Kremlin enemy was discovered. Nikolai Glushkov was a close friend and business associate of Berezovsky's and an avowed foe of Putin. He was found at his home on the London outskirts, strangled with a dog leash. Counterterrorism officers from Scotland Yard quickly took command of the investigation, but the killer had not left a trace.

Meanwhile, Sergei and Yulia Skripal were making a miraculous recovery. That was thanks to the expertise of the scientists at Porton Down and the state-of-the-art treatments they had developed for nerve-agent poisoning. Detective Sergeant Bailey, the off-duty doctor and nurse, and the children from the green were all discharged from the hospital, and when they were well enough, the Skripals were moved to a secure location to complete their recovery. A multimillion-pound military cleanup operation was under way in nine Salisbury locations that had been contaminated with the nerve agent, and it seemed for a while that the British authorities might have contained the crisis without any lives being lost. Then, four months after the initial attack, news broke that two more people in Salisbury had been hospitalized with symptoms of Novichok poisoning.

Dawn Sturgess and Charlie Rowley were a couple in their midforties who had fallen on hard times. On a balmy summer day at the end of June, Rowley had found what he thought would make an elegant gift for his girlfriend while out rifling through local trash cans and dumpsters: a gold Nina Ricci perfume box containing a small bottle with a long nozzle attached to the lid. He took it home and gave it to Sturgess, who sprayed it on both wrists.

The bottle did not contain perfume. It was the vessel that had been used by Russia's assassins to transport their Novichok to Salisbury, and Sturgess had doused herself with ten times the amount of nerve agent used on the Skripals. She died in the hospital just over a week later. Some of the Novichok had splashed onto Rowley's hands, but he narrowly pulled through and woke from his coma two days after his girlfriend had died. There were no pallbearers at Sturgess's funeral. The government's public-health watchdog had put special measures in place to protect the mourners from contamination.

Scotland Yard's counterterrorism command had deployed its finest officers to hunt the state agents who had deployed the Novichok, but for six months there was no sign that their inquiry had turned up any leads. Then, on September 5, the country's premier police force announced two men were being charged with the attempted assassination of the Skripals. They were identified as two serving members of Russia's military intelligence agency, the GRU, who had entered Britain under false names. Police released photos of both men along with CCTV stills of the grinning assassins arriving at Gatwick Airport, traveling to a shabby hotel in East London, and carrying out a reconnaissance mission to Salisbury before returning to the city on March 4 to deploy the nerve agent.

A spokesperson for the Russian foreign ministry dismissed the fruits of the British investigation as a "big fake." Then Putin announced that Scotland Yard's two suspects had been found living innocently in Russia, declaring that they were "civilians" and would be coming forward shortly to tell their story. The two men appeared in an interview aired by the Russian propaganda network RT the following day, claiming they were tourists who had visited Salisbury simply to admire its cathedral.

Later that month, the investigative website Bellingcat identified one of the suspects as a GRU veteran named Colonel Anatoliy Vladimirovich Chepiga, who had served in Chechnya and Ukraine and had been personally decorated with the nation's highest honor by Vladimir Putin. Soon after, the site identified the second man as a GRU doctor named Alexander Mishkin.

The Kremlin dismissed the reports just as Britain's intelligence agencies confirmed them. In a speech the following month, Putin denounced Skripal as a "traitor" and a "scumbag" before angrily denying GRU involvement in the events in Salisbury.

In the corridors of Whitehall and the riverside headquarters of the security and intelligence services, officials were asking themselves how it had come to this. The propensity of Russia's enemies for dying strange and sudden deaths in Britain had long been regarded with a degree of indifference. If you were a Russian robber baron who got rich on the spoils of the fallen Soviet state or a dirty financier who helped launder an ill-gotten fortune in the West, and if you met a sticky end—well, then, maybe you got what you paid for. Even after the West began to wake up to the menace of the man in the Kremlin, the deaths were seen as individual cases unworthy of much consideration by officials playing catch-up from years of inattention and struggling to get to grips with bigger issues like Russia's new nuclear capabilities and its troop movements in Ukraine. But now that hundreds of British citizens had been exposed to a nerve agent, and there was no sign of remorse from the Kremlin, it was hard to deny that

Putin's killing campaign had been allowed to spin out of control. How could he be stopped?

Vladimir Putin's covert war was, finally, in the spotlight. But for all their flustered protestations, Britain's leaders could not claim with any sincerity to be surprised. They knew they had turned away as Russia's assassins stalked the streets. They knew they had stood by as Putin's enemies and their British fixers died.

This is the story of the men who lived and died in the Kremlin's crosshairs on British soil—and the secrets, buried with them, that successive governments never wanted to be told.

PART ONE

TWO WORLDS COLLIDE

I

London—1992

The flamboyant young lawyer always made it his business to get a seat up front on the Concorde flight from New York to London. The first three rows of the supersonic jet were reserved for the most significant people on the plane, and he liked to number among them. He'd sat next to Jackie Onassis on one occasion, and another time his neighbor was Eric Clapton, so he always watched the other passengers boarding with a frisson of anticipation, eager to spot which notable might be joining him next.

The young couple who settled across the aisle in seats 1B and 1C captivated him instantly. It was a crisp autumn day, and the man, who didn't look much older than thirty, was sporting an Armani couture coat with a magisterial brown fur collar. He was tall, tanned, and athletic, with designer stubble and a cloud of dark curls framing an appealingly open face. His slight female companion had pointed features, with waves of blonde hair tumbling over the shoulders of a soft leather jacket, and a newborn baby asleep in her arms. The lawyer thought them fabulous—and clearly very much in love. They must come from very important families, he hypothesized, since British Airways had seen fit to discriminate in their favor by placing them in row 1.

Not until the jet was soaring over the Atlantic did the tall man lean across the aisle and proffer his hand to the lawyer. "Scot Young," he said with an unexpected Scottish lilt. "Should I know you?"

The lawyer was pleased at the opportunity this question afforded. He'd been enjoying a lot of publicity lately for his work on behalf of superrich and famous clients.

"You might," he said cheerily, shaking Young's hand. "I've been on the television recently. I'm a lawyer."

Young's smile broadened. His fiancée, Michelle, was busy breast-feeding their baby daughter, Scarlet, and he was bored. The family had been holidaying at the ultraluxe Sandy Lane resort, in Barbados, and had flown back via New York to do a bit of shopping en route. Young let it be known, with a confidential air, that he had paid for the entire trip—flights, five-star hotels, designer acquisitions, and all—in cash. That was a revelation that piqued the lawyer's interest. Perhaps it explained their presence at the front of the plane, he thought. But Concorde tickets cost about eight thousand pounds each for a round trip. What sort of people paid for them in cash?

The two men passed the rest of the flight chatting pleasantly, and when they had landed at Heathrow and the bridge was being at-tached, Young asked for the lawyer's card.

"I've got a little tax issue I'd like to talk to you about," he explained as they stood and stretched their legs.

A fortnight later, Young strode into the lawyer's central London of-fice and closed the door.

"I've been robbing banks all over Europe," he said matter-of-factly. "And every time I try to spend my money in the UK, the tax man wants to know where it came from."

This struck the lawyer as an unusual predicament. Most of the criminal clients he had so far acquired—a group he referred to affec-tionately as "my crims"—tended to confine their activities to the UK. Young, it appeared, was a man of more international ambitions; an al-together more interesting class of crook. He assured his new client that he could help straighten things out. But first he would need to know more.

* * *

Young was a man who seemed to have been born in a hurry. Ever since he could remember, he'd wanted to put as much distance as possible between himself and the tumbledown tenement block where he grew up in the gritty Scottish port city of Dundee. He had dropped out of school early and started dealing drugs in the pubs and clubs of his home city before making his way to Edinburgh to ply his trade on a grander scale in the smoky cellar bars of the Scottish capital. What Young lacked in formal education he made up for in charm, eloquence, and cunning. He could talk almost anyone into anything, and his great gift was the art of making a deal. It was this talent that would eventually set him on the path to becoming a self-styled "superfixer" for some of the world's richest and most politically exposed men. But first he needed to make it big on his own.

From his earliest days in Dundee, Young had an irrepressible habit of making dangerous associations. His first mentor was a gun-toting casino king named Alex Brown, who wasn't afraid to settle a pub brawl with a shotgun and whose venues had a strange tendency to burn down in unexplained fires. Brown would eventually be found dead, floating facedown next to his luxury yacht in a Spanish marina, but that was long after Young had made enough money to leave Scotland for the brighter lights and bigger deals that London had to offer. And when he got to the capital, the young hustler set about forming an altogether more treacherous alliance.

Patsy Adams was one of three brothers who ran Britain's most feared organized crime gang, and he was famed as one of the most violent figures in London's underworld. The Adams family, or the A-Team, as they liked to be known, had amassed a fortune worth hundreds of millions of pounds through their profuse crimes. Patsy was the family's enforcer: high-speed motorcycle shootings were his hallmark, and Scotland Yard had linked him to as many as twenty-five gangland hits. Young wangled an introduction to the gang boss when he got to London and worked hard to win his trust. He soon started working for the family—and that was when the cash really started flowing.

The A-Team distinguished themselves from Britain's lesser crime gangs not only by their propensity for extreme violence but also by their international outlook. Scotland Yard had tracked the family's connections with both the Colombian drug cartels and the powerful Russian mafia groups shipping their heroin and cocaine into St. Petersburg. The brothers were suspected of doing a brisk business trafficking those narcotics into Europe, on top of their healthy trade in racketeering, extortion, bribery, sex trafficking, money laundering, smuggling, fraud, gun running, theft—and armed robbery.

Young didn't mention his association with Patsy Adams to the lawyer. But he did explain that he had teamed up with a crew of armed robbers who had made millions hitting banks across Europe. Most of the loot was stashed in bank accounts in Switzerland and Liechtenstein or in suitcases filled with more cash than they knew what to do with. But every time Young tried to splash out in the UK, he got questions from Inland Revenue that he didn't know how to answer.

The problem had become more pressing since he had fallen in love. He had met Michelle when she was a successful fashion buyer in her early twenties and told her on their first date that he knew she would be the mother of his children. Now that had come true, and she'd agreed to become his wife, too. His fiancée certainly had a taste for the finer things in life, but she had no inkling that he was anything other than a legitimate businessman. He needed to find a way to spend his money in the UK freely so he could lavish her with the kind of luxury they both felt she deserved without arousing suspicion.

It struck the lawyer that there was a touching kind of naive candor about his new client. He wanted to be accepted into the wider community. It was nice, he thought, to see a young couple so much in love and moving up in the world.

He told Young he knew just the man to help get him on the straight and narrow. They needed to talk to a tax barrister.

When the lawyer ushered Young into the senior barrister's chambers, they were met at the door by an eager clerk.

"This is going to cost you £3,500 an hour" was his greeting. That seemed like an eye-watering sum, but Young was desperate. He nodded, and they were shown through.

The barrister perched behind his desk and listened attentively as Young explained the whole story. When he finished, the barrister nodded, twiddled his thumbs, and asked some supplementary questions while the clock ticked. Then he leaned back in his chair and dispensed his prized advice.

"You should tell the tax man where you got the money," he said. Young goggled at him. Confessing his crimes to the authorities was not a piece of advice he felt like paying for. But the barrister elaborated. It just so happened, he said, that the schedules of taxable earnings in the Income and Corporation Taxes Act of 1988 did not make any mention of money stolen in bank heists. Technically speaking, that meant Young was not liable to pay a penny on the proceeds of the robberies. Better still, the law protected people from incriminating themselves when making tax declarations—meaning Inland Revenue couldn't turn him in to the police.

"They don't want to stop money coming to London," the younger lawyer chimed in sagely. If Young simply declared that all the cash was stolen, and if he agreed to pay tax on the interest he had earned and any future profits he made by investing it, the authorities would be happy.

To Young's astonishment, that advice proved correct. He became a regular visitor at the lawyer's grand Georgian house on the edge of Epping Forest, spinning up the drive in his Porsche each morning for another painstaking day sorting through his tangled finances and getting ready to come clean. After three months, the process was complete. As predicted, Inland Revenue accepted the declaration, and Young suddenly had millions of pounds sitting in his UK bank accounts.

On his final visit, Young pulled up in his Porsche and rang the bell carrying a large polished wooden box. Once inside, he sat on the sofa sipping a cup of tea and passing the time of day while the lawyer eyed the mystery object keenly. Only when he was getting ready to leave did Young hand the gift over.

"I wanted to thank you for what you've done for me," he said with what the lawyer felt was a look of touching sincerity. "Why don't you open it?"

The lawyer lifted the lid, and his mouth fell open. Inside was a solid-gold Rolex Daytona, brand new and sparkling, with a brown leather strap. Young took the watch from the box and fastened it to the lawyer's wrist—where it remains to this day. Then he said goodbye and set off into the world a new man.

Oxfordshire, England—1996

From the window of the study overlooking the expansive grounds of Woodperry House, a Porsche could be seen gliding up the long gravel drive. The sleek vehicle purred to a stop outside the golden stone frontage of the eighteenth-century Palladian mansion—named after the Old English "wudu-pyrige," meaning "the pear-tree near the wood"—and a tall, expensively dressed stranger climbed out. Hearing a knock, the Iranian academic arose from the paper he was finishing inside and made his way to the door, where he was greeted with a wide grin and an outstretched hand.

"Scot Young," said the man outside. "I was on the way to Heathrow, and my wife said we've got to buy that house," he continued, gesturing at a slender blonde woman waiting in the passenger seat. "If you want to sell it, I'd like to bid."

Woodperry's owner, the eminent Oxford University law lecturer Kaveh Moussavi, had not been planning on selling. But there was something strangely compelling about the man on the doorstep, and he found himself agreeing to a meeting in London a few days later to talk terms.

When Moussavi arrived in the plush bar of the Dorchester Hotel in Mayfair, Young presented him with a flute of Champagne already poured from a bottle on ice by the table and raised his own for a toast.

"What are we celebrating?" Moussavi asked.

"I'm going to make you a deal you'll be very happy with," said Young with a flash of his engaging grin. "I'm going to buy your house in cash." He pulled out a briefcase from under the table, and Moussavi's eyes widened as he opened the lid. Inside, stacked to the brim, were rolls of fifty-pound notes.

Four years had passed since Young had reached his entente with the tax authorities, but he had not lost his taste for the thrill of a dangerous deal. He had continued his involvement with the Adams brothers, but he had recently set his sights on even loftier treasures. He and Michelle were now married with two small daughters, Scarlet and Sasha, so he had a whole family to think of. He'd been busy making new associations, and he wasn't just dealing with the odd million stashed in this Swiss account or that suitcase anymore. The stakes were much higher.

Young said he'd pay £10 million—double what Woodperry would be worth on the open market—if Moussavi was prepared to accept cash. Then they'd declare a sale price of £2 million on paper, keeping the remainder off the books and tax free. Moussavi didn't like that idea, but he'd come around to the notion of off-loading Woodperry, and he told Young he'd happily accept market value if the money came by bank transfer.

It didn't take the Oxford academic long to spot that something was amiss once the deal got under way. The first clue came at the Dorchester, when Young pulled £45,000 out of his briefcase to jump-start the sale but asked Moussavi to make out a receipt for £50,000. *So he's obviously accountable to someone,* Moussavi thought, *and he's taking a little bit off the top.* That alone raised enough questions in his mind for him to task an elite real estate agency with checking out Young's background. The agent called him back sounding perplexed.

"I've looked and looked, and there seems to be nothing there," he said. "I've no idea where his money comes from."

When Moussavi asked Young directly about his wealth, the Scotsman said he had made his first money in property and invested millions in a chip-and-PIN internet technology company with help from a brilliant Soviet mathematician. Not long after, Young turned up at Woodperry with a beetle-browed stranger who wanted to look around the grounds. The small, suited newcomer spoke in a heavy Russian accent with a hurried air. Was he the Moscow-based benefactor who had helped Young make his big technology investment? Was this the person whose money was really going into the purchase of Woodperry House?

Young was splashing cash in all directions as he prepared to take ownership of the Oxfordshire mansion. Just as claimed, he pumped £2.6 million into an internet chip-and-PIN firm, taking a 50 percent stake alongside the Finnish billionaire and Conservative Party benefactor Poju Zabludowicz, and soon after that began lining up a £2 million investment in another internet venture with the retail tycoon Sir Philip Green. He had, he liked to boast, joined the billionaire's club. But still, when the property agent chased Young for details of which bank he would be using to pay the asking price for Woodperry, it seemed he was stalling—as if he was having trouble finding a way to marshal the cash. Spooked, Moussavi phoned him and got tough.

"You've got twenty-four hours to pay, and then you're going to forfeit the asset and I'm going to sue you."

Young was unfazed. "I'm going to deposit cash into the account tomorrow," he said.

"Do you really mean cash?" Moussavi asked, still somewhat disbelieving.

"Kaveh, I mean cash. Are you sure you don't want to accept it?" Moussavi said he was sure. He wanted the money aboveboard, by bank transfer, not under the table. Lo and behold, the next day the millions arrived in Moussavi's account by transfer from Coutts—the queen's bank.

The Youngs were blissfully happy in their new two-hundred-acre mansion. They enrolled their two daughters at the ultraexclusive Dragon School, in Oxford, alongside the children of a glittering array of celebrities, and Michelle loved being the lady of the manor, overseeing a grand redecoration and marshaling armies of domestic staff to keep the house shipshape. She woke up every morning, looked out the bedroom window at the rolling grounds, and felt amazed that she was mistress of all she saw. When the snow fell in January, she bundled the girls into down-filled jumpsuits, and the family ran outside to tumble around on the marshmallow lawn.

But in the quiet rural community surrounding their stately home, the Youngs were causing a stir. When they hired an upscale local architecture outfit to redevelop Woodperry, the firm's owner rang Moussavi, an old acquaintance, in a state of consternation.

"Mr. Moussavi, there's something that smells very bad about these people," he said. "I've seen their furniture! This is clearly new money. Where did they get it from?"

Meanwhile, Michelle was ruffling feathers at the school gates by boasting of her extravagant lifestyle—the exotic holidays and diamonds and twice-weekly dinners at Raymond Blanc's double-Michelin-starred restaurant, Le Manoir aux Quat'Saisons. Young wasn't making things any better by tearing around the country lanes at top speed in his Porsche, often leaving the engine running noisily outside the quiet local pubs. Those who did welcome the wealthy new family into the community on first appearances quickly began to smell a rat on closer inspection. Young's claim to have been educated at Stowe—one of Britain's most exclusive boarding schools—was belied by his habit of passing the port the wrong way at dinner.

Moussavi was becoming increasingly suspicious when one day, around a year after the sale of Woodperry went through, he received a knock on the door of his new nearby home from a plainclothes detective. The man was from Special Branch, the national security wing of Scotland Yard, and he wanted to talk about Young. The Yard had suspicions, he said, that the buyer of Woodperry was involved in the laundering of Russian money. Might Moussavi know anything about that?

The academic said he didn't—though he spilled the beans about Young's proposal to buy Woodperry off the books in cash—but he privately resolved to find out more. He began making his own inquiries into how Young had really come into his fortune. When he put that question to a mutual acquaintance—a local wheeler-dealer who had become friendly with the new arrivals—his question met with a look of surprise.

"Don't you know?" the man asked with amusement. "Scot is Boris Berezovsky's bagman."

Suddenly the picture got a lot clearer. Moussavi knew all about Berezovsky, the notorious Russian oligarch who had made a vast fortune buying up state assets at rock-bottom prices under the country's increasingly drunken president, Boris Yeltsin, and had siphoned much of it offshore to buy himself lavish properties and yachts all over Europe. *So that's where all the money came from,* Moussavi thought. Young was, in his estimation, just a greedy barrow boy who knew how to bullshit his way in the world, but getting involved with the Russian robber barons was a dangerous business. From then on, Moussavi had a strange premonition about the new man in his mansion. *It's mathematically probable,* he thought, *that Scot Young will end up dead.*

II

Moscow and St. Petersburg—1994

The Moscow sky was choked with snow as a small, stout tycoon climbed out of his limousine, his black eyes glittering with restless energy. Boris Berezovsky hastened toward the grand prerevolutionary mansion that served as his command center, followed by a phalanx of bodyguards. The godfather of the oligarchs was rarely unhurried, and today was no exception. Berezovsky was expanding his empire.

The building, a restored nineteenth-century merchant's residence, was set in an exclusive enclave of central Moscow close to the Bolshoy Ustinsky Bridge, over the frozen Moskva River, from which the Kremlin's domes could be seen blooming brightly against the iron sky. Berezovsky had shut off the road leading to his headquarters by blocking it at both ends, turning it into a private club for Moscow's emerging business and political elite. Inside, it was smoky and sumptuous, with stuccoed ceilings, grand chandeliers, and ornate Italian furniture arrayed around a bar stocked with the finest wines rubles could buy.

The renowned Soviet mathematician, engineer, and chess obsessive had transformed his fortunes since the fall of the USSR, and now, in his midforties, he could call himself rich for the first time. As soon as the Iron Curtain came down, he seized the moment to start importing German cars and the enterprise exploded as Russia opened up for business. Berezovsky soon became the biggest distributor for the state-owned car manufacturer, Avtovaz, profiting massively by acquiring its Ladas in bulk on consignment and paying for them later, once the money had been devalued by rampant hyperinflation sparked by the sudden removal of Soviet price controls. His company, Logovaz, had made hundreds of millions that way, and it had become the official Russian dealer for Mercedes-Benz, Chrysler, Chevrolet, and several other prestigious Western marques. Logovaz was among the first big success stories of the new capitalist Russia. But Berezovsky always wanted more.

As he strode through the grand entrance of the Logovaz Club on this biting January morning, the businessman's prized possession—his hulking mobile telephone—began trilling insistently. The caller was Logovaz's general director, Yuli Dubov. He was overseeing the company's latest grand expansion, and he had hit upon a major problem.

The city government of St. Petersburg was refusing to issue the papers confirming that Logovaz owned the site of the new flagship service center it was building for Mercedes in Russia's second city. Opening without the right documentation would make the center a sitting duck for extortion by the city's notoriously corrupt officials and marauding criminal gangs, and the date when the German car giant was expecting it to be up and running was fast approaching.

"Our people can't do anything," Dubov said, sounding desperate. "And this could really damage our relationship with Stuttgart."

Berezovsky knew exactly what needed to be done. "You'll have to go and see Putin," he said.

Dubov was mystified. "Who the hell is Putin?"

As the limousine swept through the snow-cloaked St. Petersburg streets, past the golden domes of the Kazan Cathedral and the gleaming columns of the Winter Palace, Dubov reflected on what little he knew about the man he was getting ready to meet for lunch. Vladimir Vladimirovich Putin, Berezovsky had explained, was the city's deputy mayor—an unfailingly loyal but ever more powerful lieutenant to the aging Anatoly Sobchak—and these days he was the one who ran the show.

"He's a really good person," Berezovsky had told him. "And he's really in charge of what's going on in the city." Dubov had entertained many politicians in Moscow as Logovaz built its business, and he was in little doubt about how the meeting with Putin would go. He would have to spend hours plying the deputy mayor with delicious food, fabulous wine, and plenty of vodka before they turned to the problem at hand and what it would cost to solve it.

As he strode into the restaurant, brushing the snow from his coat sleeves, Dubov saw two men in gray suits seated in the lounge. They rose as he entered. The smaller man, who introduced himself as Vladimir Vladimirovich, was slight and mousy with a cautious manner to match his sober tie. *If you put him next to the wall,* Dubov thought, *you wouldn't see the difference.* The other man, who was introduced as Putin's secretary, Igor Sechin, stood to attention at his side with an attaché case in one hand and a large mobile telephone in the other. Dubov thought them an oddly austere pair.

The two men declined a drink and stayed standing. With ten minutes to go until the table was ready, Dubov ventured a few comments about the weather in St. Petersburg, which, he felt it fair to say, was dirty. When those efforts at conversation met with stony silence, and no other topics appeared to be forthcoming, he decided to be done with it and plunge ahead with his request.

Logovaz had already paid for the plot of land where its new Mercedes center would be situated, and the building works were almost complete, he explained. But the city government was withholding the documentation granting the company the formal rights to the site. Could the deputy mayor do anything to help?

"Give me one minute," said Putin, taking the telephone from Sechin, extending the antenna, and walking smartly to the window.

When he returned, he handed the phone back to Sechin and

turned to Dubov. "The documents will be finalized and given to you as soon as you come to the office," he said, reaching for his coat. "Goodbye."

"What about lunch?" asked Dubov, taken aback.

"I thought I was coming here for lunch," said Putin. "But it turned out I came here to resolve some of your business problems. Since I have done that, there is no need to spend time eating and talking." With that, he and Sechin spun on their heels and stalked out, leaving Dubov staring after them in blank astonishment.

"This is a very strange guy you introduced me to," he told Berezovsky back at the Logovaz Club in Moscow. What sort of politician declines a free lunch in exchange for a favor?

Berezovsky smiled. "Yes," he said. "He is very special."

A few years earlier, when he first began importing cars into St. Petersburg, Berezovsky had approached Putin, then a young functionary in Sobchak's administration, and offered him a small inducement to help smooth over a few administrative matters. To his astonishment, Putin declined. He was, to Berezovsky's knowledge, the first Russian official who didn't take bribes. The experience had made a huge impression, and since then he had made a point of swinging by Putin's office for a chat whenever he was in St. Petersburg. It was a useful alliance for Berezovsky when he needed to pull strings in Russia's second city. And the reach of Putin's influence didn't seem to stop at city hall.

The punctilious young deputy mayor appeared to hold significant sway over the powerful organized crime groups that terrorized St. Petersburg. The Russian mafia had mushroomed into the vacuum created by the implosion of the Soviet security state, and the car industry was a particularly gangster-infested line of business, with hoodlums using brute force to steal whole consignments of new cars and seize control of lucrative dealerships. That made opening a shiny new Mercedes service center in the heart of St. Petersburg a perilous game. But Putin had sufficient status with the city's most powerful mafia group—the Tambovskaya Bratva, known as the Tambov gang—to guarantee the security of Berezovsky's operations as well as help smooth over bureaucratic glitches with the city government.

Berezovsky was sure Putin was special. How else could he have risen up through the corrupt ranks of St. Petersburg officialdom and acquired such standing with the mob without tarnishing his seemingly spotless morals? Why else would he be so helpful without wanting anything in return?

But the fact was that Putin did want something very much indeed, and Berezovsky was uniquely well placed to give it him. It just wasn't a free lunch or a car or a bundle of money. It was the keys to the Kremlin.

Boris Yeltsin had seen off the Communists and come to power in 1991 promising to propel the Russian people out of the darkness of their totalitarian past into the dawn of a free and prosperous future. His strategy, under the tutelage of the World Bank and other bastions of Western capitalism, was to submit the country's creaking socialist economy to a radical regimen of capitalist shock therapy involving the sudden withdrawal of price controls and the mass privatization of state assets. That, coupled with a decision to plug the state's budget deficit by printing reams of rubles, prompted a prolonged period of hyperinflation that wiped out savings and plunged ordinary Russians into abject poverty. But for a fortunate few, the shock to the Soviet system shook loose a windfall of unimaginable riches.

Berezovsky had won favor with the first freely elected president of Russia by bankrolling the publication of his memoir. *Notes of a President* was a dismal commercial flop when it hit the market, in 1993, but Berezovsky made sure the author was handsomely paid, pleasing the vainglorious Yeltsin sufficiently to gain admittance to his private circle. From there, Berezovsky made a beeline for the president's influential daughter, Tatiana, lavishing her with gifts and largesse until the pair became fast friends. So it was that he became a central member of what came to be known as the Kremlin Family, the intimate group who counseled Yeltsin as he dismantled the Soviet state apparatus and carved up its assets. The businessman could hardly have profited more abundantly from his coveted place in the president's court.

Berezovsky had made a fortune out of hyperinflation at Logovaz, and now he planned to use it to buy up as many state assets as he could lay his hands on. The Soviet ban on private business had given rise to some forty-five thousand state-owned enterprises, including the country's vast oil, gas, and mineral concerns, and they were all coming up for grabs at rock-bottom prices in Yeltsin's fire sale. Berezovsky had the money and the Kremlin connections required to clean up in the auctions, but there was one more thing he needed to do. There was no way to prosper in the smash-and-grab chaos of post-Soviet Russia without getting into bed with the mob.

Gangsterism in Russia had exploded—left unchecked by the collapse of the Soviet security state, which had the multiplier effect of driving thousands of disbanded KGB officers into a life of organized crime. As the rest of the country emerged blinking from the suffocation of the Soviet system, its mafia groups were way ahead of the game. They boasted many of Russia's brightest and best businessmen (the Soviets having allowed enterprising citizens no other path to prosperity), decades of commercial experience running the country's de facto private sector—the black market—and deep political connections from years of supplying luxury goods to the Communist elite. So they swooped as soon as the auctions began, buying up swaths of Russia's energy, mineral, telecom, and transport sectors. And capitalism opened up another major revenue stream: anyone who dared to do private business in Russia without paying the mob for *krysha*—protection, or, literally, "roof"—was intimidated, run out of town, or murdered. Not for nothing did Yeltsin call his country "the biggest mafia state in the world" in 1994, warning of "the superpower of crime that is devouring the state from top to bottom." The mob had taken over—and if Berezovsky intended to survive in the hurly-burly new world of Russian business, he needed to find his way into the fold.

That was where Badri Patarkatsishvili came into the picture. The mustachioed Georgian businessman was a well-connected figure in the post-Soviet underworld, with powerful allies in the Moscow mafia and deep ties to criminal elements within the state security apparatus. He held a senior position with the state car maker in the Georgian capital until Berezovsky recognized the value of his criminal pedigree and poached him to become deputy director of Logovaz in Moscow. Patarkatsishvili's most prized connection was with the Georgian mafia boss and champion wrestler Otari Kvantrishvili, among the most powerful organized crime kingpins operating out of Moscow in the 1990s. Kvantrishvili had become something of a figurehead for the mob in the early days of mass privatization, befriending key politicians and settling disputes between rival criminal factions vying for the most sought-after assets coming up for sale. Patarkatsishvili arrived in the capital at the end of 1993, just in time to get intimately connected in the Moscow underworld before Kvantrishvili was shot dead by a sniper while walking through a parking lot.

With Patarkatsishvili on board, Berezovsky had the unholy trinity of key connections required to get rich and stay alive in post-Soviet Russia: the mafia, the Kremlin, and the security service. He had also, it turned out, met his soul mate. Boris and Badri, as the soon-to-be inseparable pair were always known, made instant sense as a partnership. Berezovsky was a man of extreme tastes and tempers—irresistibly magnetic, fantastically persuasive, and hopelessly impractical. Patarkatsishvili was the polar opposite, with his twirling white mustache and fondness for fur hats. His avuncular outward appearance concealed a ruthless inner steel, and he always got the job done. It was like two halves of a whole had come together: Berezovsky brought the ideas; Patarkatsishvili put them into practice. An extraordinary business partnership had been born.

Boris and Badri went on to acquire an astonishing array of state assets at a fraction of their true value in Yeltsin's privatization auctions, making them multibillionaires almost instantaneously. They began by parlaying Logovaz's lucrative dealership contract with Avtovaz into a controlling stake in the state-owned car manufacturer before acquiring major interests in the national airline, Aeroflot, several big banks, and much of the country's aluminum industry. The jewel in the crown came when they teamed up to help another budding oligarch, Roman Abramovich, buy the country's largest oil company, Sibneft, for $100 million—a drop in the bucket of the billions it was really worth.

Having thus enriched themselves, Boris and Badri saw another opportunity to expand their power—by buying up the mass-media companies that were flourishing in the sudden absence of state censorship. Their media interests—including the national newspaper *Kommersant* and Russia's leading television station, Channel One— gave them a portal into 98 percent of Russian households and proved an invaluable political bargaining chip.

By the mid-1990s, the old Soviet mathematician was the undisputed kingpin of a new kleptocracy emerging from the ashes of the Soviet state. But with that kind of power, inexorably, came great peril.

The early evening sun slanted under the overhanging eaves of the Logovaz Club, where Berezovsky's silver Mercedes 600 limousine was purring in readiness for his departure. The oligarch strode briskly from the rear entrance and into the armored vehicle, giving a nod to the bodyguard holding the door open as he slid into the back seat. It was a mild summer evening in 1994, and the streets were still and quiet. But as the chauffeur cleared Berezovsky's private drive and pulled onto the public road, the serenity was splintered by a massive explosion that blew the Mercedes skyward, ripping through the bulletproof door and pelting Berezovsky's face with shards of metal and glass. When the smoke cleared, he saw the headless body in front: his chauffeur had been decapitated. Clambering out of the smoldering wreckage, Berezovsky found the street strewn with the bodies of half a dozen badly wounded pedestrians and the blackened remnants of a blue Opel that had been parked by the curb. The car had been packed with half a kilo of explosives, ready to detonate by remote control as soon as he drove by.

Berezovsky spent several weeks recovering from his burns and facial lacerations at a clinic in Switzerland—a home away from home, since this was where he stashed much of the cash he was siphoning off from the companies he'd bought from the state. When he returned to Moscow, he was called to a meeting with the young state security officer who had been put in charge of investigating the blast. His name was Alexander Litvinenko.

The meticulous young official had visited the site of the explosion, spoken to witnesses, and delved through countless intelligence files tracking the activities of Russia's organized crime networks, but he had been unable to identify who had ordered the hit on Berezovsky. The only real lead was that Logovaz had recently become embroiled in a loan dispute with a bank controlled by a Moscow mobster named Sergei Timofeev—known across the city as Sylvester, thanks to a passing resemblance to Sylvester Stallone—though Berezovsky was tight-lipped on that subject. Litvinenko was coming up against a brick wall, but there was one thing he could be sure of: the attack on Berezovsky would be considered a shot across the bows of the oligarch's protectors in the Moscow mafia. If they identified the culprit, retaliation was sure to follow.

Four months after the car bomb outside the Logovaz Club, police found another burned-out vehicle in central Moscow. The smart sedan had been decimated by a bomb attached to the underside of the chassis, and inside was a badly mangled body. It belonged to Sylvester.

Litvinenko never established for sure who was behind the attack on Berezovsky. Nor was Sylvester's murder ever solved, although rumors swirled in the Moscow underworld that he had faked his own death and skipped the country. But Berezovsky was taken with the conscientious young officer, with his keen blue eyes, boyishly short-cropped sandy hair, and exact manner. The pair exchanged telephone numbers and agreed to stay in touch.

Litvinenko was an anomaly among Russia's state security officials. He was an idealist, a teetotaler, and a stickler for law and order—all rare qualities in post-Soviet Moscow. He'd cut his teeth in the chaotic final days of the KGB in his early twenties, and after the old state security apparatus was dismantled, in 1991, he'd won his dream job as a major in the organized crime unit of the FSB.

Underneath his orderly exterior Litvinenko was a live wire, prone to fits of great excitement and passion, but his training at the KGB's academy had taught him to direct that energy with pinpoint precision. He was fanatical about record keeping, maintaining an immaculate notebook that he loved to show off to fellow detectives, and neatly filing every document he gathered as he investigated the messy business of the Russian mob.

Work had always been Litvinenko's first love, but recently he'd found another grand passion worthy of his high-octane energy. His new fiancée, Marina, was a hypnotically elegant ballroom dancer with smoky blue eyes and high Slavic cheekbones, and he'd pursued her with all his boyish vigor after they met at a friend's apartment, turning up unannounced with gifts of flowers and bunches of bananas, her favorite fruit. After a dizzying romance, she had just given birth to their son, Anatoly, and now the couple were getting ready to marry. But just as life at home was settling perfectly into place, all his security in the job he loved started suddenly to unravel.

Litvinenko was gathering mountains of explosive dirt on the activities of Russia's biggest mobsters as he eavesdropped on their phone calls, recruited informants from within their closest circles, and studied their connections with politicians and officials. And as he delved into the activities of one particularly powerful criminal network, he made a series of disturbing discoveries that shook his faith in the new Russia.

Litvinenko had unearthed evidence that the Tambov gang was

working in cahoots with state security officials to smuggle heroin into the St. Petersburg seaport and onward to western Europe, operating under the protection of powerful figures within the city administration. As he dug deeper, one name kept coming up: Vladimir Putin.

Putin was a KGB man in his blood and bones. He had dreamed of joining the Committee for State Security since he was a little boy hooked on the Soviet spy series *The Shield and the Sword,* and he got a place at the KGB academy in his hometown of Leningrad (the Communist name for St. Petersburg) as soon as he could, in 1975. After graduating, his first job was to spy on foreign diplomats in the city before he was posted to Dresden, East Germany, to work undercover as a translator. It wasn't a particularly glittering start to the career of a lifelong KGB groupie. Dresden was on the wrong side of the Iron Curtain: the real cloak-and-dagger adventure was happening over the wall, in the West, where agents could move invisibly among the enemy. Putin had hoped his spell in the East was just a precursor to greater things—but then disaster struck. When the Berlin Wall fell, in 1989, he was sent packing back to Leningrad, to a dull post grooming new recruits at the state university. From there, he watched with horror as the entire Soviet state disintegrated around him and his beloved KGB was destroyed.

As the ramparts crumbled and Russia lurched toward its capitalist destiny, KGB officers were encouraged by their superiors to forge links with the mafia. The mob understood global market forces better than anyone, and it was clear that the criminal kingpins would rank among the real rulers of the reformed Russia, so the KGB moved to align itself with the new seat of power. The evidence Litvinenko was unearthing[*] suggested that Putin and a Leningrad KGB colleague

---

[*] Much of the evidence Litvinenko gathered about the Tambovskaya Bratva was later disclosed to the Litvinenko Inquiry and published at litvinenkoinquiry.org. Both Putin and Ivanov have always denied any connection to organized crime.

called Viktor Ivanov had obeyed that diktat—by going into business with the Tambov gang.

Ivanov was a dashing young officer with an insouciant eye who boasted a more swashbuckling KGB career than Putin did, having served two years in Afghanistan during the Soviet-Afghan War. Litvinenko's information suggested that in the dying days of the KGB, Ivanov had forged close ties with the leader of the Tambov gang—Vladimir Kumarin—and he had brought Putin into the action. The Tambovs were locked in a bloody turf war for control of the St. Petersburg seaport with the rival Malyshev gang, and it seemed Ivanov had sided with Kumarin, marshaling the resources of the KGB to help him drive out the enemy and consolidate the Tambovs' control of the city. From then on, according to Litvinenko's evidence, Ivanov became a key lieutenant of Kumarin, assisting him with his operations smuggling heroin into the port as well as bolstering the gang's other lucrative lines of business: arms smuggling, human trafficking, racketeering, extortion, and contract killings. Putin, meanwhile, appeared to have been enlisted to help whitewash the profits: he was on the advisory board of a sham real estate company called SPAG, which seemed to have been set up by Kumarin to launder Colombian drug money.

When the KGB fell, in 1991, Putin and Ivanov appeared to have taken their Tambov connections with them. Ivanov went to work for its immediate successor, the FSK, and the evidence suggested he had continued to use the state's resources to help Kumarin flood St. Petersburg with narcotics. Putin, meanwhile, had won himself a place in the mayor's administration and it looked like he was using his new role in the city government to protect Ivanov and Kumarin from official scrutiny. Litvinenko was sure he had hit on something big, and he intended to keep digging. The young officer had no idea how deadly his discovery would one day prove to be.

Mayor Sobchak had warmed instantly to the sober, diligent new functionary at city hall, who kept his head down and let his boss shine.

Putin's fluency in German was a boon as St. Petersburg opened up to the world along with the rest of the country, and he was soon made the head of the mayor's committee for external relations in charge of attracting foreign investment.

St. Petersburg was by then in the grip of a crippling food shortage caused by hyperinflation—and Putin soon found that out of every crisis comes opportunity. The local government had been granted federal permits to export oil, timber, and metals to be bartered abroad in exchange for meat, fruit, and sugar for the hungry population, and it was his job to distribute export licenses to local companies. Raw materials worth $100 million were shipped out of the city under his watch—but, oddly enough, the companies to which he awarded the permits all shut down right after the cargo set sail. That left no one to hold accountable when the goods disappeared and no food ever arrived in return.

The export imbroglio caught the attention of Marina Salye, a redoubtable city council deputy who had made it her business to root out corruption in St. Petersburg. When the food failed to arrive, she opened an investigation. Salye suspected that Putin and his cronies had pocketed the goods for themselves while the people of the city starved, and her inquiry led to a city council vote recommending that prosecutors investigate him for embezzlement. But Putin angrily denied any wrongdoing, blaming the failure on the now-defunct companies, and he would never be prosecuted, because Sobchak stood in the way.

The mayor had shot to power on the back of stinging attacks on the authoritarianism of the old Communist regime, but he had quickly come to curse the new democratic mechanisms that replaced the Soviet system. There were four hundred freshly elected representatives in city hall following St. Petersburg's first free elections, and Sobchak found himself hog-tied as the rookie legislators pulled all the levers of their new powers at once. They went to war over even the most basic decisions and reveled in their new right to challenge Sobchak's every move in court.

Putin had seen his boss buffeted by the turbulent city council, and now he felt the sting of parliamentary scrutiny himself. Democracy, he learned, just gets in the way. But capitalism was an entirely different story. The market made anything possible. By the time he became deputy mayor, Putin had become a neat fusion of old Russia and new: hybridizing the authoritarian tendencies of his Soviet security training with an appreciation for the market and a kleptocrat's taste for a criminal scheme. And as his influence in St. Petersburg expanded, his ambitions grew. So when Boris Berezovsky came knocking, Putin saw the path to real power opening up before him.

III

The windows of the opulent Swiss salon gave a warm glow onto the snowy streets of the ski resort where the global elite were gathering for the world's most exclusive summit. Inside, Boris Berezovsky was in full rhetorical flight, hunched forward as he made his impassioned case to a small but powerful audience. It was January of 1996, and on the sidelines of the World Economic Forum, the future of Russia was once again being decided by a cabal of megarich men.

Boris Yeltsin was preparing to stand for reelection at the end of his first term, and he was already careening drunkenly toward a humiliating defeat. The national misery caused by his economic shock therapy program, coupled with his increasingly shambolic public appearances, had made the president a figure of contempt among ordinary Russians, and his approval ratings were bumping along below 10 percent. To Berezovsky's deepening alarm, the Communists had swept the board in the parliamentary elections the previous month and established a commanding lead in the early presidential polls. Berezovsky knew what would happen if the Reds retook the Kremlin: the oligarchs would be destroyed. The former state assets they had accumulated would be confiscated, their wealth would be clawed back, and spells in Siberian prison would be all they had to look forward to. The full horror hit home when the Communist Party leader arrived at Davos to be greeted by a succession of world leaders and the international media as the future president of Russia. Berezovsky was not about to stand idly by and let Russia backslide. He simply had too much at stake.

The godfather had gathered his fellow oligarchs on the sidelines of the Davos summit to propose a plan to save the motherland. The men around the table must ensure Yeltsin's reelection at all costs—and when the battle was won, they would make the president pay. Berezovsky's persuasive powers did not fail him, and the group formed a secret pact to pump tens of millions into a war chest devoted to defeating the Communist threat. Altogether, the "big seven" oligarchs controlled around 50 percent of Russia's wealth and all its mass-media outlets: they would use the money, as well as their TV stations and newspapers, to wage an all-out information war on Yeltsin's behalf. Russian electoral rules forbade campaign spending of more than $3 million per candidate—but when had the robber barons ever let a little matter like the law stand in their way?

Back in Moscow, Berezovsky poured the Davos fighting fund into a slick Western-style election campaign, complete with rock concerts, celebrity endorsements, and glossy advertising, and dedicated the airwaves of Channel One and the column inches of *Kommersant* to coverage vaunting Yeltsin and painting the Communist Party as blood-crazed Stalinists. The plan worked. Yeltsin climbed steadily back from oblivion in the polls, and when the election came around that summer, he won. But the backing of the oligarchs did not come cheap.

In exchange for the money they had put into Yeltsin's reelection, the big seven acquired controlling stakes in yet more of the prized assets still under state control. As soon as Yeltsin was safely back in the Kremlin, the assets were put up for sale in rigged auctions, a move that cemented the hatred of the Russian people toward the band of kleptocrats now all but ruling the country. In 1997, the year after what became known as the Davos Pact and the windfall that followed, *Forbes* magazine named Berezovsky the world's ninth-richest entrepreneur, with a personal fortune of $3 billion. And the rewards he reaped for shoring up Yeltsin's second term were not purely financial.

The godfather wielded ever more influence after the election. Yeltsin gifted him a prized job as deputy director of the Kremlin's national security council and made him Russia's point man in the breakaway republic of Chechnya. Berezovsky reveled in his new roles, which afforded him all the limelight he could wish for and plentiful chances for further self-enrichment.

But Yeltsin's health was failing fast, and his increasingly drink-sodden public appearances were making Russia a laughingstock on the world stage. Berezovsky and his fellow oligarchs knew it was time to find a successor. What they needed was a man they could manipulate—a gray, malleable functionary who would stay loyal and run Russia like a puppet chief executive while they sat above as a controlling board pulling the strings. Berezovsky thought he knew the perfect man for the job—and he had just arrived in Moscow.

Mayor Sobchak had not enjoyed the same luck as Yeltsin did in the 1996 St. Petersburg elections. Without as many rich backers to tilt the ballot in his favor, the mayor had been toppled by a former ally—and that had been just the push Putin needed to leave his hometown behind and set out for the capital. In doing so, he had declined a role in the new mayoral administration, a move that impressed his virtues on Berezovsky still further. Loyalty to one's patron: that was the quality Yeltsin most fervently desired in his successor. This would make Putin an easy sell.

What the president feared most, after nearly a decade of looting, was prosecution. He knew he and his close circle had become hated figures among the population they had cheated, so he needed to find a candidate who could be trusted to forgo the easy populist points to be gained by going after the old regime.

Putin began spending time with Berezovsky—visiting him at the Logovaz Club, skiing with him in Switzerland, staying at his villa in Spain. He soon secured a junior government job with the oligarch's help, quickly winning favor through his well-honed appearance of quiet conscientiousness. And then Berezovsky helped smooth his path to a position of real power: in 1997, Putin became the chief of Yeltsin's presidential staff. He had made it inside the Kremlin.

Moscow—1998

Berezovsky was in the hospital recuperating from a snowmobile accident when his phone began ringing off the hook. The caller was the eager young state security official who had quizzed him about the car bomb four years before. Alexander Litvinenko had since been transferred to a highly secretive department of the FSB—Russia's newly revamped security agency—and he insisted he needed a private audience with Berezovsky. There was no time to lose: it was urgent.

When the two men met, Litvinenko got straight to the point. He had received orders to kill the oligarch. The new specialist organized crime unit to which Litvinenko had been transferred, the URPO, was so secretive that it was based in an unmarked bunker outside the FSB's Lubyanka Square headquarters, and orders were given only verbally. Litvinenko had hoped his transfer augured new and exciting cases investigating matters of the utmost sensitivity, but he had quickly come to realize with dismay what the new unit was really all about. The URPO was the FSB's secret hit squad.

As Yeltsin's grip on power weakened and the mob tightened its grip, the president had poured more money into the retooled FSB. The new agency was meant to represent a departure from the barbarous old ways of the KGB, but in reality it was staffed by the same men, and there was nothing about the new Russia that they liked. The URPO had been tasked with taking out organized crime kingpins whose activities were considered a threat to the state, but it wasn't long before its top brass strayed beyond their brief and began using the unit for specialist assignments of a more political nature. That was how Litvinenko and four of his fellow officers had been called into a meeting one morning and ordered to kill Russia's most influential oligarch.

The bosses at URPO never felt the need to explain their instructions, and Litvinenko had no idea what Berezovsky had done to wind up on the hit list, but there was one thing he did know for certain. Killing a senior Kremlin adviser was an act of madness—not to mention treason. To make matters worse, that order was followed by an equally unthinkable instruction. A well-liked fellow FSB officer named Mikhail Trepashkin had uncovered a network of corrupt officers within the agency, and now the URPO bosses wanted him dead, too. Trepashkin, who had cut his teeth investigating Moscow's underground trade in stolen art and antiques before being redeployed to probe Chechen mafia groups in Moscow, was a rare comrade after Litvinenko's own heart: dogged, idealistic, and single-minded in his pursuit of the bad guys. Litvinenko and his team could no more contemplate murdering one of their own than they could countenance committing treason by going after a member of the government. They resolved to blow the whistle on both plots.

At first, Berezovsky refused to believe what he was hearing. He, too, felt sure that his place inside the Kremlin would protect him from the state's own assassins. But when Litvinenko brought the other officers from his unit to a meeting and they all confirmed the story, Berezovsky was forced to believe the unbelievable. It was time to warn Trepashkin that he, too, was a target. Over the months that followed, the unwilling assassins met secretly with their two targets as they gamed out how to blow the lid off the plot.

Their plan got under way on a cool April night at Berezovsky's sprawling dacha, in the countryside outside Moscow. Under cover of darkness, Litvinenko and his colleagues gathered to make a comprehensive video record of the orders they had been given. With that evidence safely in the bag, to be released in the event that any of them was arrested or killed after exposing the plot, the whistleblowers filed a complaint with Russia's military prosecution service.

A top-secret investigation got under way, and while they waited for the results, Berezovsky ran his own interference inside the Kremlin.

The FSB had clearly spun out of control, and it was time for a changing of the guard. In June of 1998, acting on the advice of Berezovsky and other aides, Yeltsin fired the agency's director and replaced him with a man who could be trusted to do as he was asked. Vladimir Putin's boyhood dream had come true: he had made it to the top of the Lubyanka HQ.

Berezovsky was thrilled that Putin was in charge. With his protégé at the helm, he would not only be able to foil the assassination plot but also sweep out his enemies from the FSB. He told Litvinenko to visit the new director and tell him everything. Litvinenko was uncomfortable about that instruction: he was still sitting on the evidence he had started to gather a few years earlier charting Putin's connections with the Tambov gang in St. Petersburg. But the oligarch was having none of it—he had seen the evidence of Putin's probity for himself, and they could not afford to pass up such a crucial ally—so Litvinenko reluctantly did what he was told.

The director's office inside the Lubyanka building was as gray and functional as its occupant. Putin put on his best appearance of cordiality as he came out from behind his desk to greet the visitor, but Litvinenko sized up the small man in an instant. *He's doing everything he can to seem open and likable,* he thought to himself, *but it's all for show.* Still, hewing to Berezovsky's instructions, Litvinenko sat down and spilled the beans about the goings-on inside the URPO. Putin listened attentively and thanked him for sharing his information. But Litvinenko could not shake the impression that the man behind the desk was eyeing him with cold hatred.

Soon after that meeting, Putin shut down the URPO and redeployed all its officers unceremoniously. Berezovsky claimed it as a vindication, but the truth was the new director hadn't had much choice, since the order to disband the unit had come directly from the Kremlin. When autumn came and news reached the whistle-blowers that the military prosecution service had thrown out their complaint, Berezovsky did not flinch. Certain they had the backing of the man at the top of the FSB, he declared it was time to go public.

The oligarch used the pages of his newspaper, *Kommersant,* to publish an open letter to Putin calling on him to root out corruption in the FSB. Then journalists from every paper and TV station in Moscow were called to a press conference to witness the big crescendo. Out walked four men in ski masks and sunglasses alongside a bare-faced Litvinenko to blow the whistle live on television. The broadcast riveted the nation and was beamed around the world, making it a major success in the eyes of Berezovsky. From that day forward, the oligarch never lost his love for the thrill of a dramatic press conference. But watching it up in his Lubyanka office, the new FSB director was seething. The whistle-blowers had betrayed the agency by revealing its secrets and, in the code of honor among spies that Putin cherished, there was no more cardinal sin. Litvinenko and the masked cowards who appeared alongside him must be made to pay, but Putin had to bide his time. He had a distance still to climb before it was safe to let his own mask slip.

Putin had been picked to run the FSB for reasons much bigger than just the plot to kill Berezovsky. The increasingly harried aides to the ill and embattled Yeltsin were looking for a very particular sort of candidate, someone who would protect his boss at all costs, and there was one recent episode in Putin's history that had convinced them that he was just the man they needed to take care of some unpleasant business.

Back in St. Petersburg the previous year, the old mayor, Anatoly Sobchak, had found himself under investigation for corruption by Russia's vigorous new prosecutor general, Yuri Skuratov, and Putin had ridden in to the rescue. In November of 1997, when Sobchak suffered a heart attack while under interrogation, Putin arranged for his former boss to be spirited out of the hospital on a stretcher, past his police guard, and onto a waiting private jet, which whisked him away to Paris. Sobchak was now enjoying a happy exile in *la belle* France— and those optics were pleasing to the team of advisers worrying about how life after power would look for Yeltsin. Not least because the president and his close circle were having their own spot of bother with Skuratov.

The paunchy prosecutor general was a Communist sympathizer who had publicly declared war on Yeltsin in the aftermath of the 1996 election, vowing to use his role to root out corruption in the Kremlin. He had then mounted an investigation into the president's administration for taking bribes in exchange for lucrative Kremlin contracts. Yeltsin's team wanted an FSB chief willing to do whatever it took to get the president out of a corner. So when Putin arrived at the Lubyanka, getting rid of Skuratov was high on his agenda.

It wasn't just Yeltsin in the frame: Skuratov was going after Berezovsky with equal vigor. On a February morning in 1999, dozens of camouflaged men burst through the doors of the oligarch's Moscow offices brandishing automatic rifles. They were there on Skuratov's orders. The problems had arisen after Berezovsky installed a new chief financial officer, Nikolai Glushkov, at Aeroflot three years earlier. Glushkov was a persnickety numbers man who liked to mellow his austere appearance with a jaunty bow tie, and he soon made a dangerous discovery. The state airline had for years been operating as a front for international espionage, Glushkov told Berezovsky. Around three thousand of its staff of fourteen thousand were spies, and proceeds from its ticket sales were being diverted into a vast network of foreign slush funds to bankroll their clandestine operations. Glushkov was not prepared to give the spooks a free ride, so he fired the spies and shut down their slush funds. Then he diverted the money to Swiss companies of which he and Berezovsky were the principal shareholders and wrote to Russia's spy chiefs telling them to pick up their own tab from now on. Skuratov was now going after Berezovsky and Glushkov on suspicion of embezzling hundreds of millions of dollars, and the raids on the oligarch's offices caused a sensation in Moscow. Might the king of the robber barons finally be getting his comeuppance?

Not on Vladimir Putin's watch.

Days after the raids, the FSB director showed up at a private party for Berezovsky's wife wielding a huge bunch of roses to make it clear exactly whose side he was on. Then, the following month, the FSB struck against Skuratov. The state-controlled Russian TV channel used its prime-time slot to air grainy footage of a rotund man bearing a striking resemblance to the prosecutor general rolling around in bed with two prostitutes. It was a classic honey-trap operation straight out of the KGB playbook, and in case anyone missed the message, Putin personally held a press conference to tell the world that the man in the video was none other than Skuratov.

The lurid footage forced the prosecutor's resignation. When the largely Communist parliament rallied to reinstate him, Yeltsin opened a criminal investigation into Skuratov's use of prostitutes and used it as a pretext to sack him for good.

Yeltsin doubled down on Skuratov's dismissal by sacking Russia's prime minister, a potential presidential challenger who had been a staunch ally of the prosecutor general. The threat of prosecution thus averted, the Kremlin Family turned their attention to succession planning. They knew Yeltsin could not go on much longer, so they needed to find a replacement prime minister who had what it took to become president—and sooner rather than later. They did not have to look far. Putin had demonstrated his loyalty, his pliability, and his willingness to play dirty to protect his patrons.

Berezovsky was dispatched to Biarritz, where the FSB director was holidaying with his young family, to make the proposal. On August 9, 1999, the people of Russia woke to the news that not only was Vladimir Putin their new prime minister, he was also Yeltsin's chosen successor.

*　　*　　*

Putin had not been in his post for a month when the bombings began. One by one, in early September of 1999, a series of massive explosions in Moscow and two other major Russian cities reduced four apartment buildings to smoldering rubble in the depths of night, blowing residents to shreds as they slept. Firefighters pulled a thousand people free from the ruins with terrible injuries, but almost three hundred were killed. Many of the blackened bodies they found buried in the wreckage were those of children.

The wave of terror attacks, some of the most deadly the world had known until the September 11 attacks in New York, two years later, were quickly blamed on rebels in the breakaway region of Chechnya, spreading fear and alarm throughout the land. And that was exactly what the new prime minister needed to make good the next stage in his ascent.

Putin's gray-man image had served him well in convincing his various patrons that he was no more than the dour and dutiful stuffed shirt they needed to do their bidding. But what had gotten him this far was the very thing that would hold him back. It was no good just being anointed Yeltsin's heir by the hated kleptocrats in the Kremlin; he also needed to win over a deeply disillusioned electorate. That meant striking a new and more powerful pose.

The Russian people were in a state of collective identity crisis after the capitalist dream they had been sold gave way to years of poverty and rank inequality. They didn't miss the drab authoritarianism of the Soviet era, but the orgy of looting and cronyism under Yeltsin had instilled a fundamental distrust of the alternative. All that was left behind was a longing for a lost sense of greatness—a nostalgia for the time when Russia could really call itself a superpower. What they needed in a leader, Putin intuited, was a man of action to satisfy the national yearning for a strong and sure-footed Russia. That was the new posture he needed to pull off, and the apartment bombings provided the perfect opportunity.

In the wake of the attacks, Putin leaped into action, ordering air raids that reduced swaths of the Chechen capital to rubble and triggering the outbreak of a war that killed tens of thousands of civilians. What really stuck in the national consciousness was the television address in which Putin issued a blunt warning to the region's rebels. "Wherever we find them, we will destroy them," he vowed. "Even if we find them in the toilet, we will rub them out." It played perfectly with the people, and Putin's popularity ratings soared.

But critical observers of the apartment bombings and their aftermath noticed several things about the official picture that looked all wrong. The first sign was a strange declaration by the speaker of the Russian parliament, who announced soon after the third attack that a bomb had destroyed an apartment block in the city of Volgodonsk, a thousand kilometers south of Moscow. The problem was that there hadn't been an explosion in Volgodonsk—not yet at least. That fourth bomb went off three days after his announcement, killing another seventeen people. Then, the following week, residents of an apartment building in another city spotted men planting explosives in the basement and raised the alarm, sparking a national manhunt by the local police. The issue this time was that, when the cops caught up with the culprits, they turned out to work for the FSB. The agency's new director had to claim hurriedly that the bomb had only been a dummy and the agents had been involved in a training exercise to test local vigilance. But in some skeptical quarters, that story just didn't wash.

Litvinenko had by then been fired from the FSB for revealing agency secrets, but he had gone to work as a private security consultant for Berezovsky, and he was still tapping into his old informant networks. Based on the intelligence he was gathering, he was convinced that the bombings were an FSB plot set in motion by Putin before his departure from the agency as an excuse for bombing Chechnya to get a boost in the polls. If that was true, Russia's new prime minister was not only a gangster but also a monster who had butchered almost three hundred of his own people to get ahead in the election. But Berezovsky would not hear a word of it. He was far too busy clearing his protégé's path to power.

Just as he had done for Yeltsin, Berezovsky backed Putin by funding the publication of a flattering book. The biography—first published in the pages of *Kommersant*—was carefully designed to bolster Putin's strong-man image, while Channel One aired blistering attacks on his rival candidates. The oligarch also created and bankrolled a new pro-Putin political party, Unity, which won big in the December parliamentary elections. And he enlisted the help of Moscow's premier adman—a fast-living, florid-faced media guru named Mikhail Lesin—to run a slick advertising campaign painting Putin as the powerful president required to lead Russia into the new century.

With Putin surging ahead in the polls, Berezovsky persuaded the sitting president that the time had come to pick up and clear out. On New Year's Eve in 1999, Yeltsin announced his resignation, making the prime minister acting president, effective immediately. There was a quid pro quo: Putin's first decree, signed on December 31, 1999, granted the Yeltsin family immunity from prosecution. Having thus delivered his side of the bargain, Putin could fight the upcoming presidential elections from pole position inside the Kremlin.

Putin hardly had to lift a finger. Beyond a well-televised victory lap around the devastated Chechen capital of Grozny, he barely set foot on the campaign trail. The people of Russia were behind him—and the rulers of the West were cheerleading him, too. Britain's fashionable new Labour prime minister even jetted over to St. Petersburg to meet the presidential hopeful amid much fanfare a fortnight before polling day. Tony Blair caught stinging criticism from human rights groups for feting Putin amid harrowing reports of looting, rape, mass execution, and torture by Russian troops in Chechnya and for shunning all the other candidates before the election was decided. But as the two vigorous young politicians shared an evening at the opera in St. Petersburg, both had their eyes on a glittering prize.

"He was highly intelligent and with a focused view of what he wants to achieve in Russia," Blair told the BBC afterward with a classic Cheshire cat grin, praising Putin's desire to modernize the Russian economy and open the country to foreign investment. Putin did his bit, too, promising to welcome British involvement in the development of Russian oil and gas resources. So when Blair caught awkward questions about human rights violations in Chechnya, he leapt to the defense of his new ally. "The Russians have been subjected to *really* severe terrorist attacks," he said, referring to the Moscow apartment bombings Putin had blamed on the region's rebels.

What the public didn't know was that the prime minister's night at the opera with Russia's future president had been carefully orchestrated by the two countries' spy agencies. The arrangement had arisen when a senior FSB officer approached the head of MI6, Sir Richard Dearlove, in London and asked him to help arrange a high-profile meeting between Blair and Putin to burnish the latter's presidential credentials ahead of the election. After protracted discussions back at the River House, the spy chief had decided this was an "unusual and unique opening" for the UK and urged Downing Street to accept the invitation. Thus Britain had its hand in smoothing Putin's ascent.

Blair wasn't the only world leader who was starry-eyed about Russia's putative president. Bill Clinton had phoned the British prime minister months before polling day to express his own excitement.

"Putin has enormous potential, I think," the US president opined.[*] "I think he's very smart and thoughtful. I think we can do a lot of good with him." There was a faint note of caution—"He *could* get squishy on democracy"—but overall, Clinton was hopeful that Putin would come to the table with the right coaxing. "His intentions are gener-

---

[*] A transcript of this phone call was released by the Clinton Presidential Library in 2016.

ally honorable and straightforward," the US president said. "He just hasn't made up his mind yet."

On the contrary, Putin's mind was very much made up.

Seven days after his official inauguration, in May of 2000, Russia's new president enacted a raft of new laws all aimed at what he euphemistically called "strengthening vertical power." He replaced elected members of the upper house of parliament with Kremlin appointees, sent presidential envoys to supervise the running of Russia's semiautonomous regions, and granted his administration the power to remove local governors on the mere suspicion of wrongdoing. With the regions thus under tighter control, Putin clamped down on other competing power sources. Next in line was the free media.

Putin's media minister Mikhail Lesin, the adman who had helped secure his victory, led an assault on the independent TV stations, newspapers, and magazines that had proliferated since the fall of the USSR, using all the levers of state power to pressure their owners into ceding control to the Kremlin. Journalists and proprietors were arrested; advertisers were leaned on; offices were raided; trumped-up charges were brought. Lesin, who would go on to found the sprawling international propaganda network Russia Today (RT), so relentlessly rammed independent media outlets back under Kremlin control that he earned himself the nickname the Bulldozer.

And with the media purge well under way, Putin turned his attention to the oligarchs. Berezovsky and his fellow tycoons were summoned to the Kremlin and told that their special privileges were being revoked. While Putin would stop short of reviewing the rigged privatizations, they would no longer enjoy special access to power. In short: they would be allowed to keep their loot, as long as they kept out of politics.

Berezovsky was agog. He had rubbed shoulders purringly at Putin's inaugural ball, delighting in telling everyone how he had plucked Russia's new ruler from obscurity. So confident was he in his status as Kremlin chess master that he had gone to the new president soon after to propose an audacious deal. Putin would rule Russia, while Berezovsky would nominally head up the opposition party, thus carving up power between them, shoring up the position of the oligarchs, and making sure the presidency remained effectively unopposed. But Putin had declined that offer with icy disdain, and that was when Berezovsky first began to realize his mistake.

Putin's creeping authoritarianism had in fact been well in evidence long before his inauguration for anyone with eyes to see it. As the Chechen war raged on, he had used his three months as acting president to reverse some of the more pacific reforms of the post-Soviet era: signing a decree allowing for the use of nuclear weapons in response to major foreign aggression and ramping up spending on the armed forces. And then there were the warning signs that those who knew too much might have exactly that much to fear.

Anatoly Sobchak had returned from his exile in Paris to become a vocal if chaotic supporter of Putin's election campaign. The old mayor had struggled to stay on message: he appeared to have forgotten his liberal credentials when he hailed Putin as "the new Stalin," and he was all too fond of reminiscing about episodes from the old days in St. Petersburg that the presidential contender would rather forget. On February 17, 2000, Putin asked Sobchak to travel to the Russian enclave of Kaliningrad, between Poland and Lithuania, for a campaign pit stop. Three days later, the old man was found dead in his hotel room. The official postmortem declared that he had died of a massive heart attack—but that didn't explain why his two bodyguards had to be treated for mild symptoms of poisoning. The investigative journalist Arkady Vaksberg later published an account suggesting that Sobchak had been eliminated by a toxin smeared on a lightbulb in his hotel room—a classic KGB technique. Soon after, the journalist's car was blown up in his Moscow garage. He happened not to be inside—but the message had been sent.

* * *

As Putin lurched toward autocracy, Berezovsky decided to show his protégé who was boss, using the pages of *Kommersant* to publish a searing critique of the president's plans to centralize power. "In a democratic society, laws exist to protect individual freedom," he lectured in one of his open letters. When Putin ignored that moral lesson and continued his crackdown, Berezovsky's aides and advisers counseled the furious oligarch to let matters lie.

"You have to think, Boris! Slow down, calm down, think," one adviser beseeched him over wine and cigars in the Logovaz Club lounge against the tinkling backdrop of the grand piano. "You have access! Work with the guy. You're very persuasive, you're cleverer than he is, you put him in that position in the first place—so work with him." Badri Patarkatsishvili agreed. Why couldn't Boris just keep his head down for a moment and let things settle? After all, hadn't Putin said he'd leave the looted assets untouched as long as the oligarchs toed the line? But Berezovsky had developed a thirst for power that overwhelmed even his love of money, and he was incapable of conciliation.

"You son of a bitch," he would mutter when Putin's name arose. "I'm going to fight you."

For his part, the old Logovaz director Yuli Dubov was left scratching his head about that first encounter with Putin over the lunch that never was in St. Petersburg. In retrospect, he came to believe that the appearance of monkish probity had just been Putin's way of setting himself apart from the crowd.

"He was playing the long game," Dubov mused. "It was too early for him to begin to enrich himself, so he waited for his moment." Berezovsky's fatal flaw, in Dubov's mind, was an inflated sense of his own importance. He had believed Putin would be incapable of ruling without him, but it turned out that the new president no longer needed him—and neither did anyone else very much. Suddenly Berezovsky found himself quite friendless in Moscow's corridors of power. But undeterred, he went on the attack again.

In August of 2000, the new president found himself in the throes of his first public scandal after his botched handling of a nuclear submarine disaster left 118 naval officers to sink to their deaths unaided in the bitter waters of the Arctic Ocean. Berezovsky seized the moment, using Channel One to eviscerate Putin for his role in the tragedy.

Berezovsky was sunning himself at his gleaming white villa overlooking the sapphire waters of the Côte d'Azur when a copy of *Le Figaro* landed on his doorstep carrying a message direct from the Kremlin. Putin had given an interview to the French newspaper declaring that oligarchs who stepped out of line in the new Russia would receive "a crushing blow on the head." That warning was rapidly followed by a summons for Berezovsky to appear in Moscow for interrogation by the new prosecutor general, who had reopened the Aeroflot embezzlement case that Putin had helped squash two years before. The godfather of the oligarchs was now a wanted man and an enemy of the Kremlin.

One thing was immediately clear to him: while Putin was in power, he could never return to Russia.

IV

Wentworth Estate, Surrey, England, 2001

Scot Young was easing his Porsche up the gravel drive of his magnificent new mansion in Surrey on a breezy summer evening when Michelle came running through the topiary.

"There's a strange man inside, and I can't get him out!" she said. "Shall we call the police?"

Young marched through the grand columned entrance to find a small black-eyed man settled comfortably in an armchair.

"Welcome to my home!" the intruder boomed in a thick Russian accent, throwing his arms wide. "How much do you want for it?"

Later, Young liked to tell his friends that this was the first time he had ever laid eyes on Boris Berezovsky. The story appealed to him both because he was a great raconteur who loved to spin a good yarn and because it happened to be more convenient than the truth. Its punch line was that he hadn't known the man was one of Russia's richest tycoons, so he told Berezovsky to "fuck off." But of course Young knew exactly who Berezovsky was.

Years later, private detectives hired to delve into Young's association with the oligarch would uncover evidence that he had actually met Berezovsky's people a few years earlier on a trip to Moscow and had been secretly operating as his point man in the UK ever since, helping him stash the money he was siphoning out of Russia in spectacular British properties and investments. Since Berezovsky fled, the previous year, Young had also been visiting Moscow regularly on his behalf, handing out a business card billing himself as a consultant to Channel One. It didn't take long for the FSB to develop what the spooks called a "long-term interest" in the British businessman. The FSB surveillance team built up a picture of Young as a high-class fixer providing highly confidential assistance to the oligarch and being pampered in return. He had drunk and dined lavishly on Berezovsky's ticket at Moscow's exclusive Café Pushkin, Vogue Café, and Vanille—and he liked to end the night at Private Club Bordo, a brothel frequented by the city's political and business elite.

The Youngs had sold Woodperry House for £13.5 million earlier that year—more than double what Young had paid for it—and in turn had bought the main manor house on the celebrity-studded Wentworth Estate, in Surrey. After many months luxuriating in his vast Italianate villa on Cap d'Antibes, Berezovsky had tired of soaking up the sun and moved to England to start building his new life in earnest. The oligarch was putting down roots as he settled into a long exile— and he had set his heart on his fixer's home.

Berezovsky produced a case of exquisite red wine from behind the armchair and pulled out a dusty bottle. The two men spent a raucous night demolishing the offering as the Russian regaled Young with rip-roaring tales of the Wild East, and before long Berezovsky's offer of £20.5 million had been accepted. Young would always tell friends the true price was £50 million, the lion's share of which had been hidden offshore, but whatever the cost, Berezovsky had made Wentworth Estate his home.

The godfather moved into his new mansion with his wife and young children, displacing the Youngs to another spectacular property across the estate, and with that a new enclave was established. This lush corner of Surrey, with its follies, lakes, and roaming deer, was to become the seat of some of Russia's richest men as they waged a long-distance war on the Kremlin.

PART TWO

THE OLIGARCHS IN EXILE

V

Mayfair, London—2002

The Down Street butler was apoplectic. A small army of deliverymen was marching across the plush cream carpet, carrying trays heaped with delicacies that filled the Mayfair office with the powerful scent of stewed garlic and spice. There was lobio—beans simmered in wine and herbs; piles of khachapuri—bread oozing with cheese and runny eggs; and enough chicken in garlic and walnut sauce to sink a battleship. The butler ran the kitchen at Down Street with military precision, and this avalanche of unsolicited food would have been enough of an imposition without the affront to culinary sanitation that followed. The intruders disappeared downstairs only to reemerge with not one, not two, but *ten* whole roasted hogs, bearing them into the kitchen aloft and laying them down legs akimbo on every available surface.

This was a bridge too far. The butler quick-stepped across the office, past the sauna and the side room where the most secretive meetings were held, to rap on the door of his master's corner office. When it swung open, he was fixed for a moment with an interrogative stare before the glittering black eyes flicked over his shoulder to the bizarre procession beyond. Suddenly animated, the tiny figure barreled excitedly by to inspect the movable feast, leaving the butler protesting hopelessly behind.

"Mr. Berezovsky! There is no room for all this food in the fridge! What shall I do with ten dead pigs?"

The oligarch neither heard nor cared. The delivery slip confirmed what he already knew.

"From Badri!" he declared happily. His absent partner had sent him another taste of home.

Patarkatsishvili had initially stayed in Moscow to try to save the business empire after Berezovsky fled to England. The Georgian oligarch was the sort of man Putin had time for—politic, practical, and phlegmatic—so Patarkatsishvili was soon called into the Kremlin to be offered a sweetheart deal. Putin would let him keep everything and give him a clean slate, as long as he cut Berezovsky loose. Patarkatsishvili couldn't countenance that kind of treachery, so he declined the offer and was duly run out of Russia. Unlike his Anglophile business partner, the Georgian oligarch spoke barely a word of English, so when the inevitable arrest warrant was issued and he had to bolt, he took up exile in his hometown of Tbilisi. Boris and Badri remained in close cahoots as they plotted to rescue their assets from demolition back in Russia, but it was clear to all who knew them that the separation was painful.

Coming out of his own cramped office in the far corner, a slight spectacled man with a short salt-and-pepper beard stopped and took in the chaotic scene with a smile. Yuli Dubov had seen this fandango play out many times before. These food deliveries had become a frequent occurrence in the two years since Berezovsky's flight from Russia. Patarkatsishvili packed his private jet full of every home comfort his cooks could rustle up and had it all flown to London at regular intervals, having it picked up from the airstrip and chauffeured to Berezovsky's opulent new Mayfair headquarters in a fleet of limousines. There was no way Berezovsky could possibly eat all this food, so his staff would once again be saddled with the surreal task of hawking a family of roasted Georgian hogs around the kitchens of Mayfair. But Dubov knew that wasn't the point. The point was that Badri sent Boris his love.

* * *

The office on Down Street, in this refined London district, was Berezovsky's new command center, and the air seemed to crackle as the oligarch and his many visitors hatched their schemes. Dubov, the former Logovaz director, had fled Russia after prosecutors opened a new probe into corruption at the car giant, adding to the cases mounting up against Berezovsky. He had been given a small office in his boss's new headquarters, from which he assisted with the mission to extricate the billions Boris and Badri had left back home and wryly observed the colorful comings and goings.

Berezovsky had appointed himself the chieftain of a growing group of exiled businessmen and dissidents who had turned up in Britain after falling afoul of Putin, and the Down Street guest book read like a who's who of Russia's most wanted men. Among the most frequent callers was Alexander Litvinenko. The former FSB officer had been repeatedly arrested and imprisoned on increasingly imaginative charges after lifting the lid on the URPO assassination plot—until finally Berezovsky bankrolled an elaborate escape operation to relocate him and his family to Britain, where the defector was granted political asylum. Now Berezovsky was preparing to wage war on Vladimir Putin, and in his mind Litvinenko was a deadly weapon loaded with at least two silver bullets. The first kill shot was the proof of Putin's alliance with the murderous drug-smuggling Tambov gang, from St. Petersburg, and the second was the evidence connecting the president to the apartment bombings that had killed almost three hundred of his own people.

Berezovsky hadn't listened to Litvinenko about either topic when he was still pulling for Putin before the election, but now he intended to unmask his former protégé as nothing more than a criminal in a well-cut suit, a well-mannered monster who had aligned himself with the mob and butchered hundreds of Russians in his pursuit of power. It would be the perfect way to kick off his international campaign against Putin's presidency—but that was going to require a formidable fighting fund, so it was doubly imperative for Berezovsky to get his money out of Russia. The other entries in the Down Street guest book belonged to the elite cast of British lawyers and financiers with whom he was plotting to save his fortune. The Mayfair office was a dizzying confluence of different worlds.

Dubov crossed the lobby and passed the granite-faced security guards stationed by the exit on his way to the elevators. When he reached the ground floor and the doors slid open on the marbled reception area, he was met by a face that, secretly, he wished was less familiar.

"Hi, Yuli!" exclaimed the tall man, with a flash of his gratingly reflexive grin.

"Scot," the Russian replied warily. Dubov couldn't understand what his boss saw in this permatanned huckster, who was always trying to flog you a flashy watch or a penthouse or a fast car you didn't want. But since Berezovsky had moved to Britain and bought a mansion in Wentworth Estate, it was as if Young had become his shadow. The fixer cropped up everywhere he went—at Down Street, on board his private jet, in the back of his armored car—and Young had a particularly disconcerting habit of appearing late at night wherever Berezovsky was finishing dinner to whisper in his ear about the latest shady deal.

Dubov wasn't alone in his distaste. "He's a small-time crook," another of the oligarch's closest aides whispered after meeting Young. "You talk to him, and you see a crook in front of you." But Berezovsky always seemed pleased to see his fixer. Young's can-do spirit made an invigorating contrast to the skepticism of his longtime aides, who were forever pouring cold water on his ideas. Dubov wasn't about to try to tell his boss whom to spend time with, but for his money Young was a charlatan, and he'd resolved to give him a wide berth. He skirted past with a gruff nod and slipped out into the London throng without a backward glance.

Young wasn't fazed by the hauteur of the Russian hangers-on. He knew Berezovsky needed him. Funds coming from Moscow raised all sorts of alarms with Western banks—especially when the recipient was wanted for industrial-scale embezzlement back home—so his job was to help the oligarch spend freely in the UK without getting snarled up in red tape. Thankfully, the British financial system was full of handy loopholes, and Young knew them well. So as Berezovsky siphoned his wealth out of Russia, Young was busy plowing it into a dazzling portfolio of British properties and cars, hiding the oligarch's ownership behind an array of hastily established shell companies, and procuring exorbitant gifts for his ever-changing coterie of girlfriends. The sums of money at his disposal were mind-bending, and the role had thrust him into a new reality so exotic that nothing and no one could take the edge off the thrill.

Berezovsky moved through the world as if he owned it—emanating wealth and entitlement so powerfully that gravity seemed to shift around him—and that was what made being his fixer such a wild ride. Wherever the oligarch went, the former French Legionnaires who served as his bodyguards swarmed around him, scanning the area and muttering urgently into their earpieces. Young had learned that few things in life made a man feel more like he'd hit the big time than striding into a room surrounded by trained killers. The same went for traveling through London in a full-blown motorcade. Berezovsky was chauffeured around town in a bulletproof Maybach, followed by a backup car full of guards and countersurveillance vehicles bringing up the rear to check that he wasn't being tailed. Up front was an outrider zooming ahead on a fluorescent motorbike to scout for potential threats and try to hold busy intersections. The rider was a good-natured South African who joked privately about the number of times he'd been knocked off his bike trying to stop the chaotic traffic at Hyde Park Corner without the authority of a police badge or beacons. Berezovsky had grown far too used to being the most powerful man in town to be prepared to sit in traffic and wait.

This need for speed was equally evident in the oligarch's choice of air transport. He had bought a Bombardier Global Express—a top-of-the-line private jet that flew farther and faster than others because it climbed at a stomach-churning clip to a higher altitude, where the air was thinner. When it wasn't employed for business, Berezovsky used the plane to meet another of his needs. He sent his pilot on regular trips to the former Soviet states to pick up bevies of escorts and fly them back to Farnborough Airport, where he would climb aboard for a few live auditions in the cabin's deluxe double bedroom. The women who made the cut were ushered into the Maybach and driven to one of London's most lavish hotels, where they were kept in the regency splendor of the royal suite for as long as they captivated Berezovsky's interest. Those who didn't pass vetting were flown back from Farnborough without setting foot on the tarmac.

Young loved reclining on the Bombardier's cream leather seats, talking business and sipping chilled Champagne with Berezovsky as they climbed through the clouds. But hovering over the daily thrill was a dark threat that refused to be ignored.

Young knew his Russian connections represented a risk, if only because his wife wouldn't let him forget it. The trouble at home had begun when Berezovsky took the Youngs out for dinner to celebrate getting the keys to the Wentworth Estate house, and Michelle blew a gasket at the sight of the fleet of armored cars and bodyguards that turned up with their host.

"This shows that he's very dangerous," she hissed in Young's ear as soon as the oligarch was out of earshot. "I don't want anything to do with that, and I don't want my daughters to have anything to do with that."

Young had tried to reassure his wife that the family was in no danger—but it didn't help when Berezovsky dropped by to talk business and his bodyguards advised Michelle to remove Sasha and Scarlet from the house for their own safety. Things got worse when she read about Berezovsky's background and found out he had narrowly survived a car bomb back in Moscow. Then she came home one day saying she had been approached by a man who claimed to work for

MI6 and warned her that her husband was getting himself in too deep with the Russians.

"You're risking your life and your family's life!" she had fumed at him. "You think you're indestructible! You think you have so much power, so much money—but no one's invincible."

Still, for all her protestations, Michelle had gotten used to traveling by private jet, holidaying on yachts, and going on seemingly never-ending shopping sprees. Young's wealth had ballooned exponentially with Berezovsky's arrival in the UK—his Coutts asset schedule now showed he was worth £279 million—and he showered her with fabulous gifts on an almost daily basis, surprising her with a £1 million diamond necklace, a Range Rover packed to the roof with couture dresses, and the keys to an ever-growing array of palatial homes across Britain and abroad. Young had suddenly become such a huge player in the British property market that the elite real estate broker Knight Frank wrote letters of recommendation describing him as "the most important single private client the firm has within the UK." And he was rubbing shoulders with some of the world's most rich and famous people.

Young and Berezovsky were invited by the Finnish billionaire and Tory donor Poju Zabludowicz to a "boys' dinner" in London with Bill Clinton, and Young had also become close friends with the retail billionaire Sir Philip Green, the Ivy group owner Richard Caring, and the reality TV mogul Simon Cowell. He boasted about flying Paris Hilton to London for dinner, and he and Michelle hung out in Miami with the pop superstar Pharrell Williams. The faint hint of danger hanging low in the air could hardly dim the brilliance of a life so bright and beautiful.

Young rode the Down Street elevator up to the second floor, cheerily greeting the unsmiling guards who parted to pull open the office doors, and strode in to find himself momentarily overwhelmed by the heavy pong of roasted hog. *Badri*. With a grin at the immaculately

Chanel-clad receptionist, he crossed the lobby to knock on the door opposite Berezovsky's.

The elegant bullet-headed man who opened it was as groomed and gleaming as ever, but he greeted Young with a smile just wide enough to crease the corners of his ice-blue eyes. Ruslan Fomichev was Boris and Badri's single most trusted money man. He had been the chairman and chief executive of the bank they established back in Moscow to manage their multifarious investments, and now he was acting as their private treasurer in London. Berezovsky always said Fomichev was the one person who knew everything about his business, and as luck would have it, the financier was the only one in the oligarch's Russian circle who had taken a shine to Young.

Fomichev was younger than the others in Berezovsky's entourage—in his midthirties—and he and his wife, Katya, had only recently relocated from Moscow. Young provided them with a perfect entrée to the London party circuit. He regularly rubbed shoulders with celebrities and young royals at the capital's glitziest nightspots, blowing tens of thousands of pounds a night at Boujis on tables lined with buckets of Belvedere vodka and Dom Pérignon, and he could work his magic to get a last-minute reservation at any restaurant, backstage access at any concert, or an invitation to any high-society party he chose. The Fomichevs were witty, glamorous, and personable, and within a few years they had ascended to number 13 on *Tatler*'s annual "100 Most Invited" list—a rung below David and Samantha Cameron.

Young and Fomichev had become fast friends, and they were soon cooking up a number of joint ventures alongside their work for Berezovsky. The tastiest of them all was a prime property deal in central Moscow. Fomichev's father was a retired KGB general, so the banker could still operate back in Russia, and he wanted to cut Young in on the action. That was a risky proposition for Berezovsky's number one British fixer, but Young was more than game. He'd developed a taste for the cloak-and-dagger thrill of Russian business during his various trips to the capital on Berezovsky's behalf—and Fomichev's city-center development could be a huge win when it came to fruition in a few years' time. For now, though, the two men had their hands full with more pressing business.

Fomichev was coordinating the helter-skelter operation to route Boris and Badri's billions out of Russia into a byzantine network of offshore accounts—which, with Young's help, Berezovsky could draw down to fund his lifestyle in Britain. The pair had siphoned vast wealth out of Logovaz and Aeroflot during Yeltsin's government—much of which was already stashed safely in their Swiss bank accounts—but now the Russian prosecutor general was pursuing corruption cases against them with escalating vigor, issuing foreign arrest warrants, seeking freeze orders on their overseas assets, and sending squads of masked officers to raid their Moscow offices.

The oligarchs were facing two major hurdles as they rushed to rescue their remaining Russian fortune: Russian currency controls limiting how many rubles could leave the country at once and Western money-laundering safeguards requiring proof that funds being brought onshore were from legitimate sources. The latter was an especially tall order for anyone who had gotten rich in the smash-and-grab days of post-Soviet Russia and was even more challenging with arrest warrants looming overhead. Circumventing those obstacles had meant enlisting the help of some of Britain's most secretive lawyers—and doing a Faustian deal with one of Moscow's most powerful men.

Paris, Moscow, and London—2000–2002

On a crisp December night in 2000, two private jets landed at Le Bourget airport, in Paris. Boris and Badri descended the steps of their respective planes and enjoyed a brief reunion in the airport's VIP lounge before the blinking lights of a third jet hovered into view through the wide window over the runway. The two oligarchs readied themselves for a critical encounter. The man they were about to meet was one of the most influential businessmen in Putin's Russia, and he held the keys to a vast slice of their fortune. They were there to persuade him to risk everything to help them get their money out of Moscow.

Roman Abramovich strode across the tarmac and entered the lounge. The soft-spoken, sandy-haired tycoon knew how much he owed the two older oligarchs. Without their political backing, he would never have won the laughably lowball bid for the former state oil giant Sibneft that had made him a billionaire overnight in the '90s. Indeed, he had been repaying that debt of gratitude handsomely ever since. Boris and Badri claimed a share of all of Sibneft's profits, and on top of that Abramovich had been subsidizing Berezovsky's lifestyle—paying for his private jet travel, buying him his villa on Cap d'Antibes, and generally slinging him such substantial sums on the side that "Project Boris" became an ever-present item in the oil giant's expense accounts.

But Abramovich had a new master. He was one of the few Yeltsin-era oligarchs who had stayed in favor under Putin, having made the judicious decision to buy the future president a yacht when his star was still rising, in 1999. Maintaining business links with Boris and Badri was unacceptably risky now and he was anxious to part ways, but he needed to do so in a manner that showed unequivocally where his new loyalties lay. So he assured Boris and Badri that he would find a discreet way to cash them out of their joint interests and get their money out of Russia, but there was something he needed from them. Before flying to Paris, he had visited the Kremlin and obtained Putin's authority to buy another of their most prized assets: their controlling stake in Russia's biggest national broadcaster.

Channel One represented Boris and Badri's only remaining political capital in Russia. The former state broadcaster, which provided the platform for many of Berezovsky's most stinging attacks on Putin, reached almost every Russian household and had a global audience in the hundreds of millions. It had come under increasing pressure to surrender to Kremlin control as Mikhail Lesin's crackdown on the independent media intensified, and its journalists had grown all too used to preparing to go live with masked FSB agents ransacking the building around them.

For Patarkatsishvili, selling to Abramovich was a no-brainer. It might just take the political heat off them while they spirited the rest of their cash out of the country. But Berezovsky was not ready to cede control of his most prized political bargaining chip easily. The value of their stake was relatively small potatoes in business terms, but the independence of Channel One infuriated Putin—and there was nothing Berezovsky enjoyed more. He had been fomenting plans to turn the broadcaster over to a trust of journalists and intellectuals, preserving a lone uncontrolled star in the increasingly Kremlin-dominated Moscow media firmament. So the trio parted without signing a deal, and Berezovsky returned to his villa on Cap d'Antibes to think things over.

The following day brought terrible news. Boris and Badri's most loyal lieutenant back in Moscow—the Aeroflot CFO, Nikolai Glushkov—had been arrested for embezzlement and thrown into the FSB's notoriously brutal Lefortovo Prison. Berezovsky was beside himself. He was consumed with guilt about leaving the faithful Glushkov at the mercy of the Kremlin after skipping out of Moscow, and he knew his friend suffered from a blood disease that could become life threatening without proper treatment. Hoping that giving up Channel One would help get Glushkov out of trouble, he took to the Moscow airwaves to announce he was abandoning the plan to turn the broadcaster over to an independent trust, and then he got on the phone to Patarkatsishvili and agreed to sell the stake to Abramovich.

Berezovsky refused to have any further dealings with Abramovich from that day forward, deputizing Dubov to finalize the terms of the sale on his behalf. Meanwhile, Fomichev was dispatched to negotiate the Sibneft payment alongside Patarkatsishvili. After a series of meetings, Abramovich agreed to pay Boris and Badri $1.3 billion to sever all ties, on top of the $154 million he had already put up for Channel One. Now all that remained was to find a way to move the money from Moscow to London without raising red flags with the authorities at both ends. That was where two of Britain's most cunning lawyers came into the picture.

Stephen Curtis was a gigantic, gregarious man from the north of England who had become a lively member of Berezovsky's Mayfair circle since he was brought on board to help Fomichev. His law firm, Curtis & Co., operated out of smart offices at the top of a tall town house on Park Lane and had built up a client base comprising some of the richest and most politically exposed people in Russia and the Middle East. Curtis was outwardly unaffected and amiable, but his genius for dreaming up elaborately deceptive financial schemes for his secretive paymasters—while somehow keeping all the details in his head to avoid an inconvenient paper trail—had made him fabulously rich in his own right. He owned a huge Gothic castle on an island off Dorset's Jurassic Coast, and a six-seater helicopter to fly him to and fro.

Whenever he could, Curtis worked in partnership with his old friend Stephen Moss, a diffident man with a confidential manner, whose role as managing partner at the reputable law firm Reid Minty made him an ideal cleanskin. Moss tended to be kept out of the loop until all the dirty work had been done, at which point Curtis could bring him in to draw up all the official paperwork needed to make things look legitimate without the burden of too much knowledge.

When the deal with Abramovich was finalized and it was time to bring the money onshore, Curtis was ready with an elegant solution. Years spent shilling for superrich clients in the Middle East had yielded all sorts of valuable connections, and he had forged an alliance with a young royal in the United Arab Emirates that was about to prove spectacularly useful. Sheikh Sultan bin Khalifa bin Zayed al Nahyan was the son of the then emir of Abu Dhabi, and he was happy to use his position to make some extra fun money.

Over a lavish dinner at Mosimann's—a London restaurant resplendent with red upholstery, crisp white tablecloths, and giant chandeliers—the young sheikh agreed that a company he controlled in the Persian Gulf could be used as a cutout to funnel the money from Abramovich's accounts in Latvia to Berezovsky in London. That way it would simply look like Abramovich had paid the sheikh and the sheikh had paid Berezovsky. British banks would be more than happy to accept the funds of an Emirati royal, and the money would be meted out in multiple tranches to avoid attracting too much attention. Abramovich didn't need to be bothered with the ins and outs of the plan—he would just be given the sheikh's bank details and told that that was where the money was to be paid. The lawyers and accountants would handle the rest.

A trust called the New World Value Fund was established to take delivery of the payments. By February of 2001, around $140 million had arrived in Boris's and Badri's UK accounts via the sheikh from the Channel One sale, with the Sibneft money to follow. But surrendering the broadcaster did nothing to help secure Glushkov's freedom. The former Aeroflot director was still languishing in Lefortovo, and while the finishing touches were still being put to the Sibneft deal that spring, a bizarre turn of events plunged him into even deeper difficulty.

Glushkov was on a hospital visit for his blood condition when, as he crossed the courtyard in his slippers, he was accosted by a man he remembered as an employee of Aeroflot. The man said he was there to get Glushkov out of jail, but as they hurried toward a car parked outside the hospital gates, a squad of plainclothes FSB officers swooped in and handcuffed them. Glushkov was charged with attempting to escape. Boris and Badri's former head of security at Channel One, a former KGB officer named Andrey Lugovoy, was later arrested for organizing the operation. Then a warrant was issued for Patarkatsishvili's arrest on suspicion of ordering the plot.

Glushkov said he had been framed, insisting that the escape attempt had been staged by the FSB to incriminate him and Patarkatsishvili, but this was the incident that sealed his fate. Though he would eventually be cleared of the original embezzlement charges, he was found guilty of the attempted escape, spending four years behind bars in Moscow before he was eventually released and fled to England to join Berezovsky in exile. Another of the accused would also show up in London after serving time for his role in the attempted escape. Andrey Lugovoy, too, would take up a trusted place in Berezovsky's circle.

As for Channel One, almost as soon as the sale was complete, the Kremlin assumed control of the airwaves. Berezovsky could not have felt more betrayed—or more determined to exact his revenge. By then, the Sibneft money was flowing onshore via the sheikh, and Berezovsky's UK accounts were flush. Russia's public enemy number one was angrier than ever—and he had the fighting fund he needed to declare war.

VI

Tony Blair had been in such a hurry to cement his special relationship with Putin after their preelection night at the opera in St. Petersburg that, unable to contain himself until after the official inauguration, in May, he invited Russia's president-elect to Downing Street almost as soon as the ballots closed.

"Vladimir Putin is a leader who's ready to embrace a new relationship with the European Union and the United States," the British prime minister declared after the meeting, in April of 2000, doing his best to ignore the disorderly band of Chechen War protesters being carted off in police vans outside Downing Street.

Putin received similarly rapturous receptions from other world leaders. Bill Clinton flew to Moscow to greet Russia's new strongman as one of his final acts as US president, brushing aside concerns over Chechnya to declare Putin "fully capable of building a prosperous, strong Russia while preserving freedom and pluralism and the rule of law." And when Clinton's successor, George W. Bush, followed suit the next year, he, too, fell hook, line, and sinker.

"I looked the man in the eye," he told reporters. "I found him very straightforward and trustworthy—I was able to get a sense of his soul."

Berezovsky was determined to disabuse the Western dupes of their trust in his former protégé. He established the International Foundation for Civil Liberties to campaign against Putin—distributing hundreds of grants to protest groups across Russia and taking out banner ads decrying the regime's human rights abuses in the international press—and hired Lord Tim Bell, Margaret Thatcher's favorite spin doctor, to help fire out his anti-Kremlin message. Now he just needed ammunition—and that was where Litvinenko came in.

The former FSB detective had been tasked with digging deeper into Putin's links to the mob and the Moscow apartment bombings with the help of two other regular Down Street visitors. Litvinenko was to work closely with Akhmed Zakayev—none other than the leader of the Chechen rebels accused by Putin of orchestrating the bombings—who had numerous sources on the ground and was determined to prove that his fighters had been framed. Zakayev, whose jagged features and ferocious beard made him look almost as fierce as he really was, had escaped Chechnya to join the growing group of dissidents living on Berezovsky's tab in England, and he was now fighting a political war remotely from a modest home in Muswell Hill, just a few doors down from Litvinenko. The other collaborator was the brilliant if endearingly clodhopping Russian historian Yuri Felshtinsky, who was there to help compile and write up the evidence.

By March of 2002, the investigators had provided Berezovsky with his first round of firepower, and the oligarch held a press conference in central London to present compelling new evidence linking Putin's security service to the Moscow bombings. Litvinenko and Felshtinsky had laid out their findings in an excoriating book titled *Blowing Up Russia,* which was serialized across twenty-two pages of the Russian investigative newspaper *Novaya Gazeta,* and it was accompanied by a documentary, the no less ambiguously titled *Assassination of Russia,* which Berezovsky screened exclusively for the assembled journalists.

A central plank of the case against Putin rested on the explosives used in the apartment blasts. After the first bomb went off, the FSB announced that traces of the highly explosive chemical hexogen had been found—an eyebrow-raising admission, given that the military-grade chemical could only be obtained from government facilities under the security agency's own control. It hadn't taken long for the FSB to realize that gaffe and change its story, but then crime scene investigators made another damaging discovery.

Explosives experts had visited the apartments in the city of Ryazan where residents had spotted two men placing fifty-kilogram sacks of powder wired to detonators in the basement, and they announced that these, too, contained hexogen. After local police had caught the two culprits and identified them as FSB officers, the security agency announced that the whole incident was a training exercise and the bags contained nothing but sugar—but the publication of *Blowing Up Russia* ripped a huge hole in that story.

The book laid out evidence that government-controlled hexogen had indeed been found in the sacks planted at Ryazan as well as in the four other bombs that had been detonated successfully elsewhere. It included testimony from a soldier who had been posted to Ryazan in the autumn of 1999, a few weeks before the bombings, to guard a government arms depot that, oddly, seemed to contain nothing but fifty-kilogram sacks labeled SUGAR. The private had used some of the white powder in his tea and was so repulsed by its acridity that he had a team of specialists test it to make sure it wasn't poison. The results, he said, revealed that the substance was hexogen.

Berezovsky told the assembled journalists that four separate explosives experts from Britain and France had independently examined the evidence from the Ryazan incident and concluded that the bomb the FSB officers were seen planting was real. Then he introduced a former director of a Russian government explosives facility who confirmed that the security service had purchased a bulk load of hexogen in the period directly before the attacks. "At a minimum Vladimir Putin knew that the FSB was involved in the bombings," Berezovsky declared.

The allegations that the Russian president had colluded in the slaughter of almost three hundred of his own people ricocheted through the British and international media. Back in Moscow, prosecutors accused Berezovsky of "financing terrorist activity" in the wake of his press conference. The book was banned and added to Russia's official list of extremist materials, and the FSB used all its powers to stop the public from learning of its incendiary contents. Theaters that attempted to show the film were shut down and their proprietors beaten up, while trucks carrying consignments of the books into Russia were pulled over by the FSB and had their cargo confiscated. But through it all, the leaders of the West remained silent.

In the corridors of intelligence agencies on both sides of the Atlantic, there was glum acknowledgment that Putin was almost certainly behind the explosions, but there was no appetite for a fight. Six months before Berezovsky's press conference, the world had been rocked by an atrocity that dwarfed the Moscow bombings—the worst terror attack on Western soil in living memory—and no one had capitalized on the fallout more effectively than Vladimir Putin.

The Russian president had been the first world leader to telephone George W. Bush to offer his condolences after the planes hit the Twin Towers on September 11, 2001.

"Russia knows directly what terrorism means," he declared in a televised address after the call, likening the Al Qaeda attack to the apartment bombings in Moscow, which he blamed on Chechen Islamists. "Because of this we, more than anyone, understand the feelings of the American people."

Two days later, in a move that would have been unthinkable during the Cold War, NATO and Russia issued a joint statement vowing to fight the scourge of terrorism. And when President Bush declared his "war on terror," Putin immediately pledged his full backing, supporting the invasion of Afghanistan by allowing the United States to ship supplies through Russia and, equally unthinkable, to use the military bases of the former Soviet Union in central Asia. At a time when the West was uniting against a terrible common foe in the form of Al Qaeda, Russia's cooperation was warmly welcomed. Putin had positioned himself at the forefront of a global fight against Islamist terror—and it played perfectly into his narrative.

In the wake of 9/11, the Russian president announced that Islamist rebels in Chechnya were being trained and funded by Al Qaeda, repeatedly likening Zakayev and other prominent separatists to Osama bin Laden. The Kremlin had long characterized its bloody suppression of Chechen separatism as a conflict with jihadist terrorists, and portraying the largely Muslim region as the first battlefield in a new global war was the perfect way to justify the brutality as reports of rape, mass slaughter, looting, and torture continued to flood out of Grozny. And the West bought it.

When Putin visited Bush at Camp David in the aftermath of the 9/11 attacks, the US president praised him for building a Russia "at peace within its borders, with its neighbors, a country in which democracy and freedom and rule of law thrive." And when Tony Blair received the Russian president at Chequers in December of 2001, he drew his own comparisons between 9/11 and the Moscow apartment bombings as the two leaders announced an intelligence-sharing deal to combat terrorism.

Putin's pivotal role in the US-led counterterrorism coalition paid many dividends—not least of which were the establishment of the NATO-Russia Council, Russia's full membership in the G8, and Western support for the country's long-sought accession to the World Trade Organization. But among the greatest rewards of Russia's centrality in the war on terror was the incentive it gave the global community to swallow the story that Chechen Islamists, and not Putin's own state security agency, were to blame for the Moscow bombings.

On the one-year anniversary of the New York attacks, six months after Berezovsky's press conference unveiling Litvinenko's findings, Putin called President Bush to renew his condolences. Then he took to the airwaves to speak directly to the Russian people.

"Recently we commemorated those who were killed in a string of blasts in apartment buildings in Moscow three years ago, and today we are also remembering those who died in Washington and New York," he said. "In Russia, they say that time cures. But we cannot forget."

The truth, as far as Alexander Litvinenko was concerned, was just the opposite. In the wake of 9/11, his evidence linking the Russian government to the mass slaughter of its own people was simply too inconvenient. And so it was that the world forgot.

London, Tbilisi, and Moscow—2002

Whether or not the West was listening, Berezovsky and his band of investigators were far from finished. After the launch of Litvinenko's findings, the group gathered in secret at Down Street to plot the next phase of their campaign—and they were joined by some valuable new allies.

In the room with Berezovsky, Litvinenko, and Felshtinsky was a pale-faced man in a rumpled suit whose permanently parted lips and wide blue eyes gave him a look of perpetual astonishment. Sergei Yushenkov was a leading light of Russia's postperestroika revolution—having organized the "living chain" of civilians who united to protect their parliament from Soviet troops during the attempted coup of 1991—and he had served energetically as an MP since the earliest days of Russia's new democracy, campaigning against human rights abuses in Chechnya with particular vigor. The veteran MP shared Berezovsky's suspicions about Putin's hand in the Moscow apartment bombings, and so he had joined Liberal Russia—a new opposition party that the oligarch was bankrolling. Three parliamentary motions for an official inquiry into the apartment bombings had been stymied by members of Unity, the party Berezovsky had established to back Putin in the 2000 election, and the oligarch was determined to rectify that mistake by using Liberal Russia to raise hell over the FSB's role in the blasts.

Yushenkov had already volunteered to use his parliamentary immunity to help distribute *Blowing Up Russia* and the accompanying documentary in Moscow, and when he arrived at Down Street, he was charged with a further mission. Since attempts to secure an official inquiry into the bombings were leading to a dead end, Yushenkov would go back to Moscow and assemble an independent commission of politicians, lawyers, and journalists to investigate the blasts under its own steam. Litvinenko and Felshtinsky would continue their investigation and supply the commission with evidence, and Yushenkov would air their findings in parliament.

There was another new collaborator to welcome to the group. The discussion had been quietly observed by a woman who was introduced by Litvinenko and Felshtinsky as Tania Morozova—a thirty-one-year-old Russian emigré to the United States whose mother had been killed in one of the Moscow blasts. Felshtinsky had found Morozova living in Wisconsin and persuaded her to come to London for the film screening. Having seen the evidence the investigators had amassed, she was convinced her mother had been murdered by the Russian government, and she signed up to help them expose the crime. As Litvinenko explained to the assembled plotters, Morozova was officially considered a victim of the attack because she had lost a relative in the blast, which gave her the right under Russian law to review the FSB's case files and to present evidence in court should any of the perpetrators ever come to trial. Her cooperation would give the plotters an inside track on the state's case.

There was one more newcomer whom Litvinenko wanted to bring into the circle of trust. It was Mikhail Trepashkin—the dogged former FSB officer whose discovery of a corrupt cabal inside the agency had made him a target of the URPO assassination plot alongside Berezovsky. Trepashkin was a phenomenal investigator who had not forgotten that he owed Litvinenko his life, and he had been helping gather local intelligence about the bombings on the ground in Moscow. He had also recently qualified as a lawyer, so it was agreed that he would become an attorney to the independent commission Yushenkov was going to set up. At the same time, Trepashkin would take on Morozova as a client, allowing him to apply for access to the FSB's files and submit evidence in court on her behalf.

Yushenkov flew back to Russia armed with dozens of copies of *Assassination of Russia,* which he distributed to reporters who met him off the plane at Moscow's Sheremetyevo Airport. "It demonstrates how the secret services deceived Russian citizens," he told them. Then he set to work assembling his commission.

In London, Litvinenko and Felshtinsky were on the cusp of a seismic breakthrough. By that time, the FSB had named its prime suspect in the bombings: a man called Achemez Gochiyayev, who had rented space in all the apartment buildings that were blown up, and shortly after Berezovsky's press conference the investigators were approached by a Chechen intermediary with a message from Russia's most wanted man. Gochiyayev was innocent, the messenger said, and he wanted to talk to the authors of *Blowing Up Russia.*

Felshtinsky, who had been handling the communications with the intermediary, met with Litvinenko, Berezovsky, and Zakayev at Down Street to brief them on the approach. The bespectacled historian was frightened. The intermediary had demanded that he travel to the lawless Pankisi Gorge, between Georgia and Chechnya, where Gochiyayev was in hiding under the protection of a band of separatists. What if this was an attempt to kidnap him and demand a ransom from Berezovsky, or an FSB trap, or a murder plot?

Unruffled, the oligarch turned to Zakayev and asked whether the Chechens were likely to murder Felshtinsky.

"I do not think they would kill him," the rebel leader replied assuringly—adding, after a moment's reflection: "They could cut his ears."

Felshtinsky's fingers flew to his earlobes. "Boris, will you pay ransom for me if I am taken hostage?" he asked anxiously.

"Of course," replied Berezovsky. "But here is the deal." Litvinenko was to go with Felshtinsky to watch his back, and Patarkatsishvili would be in charge of their security at all times on the ground in Georgia. "This is his territory—you do what he orders," Berezovsky told the two investigators firmly. "Agreed?"

"Agreed."

When Litvinenko and Felshtinsky touched down in Tbilisi late that night, they were met off the plane by a security team sent by Patarkatsishvili to guard them around the clock. Ever the professional detective, Litvinenko had insisted that they stop at a department store on the way to the airport to buy smart new briefcases in anticipation of the incriminating documents he hoped they would receive. The pair were introduced to a driver sent by Patarkatsishvili to chauffeur them everywhere, and the man conveyed them in a mini motorcade to the five-star Sheraton Metechi Palace, where guards with Kalashnikovs flanked the entrance.

Soon after they arrived, they came face-to-face with a furious Patarkatsishvili, who was livid to discover that Litvinenko had traveled to Georgia with Felshtinsky. It was one thing guaranteeing the security of an academic, but guarding an FSB defector in Russia's backyard was another task altogether. Berezovsky's loopy schemes would be the death of them all one of these days: he was sure of it. He told the two visitors he would do all he could to keep them safe in Tbilisi, but if they strayed outside the city they were on their own. Traveling to the Pankisi Gorge, the hideout of at least half of Chechnya's sizable population of guns for hire, was absolutely out of the question. They would have to get to Gochiyayev another way.

The following day, Patarkatsishvili's driver took Litvinenko and Felshtinsky to a rendezvous point in Georgia's grand central square—under the towering Freedom Monument, depicting Saint George slaying a gilded dragon. Felshtinsky tucked a copy of the *International Herald Tribune* under his arm and waited while Litvinenko and the driver kept watch from a safe distance. They were looking for a man in a green baseball cap.

When the go-between arrived, Felshtinsky promptly informed him that he could not travel to the Pankisi Gorge: Gochiyayev would simply have to come to Tbilisi. That request was flatly refused. Georgia was crawling with FSB agents, and the gorge was the one place that was too dangerous for them to go, which was what made it the only place that was safe for Gochiyayev. They were being watched right now, the man in the cap said, pointing out several cars stationed around the meeting point. To get around the stalemate, it was agreed that the go-between would take a list of questions back to the gorge and bring a videotape of the fugitive's answers back to Tbilisi the following day.

Felshtinsky and Litvinenko had a night to kill in Tbilisi, so they took their driver and security guards out for a sumptuous dinner while they waited to hear from the messenger. When the call came, the go-between told them he had been tailed most of the way back to the gorge by two cars—but he had managed to give them the slip, and the tape containing Gochiyayev's answers would be with them the following day.

Litvinenko and Felshtinsky tucked themselves into their crisp white hotel bedsheets full of anticipation. But the following morning, the two investigators were woken by their guards with infuriating news. They needed to get out of Georgia at once—on Patarkatsishvili's orders.

"I am not leaving," Felshtinsky informed them indignantly. "I am waiting for some materials. Call Badri, please."

The guard complied and handed the phone to Felshtinsky. Patarkatsishvili sounded stern. "Come to my place immediately, with your belongings."

When Litvinenko and Felshtinsky entered the ornate Georgian mansion, the oligarch's face was grave. "You should leave immediately," he said. "I have information that your life is in danger."

He had been tipped off that a contract had been taken out to kill the two investigators, and there was no time to lose.

Felshtinsky was desolate. It was too galling to have to turn back now, just as they were on the brink of hearing Gochiyayev's story. But then he had a brain wave. Perhaps the driver Patarkatsishvili had assigned to them could be sent to collect the tape from the emissary. He knew what the man looked like, after all, having taken them to the meeting the previous day.

Patarkatsishvili shook his head. "Your driver disappeared," he told them. "He brought you to the hotel yesterday, and that is the last time he was seen. We are looking for him now."

Felshtinsky froze. If the driver had been captured by the FSB, he might have spilled the beans about the reason for their trip to Tbilisi. There was no longer any doubt that they needed to get out of Georgia immediately. Patarkatsishvili ushered them into a Jeep he had waiting outside, and they sped to the airport in a security convoy, boarding the first available plane.

The next flight out of Georgia happened to go to Frankfurt, and as soon as it landed in Germany, Felshtinsky got straight on the phone to Berezovsky. They had been forced to flee without the tape, he told the oligarch ruefully, but they were on safe ground now and everything was fine.

"It is fine with you," Berezovsky replied. "But your driver was found dead."

Despite escaping with their lives, the two investigators could not shake their disappointment that they had come back empty-handed. But, days later, Gochiyayev's emissaries made contact again. The pair were invited to a meeting in Paris, where, in the grand atrium of a hotel on the Champs-Élysées, Felshtinsky was handed an envelope containing a statement in Gochiyayev's handwriting. The story of the man accused of orchestrating the Moscow bombings, when they finally read it, was every bit as devastating as the investigators had hoped.

Gochiyayev said he was innocent and had only gone on the run be-cause he feared for his life. He insisted that he had rented rooms in the apartment buildings at the request of a business associate, who had told him he needed the space to store construction materials, and he now suspected that man of working for the FSB. After the second blast, he said he had called the police to warn that there might be explosions in two other buildings where his associate had asked him to rent a room—but his information was ignored, and the associate was never named as a suspect. If that was true, it looked like Gochiyayev had been framed.

Litvinenko and Felshtinsky needed a way to present their new evidence to the public, and Yushenkov's independent commission provided the perfect forum. The politician had persuaded the ven-erated MP and human rights campaigner Sergei Kovalyov to head up the inquiry, lending independence and credibility to its work, while Yushenkov served as its vice chairman. Then he had enlisted five other MPs, along with around a dozen journalists, lawyers, and academics. Yuri Shchekochikhin, the investigative journalist who had serialized *Blowing Up Russia* in *Novaya Gazeta,* was a particularly ac-tive member, and Trepashkin was hard at work as the commission's investigative attorney.

Litvinenko and Felshtinsky testified before the commission by video link for two hours in July of 2002, revealing Gochiyayev's story in front of an audience packed with journalists. The hearing caused a sensation in Moscow. How had these two lone operators managed to hunt down the FSB's most wanted man when the entire state security apparatus had failed?

Kovalyov was at pains to be impartial—stressing that the com-mission was nowhere near a ruling on whether either Chechen Is-lamists or the FSB were responsible for the bombings—but he said Gochiyayev's statement was "of extreme interest" and must be thor-oughly examined. The task of seeking to verify the fugitive's account was assigned to Trepashkin, who had by then gained access to the FSB's case files thanks to his status as Morozova's lawyer.

Soon after the commission hearing, Litvinenko dropped another bombshell. His second book, *The Gang from the Lubyanka,* meticulously documented Putin's connections with the Tambov gang in St. Petersburg and the transformation of the FSB into a criminal organization—and it chronicled the latest discoveries in the apartment bombings investigation, including Gochiyayev's account. Trepashkin helped smuggle the text into Russia, meeting a truck carrying ten thousand copies of the book on a lonely motorway interchange from Riga one wet August afternoon and stashing the cargo in a secluded warehouse. Within days it was selling fast across Moscow. When the Kremlin banned the book and the FSB began confiscating it from retailers, Litvinenko authorized its distribution free of charge. Copies spread like wildfire across the city.

By then, thanks to the riveting public hearings of Yushenkov's commission, the theory that the FSB had carried out the apartment bombings was gaining serious traction in Moscow, even if the outside world seemed oblivious. Putin was, finally, feeling the heat. And that was when disaster struck the city again.

Moscow—October 2002

As snow fell across Moscow one night in October of 2002, almost a thousand people gathered in the warmth of the city's Dubrovka Theater to watch a popular musical. The show—an adaptation of an old Soviet story charting an orphaned boy's Arctic adventure—was enjoying a smash-hit run, and the auditorium was sold out. When the lights dimmed and the curtain rose, the stage was stormed by more than forty camouflage-clad Chechen terrorists. The militants took the entire audience and cast hostage and packed the hall with explosives before releasing their demands on videotape. Russian troops must withdraw immediately from Chechnya—or everyone would die.

The hostage taking sparked a three-day siege, with armed FSB officers surrounding the building. Zakayev appealed for calm from

Copenhagen, where he was hosting the World Chechen Congress, urging the militants to spare their captives and "refrain from rash steps." But after fifty-seven hours trapped inside, the hostages began to realize they couldn't breathe. A woman on the phone to the Echo Moscow radio station broke the news to the outside world. "They're gassing us!" she cried. "All the people are sitting in the hall. We really beg not to be gassed!"

A powerful opiate was being pumped into the auditorium from outside, knocking out the hostage takers and all their captives. When the building was silent, the FSB stormed in, shooting the unconscious militants in the head at point-blank range. Firemen and police officers carried the slumped bodies of the theatergoers out into the snowy street in their evening dress. Realizing that scores of the hostages had suffocated, swallowed their tongues, or choked to death on their own vomit, officers began throwing their bodies into buses to hide them from the television cameras. More suffocated as the dead were heaped on top of the living.

The militants had shot two hostages during the three-day siege. The remainder of the dead piling up outside the theater—more than 130 women, men, and children—had suffocated on the gas, which was pumped into the hall by the FSB. The order had come from the top.

"We have not been able to save them all," Putin acknowledged in a televised address announcing the end of the siege, which he blamed on the scourge of international terrorism. Then Tony Blair called to congratulate him on his handling of the crisis before issuing a public statement supporting the decision to gas the auditorium. "A deadly mixture of religious and political fanaticism is being pursued by those who have no compunction about taking human lives," the British prime minister said. "I hope people will understand the enormity of the dilemma facing President Putin as he weighed what to do, in both trying to end the siege with minimum loss of life and recognizing the dangers of doing anything that conceded to this latest outrage of terrorism from Chechnya."

President Bush followed suit with a public statement of support, and the coverage in the international press drew countless comparisons to 9/11. Putin awarded the FSB chief who managed the operation the title of Hero of the Russian Federation and ramped up his anti-Islamist rhetoric, vowing to strike back at "all the places where the terrorists themselves, the organizers of these crimes, and their ideological and financial inspirers are." Zakayev was accused of plotting the attack, and an Interpol Red Notice was issued for his arrest.

The rebel leader was briefly detained by the Danish authorities before being allowed to return to Britain on bail, and Russia immediately demanded that the UK government extradite him to Moscow to face trial. When Berezovsky pledged to fund Zakayev's legal fight against being sent back to Moscow, Russian prosecutors followed up with a demand for the UK government to extradite the oligarch, too.

Zakayev was furious that the terrorists had struck so savagely in the name of Chechnya, just as exoneration for the apartment bombings had seemed at last within reach. But then, as he read the coverage of the attack in the Moscow press, it began to strike him that certain key aspects of the story just didn't add up.

For a start, the men who had carried out the attack were known extremists who were kept under constant surveillance by the FSB—so how had they been allowed to travel to the capital, armed to the eyeballs with assault rifles and TNT, and muster outside a packed theater without being intercepted? Whichever way he looked at it, that just didn't square. Then, as he read through a list of the forty hostage takers that had been published in the Moscow press, his eye locked on a single name.

Khanpash Terkibaev was a notorious figure in Grozny, a shadowy character who had wormed his way in and out of so many separatist cells, both in Chechnya and its foreign diaspora, that the region's leaders strongly suspected him of working for the FSB as an agent provocateur. When Zakayev put out feelers on the ground in Grozny, he got word that Terkibaev had resurfaced soon after the siege, attempting to infiltrate another separatist faction by boasting of his role in the hostage taking. The official story was that all the militants had been killed when the FSB stormed the building—but it seemed that Terkibaev was the one who got away. If he really was a state agent and had been allowed to escape to continue his work, then it looked like the FSB had left its fingerprints on yet another terrorist atrocity in Moscow.

At Berezovsky's request, Yushenkov's commission announced that it would be expanding its inquiry to examine evidence of possible state involvement in the Moscow theater siege. Zakayev had passed all his information about Terkibaev to Litvinenko, who set about making his own inquiries, and when Yushenkov traveled to London in April of 2003, the defector handed over a file of evidence he had assembled on the suspected agent provocateur. What they needed to take the investigation further was someone who knew how to operate in Chechnya's treacherous rebel strongholds and who had the guts to go after a violent extremist with disturbing state security links. Everyone agreed there was only one woman for that job.

Anna Politkovskaya worked for *Novaya Gazeta,* which by then was one of the country's few remaining truly independent publications. The wiry, iron-haired reporter had spent years filing dispatches from the front line in Chechnya and had an unparalleled source network on the ground. During the siege, she'd used the trust she'd built among the separatists to get inside and interview the leader of the hostage takers, entering the theater shouting, "I am Politkovskaya! I am Politkovskaya," and then stayed on the scene to aid the negotiations by passing messages from the militants to the FSB lines outside. There was no one bolder. When Yushenkov returned to Moscow, he gave her Litvinenko's Terkibaev file and she got going on the story. Then he went back to work for his commission, which was now examining government links to not one but two terrorist atrocities in the Russian capital.

Days later, as the MP parked his car outside his Moscow apartment building and stepped out into the April sunshine, three shots were fired without a sound. When police arrived, they found the pistol and its silencer on the pavement next to the lifeless body of one of the Kremlin's most vocal critics.

Ten days after the assassination of Sergei Yushenkov, Politkovskaya published her story. She had succeeded in tracking down Terkibaev and persuaded him to give her an interview. The last militant left standing after the Moscow theater siege had blown the lid off everything.

Terkibaev confirmed that he had been in the theater. He said he had led the terrorists into the auditorium and ducked out just before the attack. He told Politkovskaya up front that he was an agent of the FSB. And then he went even further than anyone suspected he would. He was, he said, a consultant to the Kremlin.

No one quite understood what had possessed Terkibaev to take his life into his hands by giving up the goods to Politkovskaya. Eight months after the interview, he was killed in a car crash in Chechnya— but his story was already out there. If what he told Politkovskaya was true, it would suggest the Moscow siege had been whipped up by the FSB to vilify the Chechen rebels and burnish Putin's strongman image as he vowed to strike back.

That suspicion was impossible for the leaders of the West to stare in the face, even if they wanted to. How could they credit it when they had already praised Putin's handling of the siege? How could they countenance the idea that the Russian government might have incited the attack when they had already justified the decision to gas 130 Russians as a proportionate response to the bloodthirsty actions of Islamist terrorists?

In June, two months after Yushenkov was shot dead, Putin was welcomed to Britain on a state visit. The Russian president received a twenty-one-gun royal salute before riding down the Mall to

Buckingham Palace next to the queen in a gilded horse-drawn carriage. It marked the start of four days of sumptuous state banquets, guards of honor, and royal processions—the first time a Russian head of state had received such a welcome since Czar Nicholas I traveled to London in 1844. The coverage in the now thoroughly tamed Moscow media was rapturous. "The kind of reception President Putin is enjoying in Britain is truly fit for a king," one tabloid gushed. "Neither Boris Yeltsin nor Mikhail Gorbachev had the honor of being invited by the queen herself." All the pundits agreed that the spectacle was a major boon to Putin's hopes of reelection the following year.

There were a few attempts to spoil the party. Amnesty International and other human rights groups strained to be heard over the pomp as they tried again to highlight the reports of rape, torture, and mass killing by Russian forces in Chechnya. But no one who mattered was really listening.

Blair and Putin held private talks at Downing Street and attended an energy conference in London focusing on opportunities for British firms in Russia, including plans for a gas pipeline from Siberia to western Europe. The British prime minister was bright-eyed with brio at the end of the four-day visit. "President Putin's leadership offers hope to Russia and the whole world," he enthused afterward.

Back in Moscow, the clamor for answers over the FSB's hand in the two terror attacks was noticeably subdued. Yushenkov's death was widely acknowledged as a political hit, and few people were prepared to pay that high a price for the truth. The work of his commission had already slowed to a near stop when, three months after his assassination, death struck again.

Yuri Shchekochikhin, the *Novaya Gazeta* journalist who had serialized *Blowing Up Russia* before becoming a key member of Yushenkov's inquiry, was stricken by a mysterious illness. Red blotches appeared all over his skin, his hair fell out, and his internal organs began to fail.

When he died, sixteen days later, the authorities seized his body and his autopsy was conducted in secret at an FSB hospital. His family was told he died from an allergic reaction, but they were denied access to his medical records, which had been classified.

With two of its key members dead, the commission saw its work investigating the apartment bombings grind to a halt. Only Trepashkin continued his solitary quest for answers.

The FSB's prime suspect had gone dark, but Trepashkin kept digging through the agency's case files on Gochiyayev. After the blast on Guryanova Street, in which Morozova's mother had been killed, local police had produced a sketch of a man suspected of planting the bomb, based on a description provided by the manager of the apartments. But Trepashkin noticed it had rapidly been withdrawn and replaced with an image of an entirely different face. The second sketch was now famous: the man it depicted had quickly been identified as Gochiyayev, whose image had been plastered all over every newspaper and TV station when he was named as the mastermind of the bombings. But strangely, all copies of the original police sketch had vanished from the FSB's files.

Trepashkin was determined to track down the first drawing, so he began delving through old press clippings in case it had been published anywhere when it was first released. After much trawling, there it was: a picture of a dark-haired bespectacled man in his midthirties printed on the yellowing pages of a newspaper published the day after the first blast. With a jolt, Trepashkin realized that he recognized the face. It was one of his former colleagues from the Lubyanka.

Vladimir Romanovich was an FSB agent who specialized in cracking Chechen cells in Moscow's criminal underworld, and he had been part of the corrupt network Trepashkin had stumbled upon before being added to the URPO hit list. In front of him, in black and white, was evidence that the man initially suspected of planting the bomb on Guryanova Street had worked for the FSB.

There was no hope of compelling Romanovich to confess his role in the attack, because he, like Terkibaev, had since been killed in a car crash. But Trepashkin tracked down the building manager whose description had been used to create the sketch and asked him which of the two men he had really seen. Not only did the witness confirm that Romanovich was the man he had spotted acting suspiciously before the bombings, he also made another striking revelation. Two days after he provided the description to the local police, he was apprehended by officers from the FSB, who dragged him to an interrogation suite at Lefortovo Prison. There they showed him a photograph of Gochiyayev and compelled him to give a new statement declaring this was the man he had seen.

This was the strongest evidence yet that the FSB's main suspect had been framed. Trepashkin had an opportunity to present his findings on Morozova's behalf at the trials of two suspects that Russian prosecutors had charged with plotting the bombings alongside Gochiyayev, which were scheduled to start in October. But he knew how the FSB worked after decades in its service, and he was braced for trouble. As an insurance policy, he handed all his files to a journalist he knew in Moscow with the instruction to publish them if anything should happen to him before the trials.

Sure enough, a week before the hearings began, Trepashkin was arrested. FSB officers swooped in on his car and announced they had found an illegal firearm. Trepashkin insisted it had been planted there, but then he was thrown in jail on a separate charge of "revealing state secrets." He would remain behind bars for four years.

The journalist published the evidence about Romanovich as requested, but the story barely raised a whimper in the wider Russian press. Mikhail Lesin's media crackdown had put almost every big newspaper, TV channel, and radio station under Kremlin control. The trials went ahead in secret, and without a jury. The two men the FSB had accused of perpetrating the bombings were sentenced to life in prison.

With so little fuss in the Moscow media, the trials tidied away be-hind closed doors, and no one to take up the cudgels in the Russian parliament, it was easier than ever for world leaders to continue their backslapping diplomacy with Putin. But Litvinenko's investigation was beginning to make waves in other quarters. Inside their green and gold headquarters on the banks of the river Thames, the Russia watchers at MI6 were paying attention.

VII

London—2003–4

The graying charcoal-suited ops boss had worked for Britain's secret intelligence service since his early twenties. He had that in common with most of his graying charcoal-suited colleagues: they had almost all received the tap on the shoulder at Oxbridge and seen their whole adult lives swallowed up by the service. Spies had to blend in, which was why everyone he passed in the corridor was so uniformly faceless. It was a funny thing, to be handpicked to serve queen and country by virtue of being utterly unremarkable—but that was the nature of the job. And everyone inside the River House knew full well that they were unremarkable in appearance alone.

The headquarters of MI6 at 85 Albert Embankment housed some of the most capacious minds in the country. The men and women who worked there were entrusted with collecting and analyzing impossible quantities of information about the state of the world, helping the government advance British interests, and, most critically, guarding against threats to the nation. It was their job to know just about everything—and to find out about everything else.

The ops boss had done his time spying for Britain all over the world before returning to London to join the ranks of the desk jockeys. His new job involved overseeing the increasingly thorny business of intelligence capture on Russia, and he didn't like the way things were going in Moscow. The problem was that no one in central government wanted to hear it.

In the aftermath of 9/11, ever more national security resources were being swallowed up by what he described privately as the "relentless maw" of counterterrorism, and the Russia desk was having to do more with less. Budgets were being slashed, country experts were being redeployed to monitor the Middle East, and ever fewer new recruits were Russophones as the building filled with speakers of Arabic, Urdu, and Pashto. Central government's sole security focus was on protecting the public from a major Islamist attack on British soil, making it a constant battle to persuade Whitehall to spend serious money on gathering intelligence inside Russia. The ops boss couldn't fault the focus on the clear and present danger posed by Al Qaeda, but he had his eye on the Moscow horizon, where he was sure a deadly storm was forming.

He and his colleagues had been gathering string on the Moscow bombings and observing Litvinenko's work with keen interest. They were as sure as they could be, without intercepting an outright confession, that Putin had a hand in the attacks. That, along with the new president's media crackdown, his assault on Russia's young democratic mechanisms, and his brutal suppression of Chechen separatism added to the emerging picture of an alarmingly ruthless new autocracy. And it was all too clear to the ops boss that the global glad-handing of Putin was misconceived. The intelligence from sources close to the Kremlin indicated that the man inside had nothing but hatred for the West. He might be smiling and shaking hands today, but what was he plotting for tomorrow?

There was no doubt that Putin was using targeted assassination as a tactic to silence his critics at home, but what really worried the ops boss was the evidence that the Russian president was laying the groundwork for a wider campaign of killing. The intelligence from Britain's dwindling listening posts and sources in Russia showed that Putin was personally overseeing a program to adapt Soviet-era weapons of mass destruction for use against individual enemies of the state.

Russia had promised to destroy its forty-thousand-ton arsenal of chemical and biological weapons in 1993, when it signed on to the Chemical Weapons Convention, but MI6 had known for years that the Kremlin was cheating on that promise. Attempts to use the stockpile in battlefield conditions had been abandoned after it turned out that airborne chemicals were too easily blown off course by the weather, making them hopelessly imprecise as weapons of war, while the bugs and germs in the biological arsenal didn't take well to being propelled through the air and landing with a bang. But the Russia watchers had been studying the goings-on at a top-secret FSB lab outside Moscow, where it was clear that the government's army of military scientists was moving quickly toward developing a suite of chemical, biological, and nuclear weapons for use in targeted assassinations.

The use of elaborate poisons to liquidate enemies of the state had long been in the KGB playbook, but this new program the FSB was advancing under Putin's aegis was much more sophisticated. The nerve agents, deadly germs, and radioactive poisons being refined in the lab were designed to kill without leaving a trace. They could be administered orally, in sprays, or in vapors to trigger fast-acting cancers, heart attacks, or multiple organ failure, allowing the FSB's specialist hit squads to eliminate a target while making it look like the victim had simply succumbed to a sudden illness or died a natural death. It seemed unlikely that Putin would go to all that trouble just to do a bit of weeding in his own backyard. The Russian president must be preparing something big.

The ops boss couldn't help but feel that the concurrence of 9/11 with the flight of Berezovsky and his band of dissidents to Britain was deeply unfortunate timing. The UK had taken its eye off the ball just as all Russia's troubles turned up on home soil. But every ill wind blows some good—and the arrival of a wave of politically hot Russians on the doorstep of the River House made sourcing a whole lot easier in these times of budgetary constraint.

Among the hottest of the new arrivals was Litvinenko. The defector not only had recent working knowledge of Russia's all but impenetrable state security agency, he was also still being paid by Berezovsky to run sources and turn up new leads in Moscow. The Russia watchers wanted in on that action. So it was that, in mid-2003, Litvinenko received an approach from a graying man in a charcoal suit who wanted to know if he was prepared to help the country he now called home. The defector had already been thoroughly debriefed when he was accepted into Britain and granted political asylum, but now MI6 wanted to bring him into active service as a consultant on the connections between the Kremlin and organized crime.

Litvinenko leaped at the chance. His new handler introduced himself as Martin and gave him an encrypted phone. The pair began meeting regularly in locations as studiedly unremarkable as the basement café at Waterstones on Piccadilly. Once he had proved his worth, the defector was told he would receive a monthly stipend of £2,000—a tidy supplement to the income he got from his work for Berezovsky. And now he was no longer just a private sleuth pursuing an angry oligarch's personal vendetta. Alexander Litvinenko was working for queen and country.

Berezovsky was enraged by the West's refusal to publicly acknowledge the evidence his investigators had amassed against Putin. But Litvinenko's new role at MI6 was encouraging, and even if the Kremlin did succeed in hiding the truth about the apartment bombings, the oligarch still had plenty of other schemes up his sleeve.

He had become a key financier of a project to transcribe a batch of secret recordings of Leonid Kuchma, the pro-Kremlin president of Ukraine, who had been caught on tape plotting various crimes, including the kidnapping and murder of a dissident journalist. Hundreds of Kuchma's conversations had been clandestinely recorded by his former bodyguard and released publicly. The cassette scandal, as it came to be known, sparked waves of protest across Ukraine and laid the ground for the Orange Revolution, which would ultimately topple Putin's pet government in Kiev. The tapes also contained damaging references to the Russian president's links to major mafia groups, including the Tambov gang in St. Petersburg, and Berezovsky enlisted Litvinenko to help make sense of the materials.

That dovetailed very happily with the work the defector was doing for MI6. Litvinenko's handlers had deployed him to assist their counterparts in various European intelligence agencies who were probing connections between the Kremlin and Russian organized crime gangs spreading their tentacles into the West. He began passing officials in Spain and Italy information he had gleaned from the Kuchma tapes—and from his own investigations—about Putin's links to the mob.

Meanwhile, Zakayev was still digging for information on the Moscow bombings and theater siege. He established a war crimes commission to investigate the FSB's involvement in the two terror attacks as well as in Russian human rights abuses throughout Chechnya, and he enlisted Litvinenko to help. The rebel leader and the FSB defector had both become admirers of Anna Politkovskaya since her handling of the Terkibaev story, and they persuaded her to help them dig for new evidence in Moscow and Grozny. The goal was to try to gather enough proof of Putin's complicity in the attacks to bring a case at the International Criminal Court.

While those struggles continued, Berezovsky and Zakayev had another big fight with the Kremlin on their hands. The Russian government was ramping up its demands that both exiles be extradited to Moscow to face trial—Zakayev for his alleged role in the theater siege and Berezovsky on embezzlement charges. Recent events had left them in no doubt that resisting this request was a matter of life and death.

The threats started arriving almost as soon as the exiles got settled in Britain. Litvinenko was the first to receive an ominous phone call. It came from a former URPO comrade who had been instructed to pass on a message: Litvinenko must come back to Russia at once, or die.

"If you don't return yourself then you'll either be brought back in a body bag or you'll be pushed under the train," the man said.

Litvinenko kept his cool. "This is a very nice offer," he replied, "but I refuse it."

The next warning had come via Trepashkin. After meeting a source with high-level FSB links in Moscow shortly after the release of *Blowing Up Russia,* the investigator had emailed Litvinenko in haste. "He stated that you are 'sentenced' to extrajudicial elimination," Trepashkin cautioned, "meaning that you definitely will be killed after publication of your last book."

The warnings continued, but Litvinenko wasn't too worried. He had successfully petitioned the Home Office to grant his whole family political asylum within months of arriving in London, and that meant he could never be extradited to Russia, no matter how much that enraged his former colleagues. He told his friends he had never felt as safe as he did on British soil.

It was Berezovsky's turn next. A month after he held the press conference announcing Litvinenko's findings about the apartment bombings, in March of 2002, he received the first in a series of poison-pen letters from Russia. The missive was signed with the pseudonym Petr Petrovich, and it gave London's Highgate Cemetery as its return address. It included a little-known quotation from the French philosopher Michel de Montaigne—"There is no place on earth where death cannot find us"—and warned: "Try to understand that everything you have been doing recently is a pulse of death, a heartbeat of death for you and your next of kin."

Berezovsky responded flippantly, sending the letter and a reply addressed directly to Putin to *Kommersant,* the paper he had once owned back in Moscow. "The preciosity of your letter makes it absolutely obvious that you, kind sir, have become seriously addicted to Mister Hexogen," he jibed at the Russian president, in a reference to the chemical explosives used in the Moscow bombings. "Hex corrupts not less than—I would dare to say, even more than—coke and cash. It is time to get cured." The paper's new editors declined to run the risk of publishing either the original threat or Berezovsky's taunting response—but thereafter a steady stream of menacing letters from Russia kept landing on the oligarch's doormat.

"Petr Petrovich encourages his clients to imagine vivid scenarios of their own death: the sensations, the pain, the panic, the helplessness, the grief of loved ones," one threatened. "As Vladimir Putin said: 'Oligarchs spend all their lives preparing, preparing, preparing...only to meet death unprepared.'"

Berezovsky was initially unruffled by what he saw as a barrage of empty threats from the Kremlin. He was narcissistic enough to half believe he was immortal, and he had developed an ardor for the British justice system that verged on obsession, so he was convinced that the courts would shield him from the summons to stand trial back in Moscow. As long as he remained in Britain, he was sure he was safe. Not even Putin would be so brazen as to start whacking his enemies on the turf of another foreign power.

But then the oligarch's security detail received a tip—a live plot to kill Berezovsky was being set in motion in Russia. And this wasn't going to be any conventional hit: the plan was to poison him in Britain using one of the radioactive substances being developed at the FSB's lab outside Moscow. The tip came from a well-placed source with serious FSB contacts, and while it was impossible to verify, the threat was far too dangerous to be ignored. The oligarch's security team obtained a Geiger counter and began sweeping ahead to check for radiation every time he entered his car, home, or office.

And it was then, just after Berezovsky had publicly accused the FSB of involvement in the Moscow theater siege, and while preparations for Putin's state visit gathered pace in Whitehall, that the security he enjoyed in Britain began to unravel. His application for political asylum, submitted soon after his arrival in the country on the basis that his life was at risk in Russia, was rejected by the Home Office in March of 2003. And the following week, the oligarch was arrested.

Scotland Yard detectives brought both Berezovsky and Yuli Dubov in for questioning on behalf of Moscow prosecutors seeking their extradition over alleged embezzlement at Logovaz. Both men insisted the fraud charges were politically motivated, and they were allowed to leave police custody on £200,000 bail paid by Stephen Curtis and Berezovsky's PR man, Tim Bell, but they were booked to appear at Bow Street magistrates' court for an extradition hearing in early April. Suddenly the threats in those poison-pen letters felt far more real.

If the judge decided to extradite Berezovsky the following month, the oligarch would be left entirely at the mercy of the Kremlin. He was in no doubt that Putin wanted him dead—but to have any hope of remaining in Britain, Berezovsky needed to prove it. His lawyers were hurriedly preparing an appeal against the refusal to grant him asylum, but they had told him the sheaf of threatening letters was worthless without proof of who sent them. He needed to get his hands on hard evidence linking the threats directly to the Russian state. But how?

The oligarch was turning this problem over in his head one morning, when the large figure of Yuri Felshtinsky lumbered into view.

"I received a letter from FSB threatening to kill me," Berezovsky told the historian. "Do you want to read it?"

"Of course!" Felshtinsky took the letter in his big hands, and a look of recognition arched his eyebrows as he scanned its contents. "Boris," he said emphatically. "I have read this letter before."

"This is impossible," Berezovsky said sharply. But the historian was adamant. The same letter, he said, had been shown to him by Oleg Kalugin, a prominent KGB general who had moved to the United States and was now living under CIA protection in Washington. The letter received by Kalugin the previous December was strikingly similar—it referred to Petr Petrovich and included the same quotation from Montaigne—the main difference being the return address, which this time was a large public cemetery in Washington rather than London.

Berezovsky got straight on the phone to his lawyers. The fact that another enemy of the Russian state had received a nearly identical threat was, surely, evidence that both letters emanated from the Kremlin's security apparatus. His lawyer instructed an expert to examine the contents of all the letters both Berezovsky and Kalugin had received in order to map their similarities and see what could be deduced about their provenance. And then, on the eve of his court date, Berezovsky received fresh intelligence from Moscow.

The oligarch's security detail had been tipped off that the FSB had sent an assassin to kill Berezovsky when he turned up for the extradition hearing. A hired hit man was to be stationed next to the aisle in the public gallery at Bow Street magistrates' court, ready to strike when Berezovsky entered. His lethal weapon was a poison-tipped fountain pen.

The information was specific enough to be passed to Scotland Yard, which sent plainclothes detectives down to the courtroom on the morning of the hearing. The officers waited until the public gallery was full before discreetly apprehending the would-be assassin, who was removed from the building and later deported.

Buoyed by this eleventh-hour vindication, the oligarch swept into court in an immaculate black suit and purple silk tie, flanked by his army of bodyguards. "He lives in fear of assassination by those loyal to the Russian government," the oligarch's lawyer told the court, describing the case brought by Moscow prosecutors as a politically motivated "sham." Judge Timothy Workman agreed to let Berezovsky out on bail once more while his asylum appeal was processed.

The oligarch left court elated and donned a Vladimir Putin mask to barrel through the hordes of journalists outside. His motorcade swept toward the Méridien hotel in Piccadilly, where he held one of

The superfixer Scot Young
on holiday with his wife,
Michelle, and their daughters,
Sasha and Scarlet.

Boris Berezovsky (center), known in Russia as the "godfather of the oligarchs," fled to Britain after falling afoul of Vladimir Putin and used his vast wealth to fight a long-distance war with the Kremlin. *(Getty Images)*

The mansion on the Wentworth Estate that Berezovsky bought from Young after fleeing Russia in 2001.

The Georgian oligarch Badri Patarkatsishvili arriving at Berezovsky's sixtieth birthday party at Blenheim Palace. The pair were inseparable friends and business partners.

Former KGB officer Andrey Lugovoy turned up at the palace by bus, a shabby brown corduroy coat slung over his dinner suit.

Young (right) arriving at Blenheim Palace with Ruslan Fomichev—Berezovsky's chief financier—and Fomichev's wife, Katya. The pair's real estate development in the Russian capital, Project Moscow, was already on the rocks.

The FSB defector and dissident Alexander Litvinenko entering the palace with his wife, Marina.

Yuri Felshtinsky making his entrance. The Russian historian was hard at work alongside Litvinenko investigating FSB links to a series of terrorist atrocities in Russia.

Berezovsky (left) and Patarkatsishvili greeting one another as guests drank pink champagne by a roaring fire.

Young (right) embracing Berezovsky as the old Logovaz director Yuli Dubov sidled by to their left.

Young was not looking quite himself at the party. His dark curls around his collar were slightly slick with sweat, his bow tie was askew, and his eyes were glazed.

Fomichev chatted easily with the party guests, but he was feeling intense pressure from Moscow as his city-center development fell apart.

Berezovsky was in his element as the big man at the party—embracing everyone, toasting mother Russia, and showering his loyal followers with largesse.

The Chechen rebel leader Akhmed Zakayev (center) presenting his benefactor with a carefully wrapped samurai sword as the birthday festivities drew to a close.

his press conferences with a live satellite link to Moscow. He was under strict instructions from Scotland Yard not to mention the foiled murder plot at Bow Street, but he could barely suppress his glee as he told the packed room that he was grateful to live in a country with a "truly independent" judicial system, a country where the extradition request against him had "zero" chance of succeeding.

Berezovsky's lawyers, meanwhile, now had evidence of a live assassination plot to bolster his asylum appeal. They also sent the Home Office a statement from the expert they had hired to examine the menacing letters—a US-based KGB defector named Yuri Shvets, who had trained with Putin at the state security academy in Leningrad. Shvets asserted that, in his professional opinion, the missives constituted "a clear warning that if Berezovsky does not stop challenging the Russian regime and the FSB in particular, he will be killed, even if he resides in a foreign state." He continued: "Given [the] almost pathological importance given to Boris Berezovsky by the Russian leadership and security services it is not far-fetched to say that he can be easily assassinated in Britain."

In September of 2003, the home secretary, David Blunkett, granted Berezovsky political asylum. The Russian government reacted furiously to the move, accusing Britain of trampling the rule of law and refusing to drop its extradition proceedings against the oligarch.

Scotland Yard had privately informed Judge Workman that continuing to hold hearings at Bow Street posed a risk to Berezovsky's life. He threw out the extradition request—ruling that the government's decision to grant Berezovsky asylum made the proceedings moot.

Zakayev's extradition case came up before the same judge a few weeks later. The Russian government had by then racked up thirteen charges against the rebel leader, including murder and kidnapping. But the state's case began to unravel when a key witness flipped and told the court he had been tortured into signing a statement implicating Zakayev. The judge rejected the extradition request on the grounds that it was politically motivated and that Zakayev would be at risk of inhumane treatment in Russia. "I have come to the inevitable conclusion that if the authorities are prepared to resort to torturing witnesses, there is a substantial risk that Mr. Zakayev himself would be subject to torture," Judge Workman said. "It would be unjust and oppressive to return Mr. Zakayev to stand his trial in Russia." Hailing the ruling as a "small victory," the rebel leader used his moment in the spotlight to tell journalists he would not rest until Putin stood trial at the International Criminal Court for atrocities against the Chechen people.

The Kremlin lashed out at the court's decision. A spokesperson said the ruling reflected "the politics of double standards known from the period of the Cold War," accusing the British government of harboring extremists and threatening to roll back counterterrorism cooperation with London. Diplomats scrambled to explain that the government held no sway over the courts, but that was not a notion Putin readily understood.

Russia's three most prominent antagonists in Britain were now beyond the reach of prosecutors in Moscow. If the Kremlin wanted to put a stop to their relentless provocations, extrajudicial measures were the only remaining option.

Stephen Moss had become increasingly uneasy about his work for Berezovsky as the oligarch's attacks on the Kremlin grew more vociferous. The lawyer got more withdrawn as the date for the final Sibneft payment approached, and when friends asked what was troubling him, he confided that he was afraid. He wouldn't say why, but he thought his life might be in danger.

Moss left the country with his wife and young children for a welcome holiday in Italy while Berezovsky was fighting extradition. He came home shortly after the case against the oligarch was thrown out by Judge Workman and seemed more relaxed as he enjoyed an afternoon at the races in Surrey with a small group of friends. Three days later, he was dead.

The news that Moss had been killed by a sudden heart attack at the age of forty-six caused alarm in Berezovsky's circle. The lawyer's friends suspected that he had been whacked, and their fears deepened when they heard that Moss's home had been broken into soon after his death. The intruders didn't touch any of the family's valuables, they heard, but they had taken the lawyer's computers. And just as he was trying to figure out what secrets might have been stored on his partner's hard drives, Stephen Curtis started receiving menacing phone calls from Russia.

"Curtis, where are you?" said a man with a thick Russian accent in one voice mail. "We are here. We are behind you. We follow you." The messages kept coming, no matter how often Curtis changed his number. He hired a team of bodyguards and had a panic room installed inside his Dorset castle. The lawyer had more reason than most in Berezovsky's circle to watch his back: he was now deeply embroiled in the perilous business affairs of a second oligarch who had found himself on the wrong side of Putin.

Mikhail Khodorkovsky was the owner of the $15 billion oil giant Yukos, which made him the richest man in Russia, and his arrest in October of 2003 had proved that no one was too big to be brought down by the Kremlin. The oil baron's career-ending mistake had been to challenge Putin over government corruption at a public meeting, resulting in his imprisonment on spurious fraud charges in a Siberian labor camp, where he would remain for a decade. It then fell to Curtis, Khodorkovsky's longtime lawyer, to try to save Yukos as its owner fumed behind bars.

The Kremlin had frozen all shares in the oil giant and hit it with crippling backdated tax bills, threatening to wipe out almost all its value with a single stroke. Curtis had joined forces with one of the company's cofounders, Yuri Golubev, who had come to London after Khodorkovsky's arrest, and the two men were fighting a rear-guard action to defend Yukos against the Russian government's attacks.

At the same time, Curtis was helping Fomichev plow the $1.3 billion Boris and Badri had received from Roman Abramovich into a bewildering network of offshore funds and investments—keeping the details in his photographic memory to avoid a paper trail. He was making more money than ever out of his Russian clients and had acquired Scot Young's habit of splashing tens of thousands of pounds a night on vintage Champagne and private lap dances in the VIP rooms of exclusive London nightclubs. But his ballooning wealth went hand in hand with suffocating levels of stress.

Curtis's nerves—and his manners—were fraying. No longer the jovial, easygoing northerner who had first joined Berezovsky's circle, he had become increasingly irritable and imperious as the pressure mounted and the threatening messages grew more frequent. And in January of 2004, a bizarre incident served to compound his fears.

On a bracing January night in the picturesque Hertfordshire village of Furneux Pelham, an eighty-three-year-old Second World War veteran named Lieutenant Colonel Robert Workman opened the door of his clapboard cottage to a mystery caller. The man on the doorstep was carrying a sawed-off shotgun, and he fired a single shot at point-blank range. The villagers were all warmly ensconced for the night in their timber-framed cottages, so the colonel's corpse lay undiscovered until morning. By the time he was found, the killer had long since dissolved into the darkness.

The assassination in the sleepiest recesses of the home counties was a mystery that remained unsolved and perplexed the villagers of Furneux Pelham for almost a decade. No one could understand who could possibly have had a motive to murder the elderly veteran. But as Hertfordshire police struggled to make sense of the crime, they made a connection. Lieutenant Colonel Workman shared his surname with a man who made a much more likely target: the extradition judge who had recently enraged the Kremlin by refusing to send Berezovsky and Zakayev back to Moscow. Judge Workman, who lived in the nearby home county of Berkshire, was warned by detectives that he might have been the intended victim of the hit.

When Berezovsky heard of the killing, he was certain that the Kremlin had made a bungled attempt to exact its revenge on the judge who had granted him and Zakayev safe haven in Britain. After all, members of the judiciary in Russia who refused to bend to Putin's will might very well find themselves on the wrong end of a sawed-off shotgun: that was how the president had his enemies convicted of spurious crimes with such ease. If this was a state-sponsored hit, it clearly wasn't a sophisticated one, but perhaps some local hoodlum had been hired for the job and got his wires crossed. "Close connection between the FSB and the Russian organized crime is a fact," the ex-KGB man Shvets had written in his expert statement in support of Berezovsky's asylum application. "A low-level FSB officer can instruct a professional criminal to kill anybody in the UK, and it will be done without any paper trail."

Years later, the veteran's killer was finally caught. It was a local ratcatcher named Christopher Docherty-Puncheon, who was serving time for another murder when he told his cell mate that it was he who had shot Lieutenant Colonel Workman. He was a hired gun, he said, and had killed the colonel for cash. Docherty-Puncheon was convicted of the murder in November of 2012—but he never revealed who had paid him.

Berezovsky's circle was rattled by the killing. Curtis, who was receiving menacing phone calls with ever greater frequency and was certain that his car was being followed, was now petrified. By February of 2004, he was sufficiently scared to approach Britain's National Criminal Intelligence Service and offer to become an informant in return for government protection. He was assigned a handler and met the official twice to discuss what he knew about the activities of his Russian clients in London. But his fears were not allayed. At the end of the month, Curtis told a friend: "If anything happens to me in the next few weeks, it will not be an accident."

The following week, on March 3, 2004, he boarded his brand-new six-seater Agusta helicopter at Battersea Heliport on a clear spring evening and climbed into the London skies, bound for his Dorset castle. By the time the aircraft was on the approach to Bournemouth Airport, half an hour later, a light rain was falling. As the pilot radioed air traffic control for permission to land, the helicopter suddenly plunged sharply to the left, falling four hundred feet. The pilot struggled to regain control, but the Agusta nose-dived as the engine lost power, sending a thirty-foot fireball into the air as it smashed headlong into a field. Both Curtis and his thirty-four-year-old pilot were killed instantly.

Local police quickly determined that there was nothing for them to investigate. The inquest, a routine judicial inquiry to determine the cause of death, ruled that the crash was an accident—though the coroner acknowledged that the case had "all the ingredients for an espionage thriller." But despite the public insistence that Curtis's death was nonsuspicious, the Russia watchers in the River House were on the case.

The spies at MI6 were gathering intelligence suggesting that both Curtis and Moss might have been assassinated, and they asked for help from their partners in the United States. Such requests are sent by telex through security-cleared officials at the US embassy in London, and the responses come via the same route. US spy agencies confirmed that they had information linking both deaths to Russia stored in their classified databases, and they were happy to share it with their counterparts in London. The intelligence suggesting Russian involvement in the fatalities was considered "strong," the American spies said—particularly in relation to Curtis.

The problem was that the information came from the same web of sources and listening posts that were providing such a crucial portal into the development of a chemical and biological poison at the lab outside Moscow, and it was impossible to use it without risking blowing the whole network. That would nix any chance the spies had of staying ahead of Putin's long-term strategy—and so the information stayed locked away.

Berezovsky and his entourage turned out in force for the lawyer's funeral in Dorset. Horses in feather-plumed headdresses pulled a black carriage containing the coffin, adorned with a bouquet of white flowers spelling DADDY and preceded by a phalanx of footmen in tails and top hats. Curtis had been well prepared for this moment. He had planned every detail, right down to the fireworks that exploded over the bay as the Union Jack fluttered from the tower of his castle overhead.

Berezovsky was devastated by the death of his lawyer. "He was killed," he told Dubov, his black eyes glinting with anger. "I know it was an assassination." Dubov was more circumspect. In his experience, Berezovsky was always 100 percent sure about the first idea that came into his head. But he couldn't say he trusted the line taken by the British authorities much, either. The faintest suggestion of Russian involvement would completely destroy the already frayed diplomatic relationship, just as the British government scrambled to mend fences with Moscow in the wake of the extradition row. It seemed likely that no one would ever know for sure how Moss and Curtis had really died.

Less than a fortnight after the helicopter crash at Bournemouth, Putin swept to reelection with 71.9 percent of the vote. Tony Blair got straight on the phone to the Russian president to express his warmest congratulations on the landslide victory, brushing aside the election observers' allegations of ballot stuffing and bias in the state media, and publicly restating his commitment to fostering ever closer ties with the Kremlin.

It was a chilling time for Scot Young, who hastily canceled an order for an Agusta six-seater helicopter—the exact model in which Curtis had perished. The death of the two lawyers had shattered the fragile pretense he'd been maintaining for Michelle's sake that being Berezovsky's bagman in Britain was anything other than a deeply risky business, and the marriage was feeling the strain. But the fixer's financial moves were typically unsentimental.

He set about helping the oligarchs cut Curtis's family out of his share of the New World Value Fund, which held the proceeds of the payments the lawyer had helped them funnel onshore from Abramovich, and then he dived headfirst into an array of new deals with Berezovsky. Playing in the big leagues was always going to be a dangerous game—but when the stakes were this high and the winnings this big, it was impossible to walk away.

PART THREE

OCCUPATIONAL HAZARDS

VIII

———

Miami, Florida—2004

The cruise ships were steaming out to sea along the narrow turquoise cut between Fisher Island and the Miami mainland as Jonathan Brown settled at his usual waterfront table. The tanned, barrel-chested mogul looked every bit the Miami native as he drained his martini in the honeyed evening sunlight—but his penchant for tight white jeans and crocodile-skin boots hid a less glitzy backstory. Brown was a sheep farmer's son from Cumbria, in the rainy north of England, who had set himself up in the smoked-salmon business and proved to everyone who doubted him just how rich you could get selling fish. He had moved to Miami to expand his salmon empire and multiply his millions in Florida property investments, and though he liked to bellow "I'm a fish man!" at strangers as he blew thousands of dollars at the bar, he had put all the clear blue water he could between himself and his drab Cumbrian past.

Brown was at his favorite South Beach steakhouse, Smith & Wollensky, to greet a new arrival in Miami: a London tycoon who had just sailed in to look for a new waterfront mansion. The smoked-salmon mogul had been asked to entertain the visitor by a mutual friend in the Florida property trade, and he watched with interest as the yacht-bronzed newcomer strolled across the terrace toward his table, grinning at the diners who glanced up curiously as he passed.

Young still had the sort of style and swagger that turned heads, even if his hair was thinning a little these days while his waistline

127

did the opposite. He had been spending more time in Miami as life in Britain got increasingly complicated, and he had recently alighted upon the idea of moving his family out here for good. That would put his daughters at a safe distance from his risky Russian business, and it would buy himself a bit of breathing room from his increasingly strained relationship with Michelle. He was here to hunt for properties, and he was glad for a companion.

The pair hit it off instantly. When Brown suggested they write down their favorite moment in film history as an icebreaker, they swapped cards to discover they had both picked the exact same scene from *True Romance*. It was the part when Dennis Hopper is about to get whacked by the mob, and he uses his last words to hurl florid insults at his Sicilian assassins.

"Even in death, we're gonna fuck 'em!" Brown shouted happily, and Young laughingly agreed. The banter continued over a repast of dry-aged sirloin sluiced back with bottles of velvety red wine, and by the end of the night they were noisily hatching plans for future escapades.

"Come to London next week!" Young insisted. "I'll show you how to live!"

Brown had recently finished selling a big swath of his fish business, and his marriage was going stale. He was at a loose end—and he'd just bought himself a brand-new private jet that he was itching to take for a spin. *Thank fuck*, he thought as he gladly accepted Young's offer. *I've finally found someone I can play with.*

London and Miami—2004–5

Young had two Rolls-Royce Phantoms waiting on the tarmac when Brown landed at London's Biggin Hill airport the following week. He put his friend up in lavish style at the five-star Halkin hotel, in Belgravia, and they hit the town—partying until dawn at Boujis, the favorite nightspot of Princes William and Harry, where Young blew

£50,000 night after night on cocaine and magnums of Dom Pérignon that he'd shake up and spray all over the crowd.

They had such a riotous time that Brown began flying to London to stay at the Halkin regularly, and Young spent ever more time in Miami. He bought himself four Porsches to keep on the peninsula and enlisted Brown's help in hunting for his waterfront property, setting a budget of £45 million. Before long, he had bought a dazzling white villa in Coconut Grove and moved his family into their new home.

Michelle was tough to please these days, but she was thrilled with her new mansion overlooking the mangrove-fringed waters of Biscayne Bay. Young confided in his new friend that his marriage was falling apart, and the move to Miami was a way to get his girls settled into a wonderful new life before he left their mother for good. Brown wanted to help, so he pulled strings to get Scarlet and Sasha into the same exclusive local school as his own daughters. But after a few months hanging around with Young, his own marriage was hanging by a thread.

Brown had been seeing a young Russian woman during his stays at the Halkin, and he was just starting to realize that he was falling for her when she told him she was expecting a baby. Now he, too, was living a double life, with a pregnant girlfriend secreted away in a stylish London apartment, at a safe distance from his wife and daughters back in Miami. But for all the upheaval, Brown couldn't remember feeling more alive. Young's wayward charisma was intoxicating, and being with him made life feel magical. Brown would never forget the time that December when he was treating his girlfriend to a stay at the Dorchester and Young kicked in the door, burst into the room, and threw armfuls of cash at them as if it were confetti.

"Jonny! Happy Christmas!" Young yelled as Brown lay in bed laughing and the air flowed with fifties.

Still, there were some things Brown found unnerving. Young dealt almost exclusively in massive piles of cash, and there always seemed to be some stranger or other turning up at the Halkin with another bag of money. Where on earth did it all come from?

"Swear to me, Scot: you're not in fucking drugs, are you?" Brown asked when he could no longer contain his curiosity. Young scoffed at the suggestion, saying he was just taking care of a bit of money for investors he wouldn't name. But soon after that, he told Brown that there was someone he should meet.

"Boris Berezovsky? I've heard of him!" Brown exclaimed.

"Yeah," said Young. "He's ex-Russian. I help him."

The fixer invited his friend along to a discreet club on Berkeley Square where Berezovsky was waiting, flanked by two bodyguards who struck Brown as lethal-looking killers and freaked him out by following him every time he went to the loo. But the oligarch himself was instantly disarming. Brown could hardly believe that this twinkling little man dangling a cigarette between his fingers was the ferocious Kremlin enemy he'd read about.

He soon learned that the oligarch made up in sheer force of personality what he lacked in physical stature. Berezovsky was a scintillating raconteur, given to vivid flights of rhetoric about mother Russia, and Brown hung avidly on his tales of political feuds, gangland battles, and murder plots back home. The smoked-salmon mogul started spending as much time as he could with the oligarch and his fixer.

Being with Berezovsky was a markedly more civilized affair than the sorts of debauches Brown usually enjoyed in Young's company. The older man was never one to dance on the table or spray the room with Champagne, but he liked wine and music, and Brown came to think of him fondly as the sort of "weird uncle" with whom one could have long talks about the meaning of life. The oligarch had a way of making him feel important—calling him "my love" and, when soliciting his attention on a matter of any delicacy, stepping gently on

Brown's toes and leaning in close in a manner that betokened great trust.

The three men got so close that Young leased them all grand town houses on Eaton Square, in Belgravia—the capital's most exclusive address—complete with pristine white columns and balconies overlooking private gardens. Young renovated the three properties in high style and handed Berezovsky the keys to number 29, while he took number 27 and Brown had the place in between.

The oligarch kept his family at Wentworth Estate and already had a stunning array of London properties to choose from when he wanted to stay in the capital, but he had other plans for the house on Eaton Square.

"My love," he said to Brown after they had all gotten settled, treading on his toes with the tip of a polished shoe. "I cannot live in twenty-nine. But can you look after my ladies?" When Brown was shown inside, he found the house full of teenage prostitutes Berezovsky had flown in from the Baltic states.

"Boris!" he said. "They're younger than my children!" But he promised to watch over the girls while his friend was away.

Brown was increasingly enthralled by Berezovsky. He loved visiting Down Street, allowing himself to pretend he was in a film every time the security guards pulled open the doors to the oligarch's inner sanctum, with its Chanel-clad secretaries, rotating cast of Russian runaways, and constantly indignant butler. Berezovsky's almost childlike reliance on Young was another source of fascination. Brown learned just how heavily the oligarch leaned on his fixer when, one day in Miami, he answered his friend's phone for him.

"My love," Berezovsky said without waiting to hear whom he was speaking to. "Get on a plane—I need you in London. I have *lost* the Phantom of Love."

Mystified, Brown turned to Young. "What the fuck is the Phantom of Love?"

The missing treasure was a £500,000 vintage Rolls-Royce that

Young had bought for Berezovsky via an offshore shell company in Gibraltar. The vehicle featured an "audacious rococo interior that is nothing less than magnificently palatial," according to its auction house listing, with fine upholstery and a ceiling painted with naked cherubs that resembled "the throne room at Versailles." Berezovsky had given the Phantom to an eighteen-year-old girlfriend as a present, and she had called to say it had "vanished" off the street.

Young was confident he could find it. "I know someone who'll know someone who'll know where it is," he said with a wink. And, to everyone's astonishment, he did.

Brown was continually awed by his friend's ability to fix anything, anytime, while juggling huge deals that seemed to yield unbelievable profits. But for all the fun they were having, Brown had never been offered a piece of that action. And then, as they drove to the airport one morning, Young finally let him in on the secrets of Project Moscow.

The city-center development that the fixer had been cooking up with Ruslan Fomichev, Berezovsky's chief money man, was finally coming to fruition. Young explained that they had bought a swath of land in the Russian capital and were planning to build a "spectacular" complex of shops and offices, which promised "profits running into hundreds of millions." Brown was being offered a slice of that pie— and he grabbed his chance.

Coming in on the deal required the smoked-salmon mogul to keep two big secrets. First, Berezovsky was putting $6 million into the project. That had to be kept under wraps because the oligarch was a wanted man in Russia and "Putin wouldn't like it," Young explained, so he was fronting for the investment himself. The next issue was that the site they were buying contained two buildings belonging to Russia's civil defense ministry, which would require planning permission from the city government to be redeveloped, so it was important to have friends in high places. Fomichev's[*] father was an FSB general, which came with certain benefits, but you couldn't be too careful, so Young said he'd bought the backing of the city's powerful mayor to ensure that the permissions were all waved through. That was the second secret that Brown would have to keep.

"We've got the best location in Moscow; we've got the mayor paid off—it's going to be a fantastic deal," Young promised.

Mayor Yury Luzhkov[†] was then one of Russia's leading politicians, a key ally of the Kremlin, and married to one of the country's richest women, whose personal fortune was estimated at more than $1 billion. He was also, US officials alleged in one diplomatic cable, a corrupt power broker "involved with bribes and deals regarding lucrative construction contracts throughout Moscow." US analysts studying the center of power in the city identified "a three-tiered structure" with Luzhkov at the top, the FSB at the second level, and ordinary criminals at the bottom. Anyone seeking to do business there had to pay for *krysha*—protection, or, literally, "roof"—from one of these groups. "If people attempt to forgo protection, they will instantly be shut down," the cable noted.

Luzhkov was another critical reason why Berezovsky's name had to be kept out of the picture: the two men were old foes from post-Soviet Russia. The oligarch enjoyed telling everyone that the enmity began when he trounced Luzhkov at pool early in the mayor's political career. The contest was intended to foster good relations with Moscow's

---

[*] Fomichev said he had never met or had any dealings with Mayor Luzhkov and denied maintaining any links to the Russian security services. "I never had any *krysha,* never made any deals with anybody, never bribed anyone," he said, insisting that "Project Moscow was the cleanest deal you can imagine being done in Russia, ever." He denied Berezovsky's involvement in the scheme, then said he was "shocked" when he was showed documents evidencing the oligarch's secret investment. "The first time I am hearing about this is now," he said. "That was not my intention to involve Berezovsky in Project Moscow."

[†] Luzhkov strongly denied any involvement in corruption. His lawyers said in a letter that he had never met Young, had no involvement in Project Moscow, and had not accepted any payment in exchange for protection. Nor, they said, would he have sanctioned any scheme involving Berezovsky.

new ruler—it was the mayor's favorite game, and Berezovsky claimed he had never played before—but then, the oligarch boasted, he had managed to win all three games in an act of impudence that angered Luzhkov so much that he snapped his cue. Luzhkov's hatred for Berezovsky was cemented when he ran against Putin in the 2000 election and was viciously attacked by the oligarch's newspapers and TV channels. The coup de grâce was when Yeltsin's former head of security broke ranks to allege publicly that Berezovsky had tried to have the mayor of Moscow murdered. It was imperative that Luzhkov should have no inkling that his old adversary was involved in Project Moscow.

That was why Young had come up with a cunning ruse to channel Berezovsky's $6 million investment into the scheme undetected. The deal was done in the name of Berezovsky's daughter Ekaterina,[*] who "sold" Young a luxury property in London's upmarket Mayfair without any actual money changing hands. Young committed to pay later from the profits of Project Moscow, and then he took out a mortgage on the property to raise Berezovsky's capital for the scheme, ensuring that the original source of the funds was obscured.

The fixer was going halves on the project with Fomichev, and his job was to raise a total of $26.5 million by January of 2006 to get the development off the ground. He set up a network of offshore vehicles to channel further investments into the scheme, starting with the $5 million Brown had already promised to pour in. Poju Zabludowicz, the Finnish billionaire and Tory donor who had invited Young and Berezovsky to a dinner with Bill Clinton in London, threw in a few million, as did two more of Young's friends—a Monaco-based film mogul and a London money lender.

Young was so confident in his *krysha* that he personally underwrote all the investments, promising to repay the backers every penny if the

---

[*] Ekaterina Berezovsky declined to comment, but sources close to her said she had no idea her name had been used to funnel money into the project and would not have expected her father to invest in Russia through any route "because it would have put him and any fellow investors in danger."

project failed. But any protection he thought he had came as cold comfort to his London lawyer, who warned that he was placing too much trust in his Russian partner's connections. "Apart from accidents, Russia is still a dangerous place where people are kidnapped for ransom, are murdered, or simply disappear," the lawyer noted in a due diligence document. "You are bearing the risk on this because your understandings with RF [Ruslan Fomichev] are worthless if he is not around."

Young was sure all would be well—as long as no one found out about Berezovsky's secret investment. "You can't let them know," he told Brown whenever the Miami mogul came into contact with the other investors. "Nobody knows Boris is involved, Jon, but you."

"I don't give a fuck," Brown said, covering his concern with bravado. "I'm a fish man!"

But the truth was, Berezovsky's involvement scared him. The oligarch talked all the time about the fact that Putin wanted him dead—and yet he refused to stop poking the bear.

"Boris!" Brown yelled when he saw that his friend had published yet another article lambasting the Kremlin. "Don't wind the government up!" But his words fell on deaf ears. Berezovsky was in a fantasy world, Brown began to realize: he was obsessed with Russia, and he thought he was running the Kremlin out of Down Street. It felt less safe all the time being around the oligarch as his attacks on Putin intensified, and his swarms of bodyguards and armored cars served as a constant reminder of the threat. When Brown rode in the back of Berezovsky's Maybach, he couldn't help but remember the car bomb that his friend had only narrowly survived back in Moscow and think, if that happened again now, *I wonder if I'd feel it.*

As for Young, he seemed so blinded by his boss's billions that he just couldn't see the danger. Looking back, Brown would come to wish he'd done more to persuade his friend to distance himself from Berezovsky.

"Me and Scot, we can do the best we can, we make ten million, twenty million, thirty million," he would say. "We don't make billions, right? It doesn't work that way. The billions come when Boris turns up. But it comes with a cancer. And the cancer kills you."

London and Kiev—2004–5

The latest of Berezovsky's wheezes was his effort to stir up trouble in Russia's backyard. In Ukraine, the cassette scandal had sparked mass protests against the pro-Kremlin regime of President Kuchma, and by 2004 the dissent had grown into a full-blown uprising, with hundreds of thousands of orange-clad activists staging sit-ins, strikes, and marches on the streets of Kiev. The unrest was spearheaded by the strikingly handsome opposition leader Viktor Yushchenko, who had declared a state of revolution soon after the tapes were released. As usual, behind the scenes, Berezovsky was pulling the strings.

In addition to paying for the transcription of the incendiary recordings, the oligarch poured tens of millions of dollars into Yushchenko's "Orange Revolution," funneling the money through offshore companies to evade Ukrainian laws banning the foreign financing of politics. By 2004, as Kuchma reached the end of his term, Berezovsky's funds were pumped into a campaign pitting the opposition leader against the newly anointed pro-Kremlin candidate in the presidential election.

Yushchenko's presidential manifesto read like an *A* to *Z* of everything Putin most loathed: accession to NATO, European integration, and a purge on official corruption, all under the inflammatory slogan "Power to the people." Since the government controlled the election coverage on most TV channels, the opposition leader built his platform on face-to-face communication with voters, wearing out his shoe leather on the campaign trail and drawing armies of orange-clad supporters to his rallies.

A few weeks before the vote, on September 5, 2004, Yushchenko returned home from a dinner with the head of Ukraine's security service and greeted his wife with a kiss.

"Your lips taste metallic," she told him. Before long, his head and face began to swell, his skin broke out in pus-filled inflammations, and a searing pain was spreading through his body. The leader of the Orange Revolution was flown to Vienna for emergency treatment, where tests revealed he had catastrophic quantities of a powerful toxin in his body. Yushchenko had been poisoned with TCDD—the most potent contaminant in the chemical weapon Agent Orange.

The dose should have been enough to kill him, but with expert treatment from Viennese toxicologists, Yushchenko made enough of a recovery to fly back to Kiev. He appeared at a rally to address his supporters, his once-handsome face gray and grotesquely disfigured with lesions and pockmarks above his orange scarf. And then he carried on campaigning.

The election weeks later was rigged. When Yushchenko lost to the pro-Kremlin candidate, the country erupted: as many as a million protesters took to the streets of Kiev, turning Independence Square into a roiling sea of orange banners and bringing the city to a standstill. Berezovsky's funding helped sustain the demonstrations for nearly two months, with Yushchenko's campaign busing protesters in from the suburbs when reinforcements were needed.

The demonstrations drew a furious reaction from Moscow: Mayor Luzhkov described the protesters as a "sabbath of witches who have been fattened up with oranges," while Putin went on to warn that the uprising would turn Ukraine into "a banana republic where the one who shouts loudest is the one who wins." But when the revolt showed no signs of abating by the end of December, a rerun of the vote was forced—and this time it was the permanently disfigured Yushchenko who swept to victory.

The Orange Revolution was the biggest threat yet to Putin's authority, scuppering his efforts to install puppet regimes in the former Soviet states and sending a message to the population in and around Russia that corruption and vote rigging did not have to be tolerated.

The people had been shown that an authoritarian government could be toppled through peaceful protest alone.

Putin vowed to prevent a similar "color revolution" occurring on his turf. To that end, he oversaw the creation of a youth movement named Nashi—meaning "ours"—which was billed as an "anti-orange" force to "defend Russia" against prodemocracy activists inspired by events in Ukraine. The movement mushroomed to a membership of more than two hundred thousand fanatically loyal teenagers, who marched in red cloaks emblazoned with Putin's face and adopted his message of "restoring Russian greatness."

The Kremlin poured hundreds of millions of rubles into Nashi, and Putin met repeatedly with its leaders. As its membership matured, it would morph into an aggressive arm of the Russian state, launching cyberattacks against critical media outlets, putting new recruits through quasimilitary training, using agents provocateurs to gather *kompromat* on rival groups, and running campaigns of harassment, intimidation, and sometimes violence against opposition figures. And while Nashi did battle with the opposition in the street, Putin went on to crack down on the forces of change from on high, eventually passing a series of antiprotest laws restricting the right to freedom of assembly and starving NGOs and protest groups of funding by banning them from receiving money from abroad.

If Berezovsky had once been a nuisance to his former protégé, he was now an active menace. Suddenly a stream of whispers about fresh plots to kill the exiled oligarch blew into the River House from British sources and surveillance stations in Moscow. And the threat was getting closer. Across the Thames, inside the neoclassical walls of Britain's domestic security agency, MI5, counterintelligence officers had detected a significant escalation in Russian espionage on British soil. They sent a confidential report to central government in the spring of 2005 identifying thirty-two Russian spies who were operating under diplomatic cover in London. The intelligence officers had been tasked with obtaining secret information about Britain's military capabilities, its defense industry—and the activities of the men in Berezovsky's circle.

Putin's state of the nation address that spring signaled the change in the weather. After years of mouthing platitudes about building a free and democratic Russia and opening up to the West, the president had finally showed his true KGB colors when he branded the collapse of the USSR "the greatest geopolitical catastrophe of the twentieth century" and described the independence of the former Soviet states as a "genuine tragedy" that had left "tens of millions of our fellow citizens" outside Russia.

Putin's bellicose rhetoric, the fresh threats against Berezovsky, and the escalation of Russian espionage in Britain made a noxious mix that caused severe discomfort among the Russia watchers. But any hope of getting central government to confront their concerns evaporated that summer, when disaster struck London.

On the morning of July 7, 2005, four suicide bombers detonated backpacks filled with explosives on the city's crowded public transportation network, killing more than fifty people and injuring hundreds more. It was Britain's first Islamist attack—the very nightmare the country's entire national security apparatus had been cranking up to prevent—and, in the wake of 7/7, Britain wanted to pull its allies in the fight against jihadist terror even closer.

When Putin visited London for an EU-Russia summit that October, Blair came up with the most significant gesture conceivable to restore trust with Moscow. The prime minister invited the Russian president into the sacred chancel of British security: the underground bunker where cabinet ministers receive top-secret intelligence briefings during times of crisis. Inside Cabinet Office Briefing Room A— known across Whitehall as COBRA—Putin was given an audience with the country's most senior spies for a discussion on counterterrorism intelligence sharing. Few, if any, other world leaders had ever been so honored.

Still, Berezovsky had finally managed to light a real fire under

Putin's feet in Ukraine. And he was meddling in the politics of Georgia and Belarus, too, funding protest groups and forming alliances with opposition candidates. As always, the oligarch's political moves fused neatly with his business interests. As soon as Yushchenko was in power, Berezovsky deployed Young to scout for new deals in Kiev, with instructions to use his status as the secret funder of the new administration for leverage with key officials. The fixer was soon lining up an investment opportunity for Berezovsky in a major government infrastructure project, and he dived into Georgia, too, booking a private jet to Tbilisi to hunt for new business. Young was also spending more time scoping new opportunities in Russia as Project Moscow came together, sizing up a power-station deal with the Moscow government and another big property development in St. Petersburg. Berezovsky was at the peak of his provocative powers, forging ahead into ever-more explosive territory—and his fixer was right behind him.

IX

Oxfordshire and St. Petersburg—2006

A winter mist hung low over the lake as limousines streamed up the drive toward the moonlit palace. The guests climbed out in their evening finery, pausing to gaze up at the grand towers and flying buttresses overhead before ascending the steps toward the columned portico at the entrance to the great hall.

It was January 23, 2006, and Boris Berezovsky was celebrating his sixtieth birthday with a black-tie ball in the baroque splendor of Blenheim Palace—the ancestral home of Winston Churchill and the Dukes of Marlborough. Through doors guarded by red-liveried footmen in bearskin hats, a string quartet was playing as two hundred guests sipped pink Champagne by a magnificent fire. Among them were all the key players in the oligarch's global chess game.

Badri Patarkatsishvili was a picture of bonhomie, throwing his arms wide and planting kisses on the cheeks of all who passed him, while Ruslan and Katya Fomichev sashayed arm-in-arm through the crowd, Yuri Felshtinsky pontificated before a small audience, and Scot Young networked his way energetically around the hall. On the sidelines, Yuli Dubov laughed and clapped his hands with Berezovsky's youngest children while Alexander Litvinenko and Akhmed Zakayev huddled conspiratorially in the corner, deep in conversation. What nobody yet knew was that an agent of the enemy was in their midst. Vladimir Putin had, finally, gotten a pawn to the back of the board.

Andrey Lugovoy did not turn up by limousine. He was among the less glamorous guests who were brought to the palace by bus from London, arriving in a shabby brown corduroy coat slung over his dinner suit. Boris and Badri's former head of security at Channel One had finished serving his time in Moscow for the plot to spring Nikolai Glushkov out of jail, and no one thought twice about trusting him when he washed up in the UK looking for help getting back on his feet. It was Patarkatsishvili he'd called first. The Georgian oligarch was now splitting his time between Surrey and Tbilisi, having snapped up the deeds to Downside Manor, a grand residence not far from Berezovsky's Wentworth Estate house, and he'd invited the former security man to visit.

Lugovoy was as fair and boyish as he was inscrutable. His rosy cheeks, short blond bangs, and easy smile created a general appearance of wholesomeness—but for a slight tension in his gait and the way he watched the crowd from the corner of his eye. He had served in the KGB as a bodyguard before going on to work for Boris and Badri, so Litvinenko had been particularly eager to welcome him into the world of the exiles. The defector wanted to start making money selling private intelligence in London, and he was looking for a Russian partner.

The pair could almost have been brothers, with their sandy hair, watchful manner, and KGB academy ways, and they had struck up an immediate rapport. So when Lugovoy sidled into the great hall, Litvinenko hastened to join him, keen to continue their discussions about ways to make their security acumen pay in London. Lugovoy was only too happy to talk shop and smile for pictures with Litvinenko and his elegant wife, Marina. He knew this little partnership would indeed prove very lucrative.

A commotion erupted as Berezovsky entered the hall. The oligarch swept past a giant Kremlin-shaped ice sculpture and a look-alike of the queen in a red cape and feathered hat as he made a beeline for Patarkatsishvili. The old friends shared a warm backslapping embrace before Berezovsky broke away to greet his fixer. Young was not looking quite himself. His dark curls were slightly slick with sweat around his collar, his bow tie was askew, and his eyes were a touch glazed. But he broke into a brilliant grin as soon as he saw Berezovsky, throwing his arms around the oligarch and bellowing, "Boris! This is fantastic!"

The guests were soon ushered into the library for a candlelit banquet serenaded by opera singers. During the meal, Berezovsky's twelve-year-old daughter burst out of a cake and performed a belly dance in a pink sequined skirt and bra. When the repast was over, Young slugged back a large brandy as he watched Zakayev present his benefactor with a carefully wrapped samurai sword while Patarkatsishvili cavorted around the dance floor to "Brown Eyed Girl" with Marina Litvinenko and Lugovoy strolled through the crowd stealing sidelong glances and puffing on a cigar.

Berezovsky was in his element—the big man at the party, embracing everyone, toasting mother Russia, and showering his loyal followers with largesse. The evening culminated in a spectacular fireworks display over the lake before the chauffeurs brought the cars around and the guests said their flurry of goodbyes. The exiled oligarch stood on the steps of the palace, watching his guests roll away down the torchlit drive until the last of the limousines had vanished into the darkness. Then, suddenly, it was all over.

The Kremlin chose Berezovsky's birthday to fire a humiliating salvo at Britain. The Russians had discovered an MI6 portal into Moscow—a transmitter hidden inside a fake rock that had been planted on a city street. The device was being used to conduct digital dead drops: a Russian source would stroll past and beam secret information into the rock using a small handheld computer, and MI6 officials would come along a few hours later to harvest it using a wireless receiver. The FSB had known about the rock since the previous year and had been spying on the spies for months, secretly filming them and their top-secret Russian sources performing their drops and pickups.

Russian state TV revealed the find in a crowing newscast, showing images of the rock with its top sawed off to expose the transmitter inside and airing the secret film of the agents and their handlers at work. The covers of four British spies were blown, and a mole they had been running inside Russia was arrested. It was an unalloyed disaster for MI6, and it came at a particularly delicate time.

Britain had just handed over the presidency of the G8 to Russia, and preparations were under way for the group's first summit to be held in St. Petersburg that summer. Days before the spy rock scandal broke, the Kremlin-owned gas giant Gazprom had sent shock waves through European energy markets by shutting down a critical pipeline through Ukraine, threatening to cut off the heat in homes across the continent in the depths of winter. The taps had been turned back on after a four-day standoff over prices, but the crisis was a stark reminder of Russia's stranglehold on European energy, and EU leaders were anxious to lock the Kremlin into guaranteeing a secure supply of gas and oil at the summit.

Britain was eyeing another big energy prize. The London Stock Exchange was readying itself for the flotation of Rosneft, the Russian state oil company, which was scheduled to go ahead on the eve of the summit, in mid-July. Britain's Financial Services Authority had approved the initial public offering—despite protestations that the bulk of Rosneft's assets were stolen from the rival oil giant Yukos, whose owner, Mikhail Khodorkovsky, had been jailed and stripped of his riches after criticizing Putin. The flotation promised to earn the City of London a fortune, and the British oil giant BP was planning to snap up a massive stake in its Kremlin-owned rival. So the government was eager to ensure it all went smoothly, and the spat over the spy rock was not a happy development.

It was at this sensitive moment that Berezovsky chose to launch his latest broadside. Incensed by a story planted in a Kremlin-controlled newspaper alleging that he had obtained political asylum in Britain through fraud, the oligarch lashed out more ferociously than ever—

phoning in to the Echo Moscow radio station to announce baldly that he was plotting the violent overthrow of the Russian government.

"The regime is doomed, and I want to see it collapse before Russia collapses," he declared. "There is only one way out: a coup. A forced seizure of power."

Berezovsky, who claimed to have been plotting an armed uprising for eighteen months, could have made no more incendiary statement as Putin licked his wounds in the wake of the Orange Revolution. The move threatened to plunge diplomatic relations between London and Moscow further into the freezer—infuriating Blair, who had taken such pains to repair the damage after the last row over Berezovsky's asylum status.

The foreign secretary was dispatched to the House of Commons to condemn the oligarch's remarks and restate the country's "close working relationship with Russia, as a valued partner of the UK." Jack Straw stressed that Berezovsky had not entered the UK at the government's invitation, and he issued a stark warning to the turbulent oligarch.

"Those granted asylum in the United Kingdom have duties to the UK," he said. "They are advised that their refugee status can be reviewed at any time where it is considered their presence is not conducive to the public good."

The Kremlin promptly challenged Straw to put his money where his mouth was, issuing a fresh extradition warrant for Berezovsky on charges of violent sedition. But again, Judge Workman stood in the way, throwing out the request at Bow Street magistrates' court that June. Berezovsky had succeeded in landing another stinging blow on the Kremlin before ducking back behind the obdurate shield of British justice. But by then, a furious Putin had already set other plans in motion.

The following month, a new "antiterror" law passed through the Russian parliament, giving the FSB a license to kill enemies of the state on foreign soil. It was accompanied by the announcement that the Kremlin's hit list of targets had already been drawn up. The exiles soon heard from their remaining FSB contacts exactly what they already feared: Litvinenko, Berezovsky, and Zakayev were at the top of the list, along with their friend the *Novaya Gazeta* journalist Anna Politkovskaya.

Litvinenko was particularly terrified. Putin's murderous intentions were no surprise, but this amounted to a public declaration of war. At least covert killing was a hit-and-miss business, but whacking people in broad daylight would be child's play for trained assassins. For the first time since he got his British passport, the defector no longer felt safe in the land he had made his home. He turned to a new hero for help.

Oleg Gordievsky was the jewel in the crown of British espionage during the Cold War. The former KGB colonel was the most senior Russian spy ever recruited by the West, working for MI6 as a double agent for more than a decade in the '70s and '80s. During that time, by happy fluke, he was put in charge of intelligence gathering at the Soviet embassy in London, thus nullifying Russian spying operations in Britain with a single stroke while continuing to feed his handlers prized intelligence on Soviet nuclear plans and political machinations. Gordievsky was a national hero who went on to be decorated by the queen for "services to the security of the United Kingdom," and he had become something of a mentor to Litvinenko. After discussing the new laws with the younger defector, he sent a letter to the London *Times* that minced no words.

Sir,

As the seven leaders of the world's most industrially developed democracies are packing their suitcases in order to go to St Petersburg for the G8 meeting, their would-be host, Former KGB Lieutenant–Colonel Vladimir Putin, has rushed through the state Duma two new pieces of legislation.

First, a new law enabling him to use his secret services as 'death squads' to eliminate 'extremists' anywhere abroad (including in this country). Second, an amendment to existing law on fighting 'extremism', providing a much broader definition of that 'crime' which, among other things, will include now any 'libellous' statements about his Administration.

Thus, the stage is set for any critic of Putin's regime here, especially those campaigning against Russian genocide in Chechnya, to have an appointment with a poison-tipped umbrella. According to the statement by the Russian Defence Minister Sergei Ivanov, the black list of potential targets is already compiled. In keeping with the best traditions of the Soviet-era foreign policy, which always strived to make the world an unwitting accomplice of their crimes, this masterpiece is delivered precisely to coincide with the G8 meeting, which will serve to provide a semblance of approval, or at least of acceptance, by the world of this new development in the 'common fight with terrorism'.

Needless to say, this is an extremely dangerous development. Unless the Western leaders are prepared to share responsibility for murder…they must cancel their meeting, or, at the very least, should protest loudly against such abuse of the G8 chairmanship.

The summit in St. Petersburg went ahead in mid-July without a hitch. Energy was at the top of the agenda. As Blair landed in the city, he received news that the Rosneft flotation had netted the Kremlin $10.7 billion—making it the then fifth-biggest initial public offering in world history—and BP had snapped up a $1 billion stake. That didn't stop Putin from making his rancor over Britain's refusal to extradite Berezovsky and Zakayev felt during the talks at the Konstantin Palace. In response to suggestions that Russia's allies Iran and Syria should be sanctioned for harboring Hezbollah fighters, he fired a shot in Blair's direction: why, he asked, didn't the group focus instead on "other countries that harbor people who are quite obviously terrorists?" But the summit moved toward a broad agreement that Russia would guarantee a steady supply of oil and gas to the European mainland—even if Putin did manage to duck out of signing anything locking him into that pledge.

If the foreign secretary's threat to withdraw Berezovsky's political asylum had given the oligarch any pause, he wasn't showing it. Instead he had taken out full-page newspaper advertisements on the eve of the summit, portraying Putin as Groucho Marx. Underneath was the comedian's famous slogan: "I wouldn't want to belong to any club that would have me as a member."

Berezovsky's mischief making was easily ignored—and so was Gordievsky's letter. The assembled world leaders raised not a word of public protest about Russia's new laws legalizing overseas assassinations. They carried on courting Putin.

London, Moscow, and Miami—2006

Project Moscow was on the rocks. The trouble had arisen just before Christmas, a few weeks ahead of Berezovsky's birthday party, when Young missed the deadline to provide the last tranche of money he had promised to put into the deal. The usually cool and collected Fomichev sent him a furious email. "Today on thursday 22 DECEMBER!! we received no moneys from you," he wrote. "I do not feel that i have to be responsible towards you when you are not doing the same to me."

The fixer kept resurfacing with promises that the money was coming at any moment, but when he missed another payment deadline at the start of February, his Russian partner was at a loss for words. "What the........!!!!!!" Fomichev wrote.

"I am juggling," Young responded. "You will have it before 12 tomorrow."

Young's final $5 million was vital for keeping the city government on board: a raft of payments was due to officials in charge of granting permission for the development, and Luzhkov was quick to anger when his people didn't get what they were owed. "I am leaving tom to moscow and need to meet with you to discuss our position with the moscow mayor," Fomichev* emailed Young, to no avail.

The funds never materialized, and in March, Fomichev finally pulled the plug on Project Moscow.

The first Jonathan Brown heard of the trouble was when news reached him that Young had lost everything, had attempted suicide, and had been committed to the Priory "psychiatric" hospital. Brown didn't believe a word of it, and he got on the phone to Young.

"Scot, it's me," he bellowed. "You're not in the fucking Priory. Let's go to Boujis and do some blow!"

Brown's hunch was right: Young had not been committed, though he had visited the Priory voluntarily after taking too many tranquilizers and superficially cutting his wrists—something doctors noted he had done because he "wanted people to think he was suicidal." Then he had fired out a series of incoherent emails to the Project Moscow investors, to whom he owed millions, telling them he was "heavily sedated," rambling about suicide, and promising to resolve the crisis when he recovered.

Brown persuaded his friend to get on the first plane to Miami. When he arrived, it became clear that Young's suicide attempt was a sham designed to buy time with his angry creditors, and Brown soon had him chucking back cocktails at the GreenStreet Café, in Coconut Grove. But it was also clear that trouble really was brewing in London and Moscow. Young insisted that he had lost everything and was tens of millions of pounds in debt, but he wouldn't say how this had come to pass. To Brown, it seemed as if the sky had suddenly fallen in on his friend.

Young had underwritten every penny that British investors had funneled into his half of Project Moscow, and now that the scheme

---

* Fomichev said he had never discussed the project with the mayor and did not recall this email, but he said it had likely been sent "to pressure Scot" into paying the money.

had collapsed he owed them more than $20 million. On top of that, he had racked up huge loans and mortgages with various banks and a whopping bill from the UK tax authorities that he said he could no longer afford to pay. Most alarmingly of all, back in Moscow, Mayor Luzhkov's government was on the warpath.

The city administration had turned on the Project Moscow investors following the failure to pay for the required permissions to build the development, and now it was attacking from all sides in a bid to seize control of the site and all its assets. Officials were claiming a debt of "several million rubles" in back rent for the government-owned buildings on the land, and politicians were raising a hue and cry in the state parliament about unauthorized construction, demolition, and the felling of trees on the site. Then state prosecutors announced that all the investors were under investigation for "economic crimes,"* and the FSB started digging into the finances behind the development. Suddenly Berezovsky's secret investment was in danger of being exposed.

Fomichev swept in to save the day, arranging for a Russian company called Guta Group to buy out all the investors and take control of the site in an eleventh-hour deal to stave off the attacks from Luzhkov's administration. The owners of Guta Group were old friends of Fomichev's, and they had a number of other irons in the fire in Moscow, so they planned to use the site as a bargaining chip "for negotiation purposes with the government on other matters." That kept the wolf from the door in Moscow, but Young was plummeting deeper into crisis. He was being served with writs and freeze orders from creditors on an almost weekly basis; one by one his mansions in London, Oxford, and Florida were being repossessed or sold to pay his debts; and his collections of exotic cars, luxury watches, and antique furniture were all seized by angry lenders.

---

* No charges were ever brought.

Everyone remained mystified about what had caused the fixer's finances to implode so suddenly. Some friends speculated that his business empire had been a house of cards all along, built by borrowing on the back of assets he never really owned. Others heard rumors that a deal with the Russian mafia had gone bad. But Michelle had her own theory. The marriage had been in trouble for years, and she was convinced this was a ruse to hide his fortune so he could leave without paying her a penny. While Young was pretending to be in the Priory, he had instructed a lawyer to phone his wife and tell her he had lost everything and attempted suicide—adding, for good measure, that he had also been having affairs with "hundreds of girls." The call had its intended effect: shattering the marriage irrevocably and clearing the path for Young to start a new life on his own terms. But it had also filled his wife with white-hot hatred.

Michelle filed for divorce, claiming that her husband was hiding "a few billion at least." She put together a team of lawyers, private detectives, and forensic accountants to hunt for the missing money. Then she obtained a worldwide freeze order on all Young's assets, including the Mayfair property that had been used to funnel Berezovsky's funds into the scheme. So began the longest-running High Court divorce battle in British legal history, conducted in a continual blaze of media attention. And the secrets of Project Moscow were at the heart of the case.

Young went to every length imaginable to keep the lid on his Russian business dealings. He flouted repeated court orders to disclose evidence explaining the disappearance of his fortune, and he destroyed hundreds of emails he had exchanged with Berezovsky. He would even spend three months in prison for contempt of court rather than reveal the truth. And yet, somehow, he maintained a lifestyle beyond the wildest dreams of the average citizen—dining in fine restaurants, staying in penthouse apartments, dressing in designer clothes, and paying for purchases with huge rolls of £50 notes.

Brown was just as mystified as everyone else. He couldn't believe that Young's hundreds of millions had really gone up in a puff of smoke overnight, but some sort of calamity had clearly befallen his friend. He wondered whether Young's sudden financial collapse was linked to a change in circumstances for Berezovsky.

In February of 2006, just as Project Moscow was imploding, Patarkatsishvili announced that he wanted a financial "divorce" from his longtime partner. Berezovsky's increasingly savage attacks on the Kremlin were getting in the way of business. Russian prosecutors bearing down on him with embezzlement and money-laundering charges had by then enlisted the help of several foreign authorities, with the result that his properties in France had been raided by armed officers and the funds he had stashed in Swiss bank accounts were being systematically frozen. The onslaught wasn't only directed at Berezovsky: those doing business with him also risked a freeze on their accounts, and several Western banks were refusing to accept Patarkatsishvili's money under pressure from the Russian government. Berezovsky's call for armed revolution in Russia had been the final straw. The Georgian oligarch told his partner he wanted to separate business from politics, and Berezovsky agreed, telling everyone that the split was just a sham devised to take the heat off their shared investments. Patarkatsishvili would handle all the finances while he continued to campaign against Putin—and, behind the scenes, everything would still be shared.

Did Berezovsky's separation from the purse strings have anything to do with Young's sudden financial fall? Brown never did work out exactly what happened, but there were two things of which, with hindsight, he would say he was absolutely certain.

"Money went missing. And then people started fucking dying."

PART FOUR

THE PRICE

X

Muswell Hill and Mayfair, London—Summer 2006

Life had settled into a comfortably knowable rhythm inside the unassuming yellow-brick town house on Osier Crescent, the sleepy Muswell Hill side street where the Litvinenko family lived opposite the Zakayevs. The neighbors knew them as Edwin, Maria, and Anthony Carter—even if Litvinenko's thick accent and habit of feeding Russian kolbasa sausages to the neighbor's cat gave the lie to those quaint English aliases. He was a figure of some fascination to the locals, who joked privately at first that perhaps he was a KGB spy—until he dropped signed copies of *Blowing Up Russia* through their doors at Christmas and they stopped laughing.

The family had been there approaching six years. Litvinenko still spoke very broken English, but Marina had studied hard to become fluent, and she'd taken up teaching ballroom dancing to supplement the family's income. Anatoly was well settled, too, sounding more like a native Londoner as he aced his first year at the prestigious City of London School for boys on the banks of the Thames, where Berezovsky was paying for him to study. He was twelve, old enough to beat his father at chess, and he still spoke to his dad in Russian. But his memories of sledding and seeing the Moskva River freeze over in the fierce winters of his early childhood were gradually melting away, along with the last traces of his accent. The defector's son seemed to become a little less Anatoly Litvinenko and a little more Anthony Carter every day.

Litvinenko was proud to live in England, enthusing often about the rights and freedoms the family enjoyed in their new home. Soon after they arrived, he had taken Anatoly to visit Speakers' Corner and stopped to pose for a photo with two London bobbies. This was a place where you could speak up for what you believed, he told his son, and the law would protect you. He kept the front driveway obsessively well swept, strung a British flag from the balcony, and worked out vigorously every day in the makeshift gym he'd rigged up in the garage. On the weekends he went for ten-mile runs and swam with Anatoly in the local pool. Sometimes, when he felt homesick, he'd watch old Russian movies on VHS while Marina cooked comfortingly familiar recipes—spicy soup and stuffed pancakes. But most nights it was work that kept him busy.

The house on Osier Crescent was lined with the investigative case files that Litvinenko had spent years assembling in his personal crusade against Vladimir Putin. Row after row of immaculately indexed folders contained all the evidence documenting the Russian president's links to the Tambov gang in St. Petersburg, the FSB's plot to assassinate Berezovsky and Trepashkin, and the government's links to the terrorist atrocities it blamed on Chechen rebels. Litvinenko spent many evenings rereading and adding to his records, often leaping up and racing across the road to speak to Akhmed Zakayev when he happened upon a new discovery.

The defector and the rebel leader had grown to be best friends, and their two families formed a tightly knit little community on Osier Crescent—eating together, sharing holiday celebrations, and minding each other's kids. Litvinenko had a habit of disappearing for hours into the Zakayevs' house, infuriating Marina by coming home so full of Chechen delicacies that he had no room for his dinner.

The two men were still actively investigating the FSB's role in the Moscow bombings and theater siege as part of Zakayev's Chechen war crimes commission, helped by the dauntless *Novaya Gazeta* journalist Anna Politkovskaya, who was a regular guest at Osier Crescent when she came to visit her sister in London. And now the trio was gathering string on a third terrorist outrage.

Two years earlier in Beslan, a town in Russia's wild North Caucasus, armed Islamist militants had occupied a school and taken more than one thousand people hostage—most of them children. The captives were crammed into the gymnasium, where explosives were strung from basketball hoops over their heads as the terrorists demanded Russia's withdrawal from Chechnya. After a three-day standoff, Russian troops stormed in, pounding the building so heavily with tanks, rockets, and grenade launchers that the roof of the gym collapsed, crushing many of the hostages. More than three hundred people were killed in the operation—186 of them children.

The use of such deadly force carried clear echoes of the Moscow theater siege, and the Muswell Hill investigators were suspicious as soon as the news broke. Then they heard that Politkovskaya was recovering in the hospital after drinking a poisoned cup of tea on the plane as she traveled to Beslan to report on the attack. Convinced the government was hiding something, Litvinenko started digging.

His first observation was that several of the hostage takers had been in FSB custody for other terrorist offenses but had been mysteriously freed before the attack. Had they been flipped in prison? Even if not, they would have been kept under close surveillance after being released—so how had they managed to travel to Beslan armed with bombs and suicide belts without raising any red flags? It would later emerge that Putin had been warned that Islamists were planning a hostage taking at a school in the region several days before it occurred and that he had done nothing to alert the local population or prevent the attack. Litvinenko wrote a damning article for a website Zakayev had set up to chronicle Russian atrocities in Chechnya, asserting that the FSB had at best allowed and at worst provoked the Beslan school siege in another effort to tarnish the separatist movement. And he, Zakayev, and Politkovskaya carried on delving into the FSB's links to terror.

The defector's theories had found a receptive audience in the MI6 handler he knew as Martin, and their meetings in the basement café of Waterstones on Piccadilly had become part of the familiar rhythm of his London life. Whenever he had a new lead linking the Kremlin to organized crime or acts of terror, Litvinenko contacted his handler over an encrypted phone line to arrange a rendezvous. In addition to passing on information gleaned from his own investigations, he helped make sense of intelligence the Russia watchers gathered from their own sources. And now, to his delight, he had been tasked with another big assignment—one that finally made all the time he had spent digging into Putin's St. Petersburg mob connections start to seem worthwhile. The British spies had asked him to help their counterparts in Madrid unravel the Kremlin's links to a powerful Russian mafia group spreading its tentacles into Spain. The Tambov gang was on the move.

The St. Petersburg mob had extended its operations across Europe under the enterprising leadership of Gennady Petrov, a giant of a man with a face like a slab of concrete who commanded his criminal empire from a mansion in Majorca. Petrov had risen through the ranks of the Tambov gang in the '90s, while Putin was deputy mayor in St. Petersburg. He had relocated to Spain after becoming the group's leader, and prosecutors suspected him of laundering the proceeds of drug smuggling, gunrunning, and contract killings through properties in the Costa del Sol. Litvinenko had briefed Martin on Putin's relationship with the Tambov gang, and his handler had asked him to work with the Spanish authorities as they devised an ambitious strategy to "behead" the Russian mafia. So he was now making regular trips to Madrid, where he fed information to a handler called Jorge, who passed it up the chain to prosecutors building a case against the Tambovs.

Litvinenko had explained to Jorge that the Russian government, its intelligence agencies, and organized crime had merged into a single "mafia state" under Putin, in which the Kremlin used the mob to do its dirty work in exchange for official protection. He described how the president's relationship with the Tambov gang had developed during his time as deputy mayor of St. Petersburg and provided specific information about members of the group who, he suspected, still maintained deep links to Putin's government. Sure enough, when the Spanish authorities tapped the gang members' phones, they found the men to be in regular contact with a network of senior Kremlin officials.

Litvinenko's evidence paved the way for a series of raids two years later in which twenty gangsters were arrested, ultimately leading Spanish prosecutors to indict twelve suspected kingpins—including several current and former Kremlin officials—for colluding with the Tambovs. The subsequent trial ended without any convictions after Moscow stonewalled requests for evidence and allowed key suspects to remain at large in Russia. But all that was yet to come. In the summer of 2006, Jorge was arranging for him to meet directly with prosecutors as a first step toward giving evidence about Putin's links to the mob in open court.

These services to Britain and its allies were a source of deep pride to Litvinenko—but he was running short of money. The £2,000 monthly stipend he received from MI6 was nowhere near enough to keep his family afloat on its own, and Berezovsky had cut his monthly payments at the start of the year as the freeze on the oligarch's Swiss funds began to bite. Litvinenko needed to start paying his own way, and, thanks to Martin, he knew where to turn. Two years earlier, when he was first recruited as a British intelligence asset, his handler had provided him with an introduction to a key figure in the shadowy world of London's private spying industry. Now it was time to cash in.

Dean Attew worked for Titon International, an elite Mayfair-based private intelligence firm of the sort that enjoys direct lines to the River House and does odd jobs for queen and country in return. He was well connected with the Russia watchers, and Martin had introduced him to Litvinenko back in 2004, suggesting that the defector might be a useful source of information for British companies doing due diligence on opportunities in Russia. Attew had also worked in security at high-end casinos around the world, and his years studying potential swindlers around countless card tables had given him a sharp eye for the small tells on a human face. He sensed he could trust Litvinenko. But he had made it clear that the defector would be of no use to British clients unless he learned to speak some English, so when Litvinenko's money began to dry up, he signed up to take a language course and then called Attew asking for work.

The private spy boss had since offered him several paying projects probing Russia's business and political elite, but Litvinenko soon realized that if he was going to come up with the sort of fresh intelligence Attew wanted, he needed a partner on the ground in Moscow. That was where Andrey Lugovoy came into the picture.

The two former KGB officers were soon doing brisk business. The division of labor was simple: Litvinenko hustled for jobs in London from Titon and several other Mayfair firms, and Lugovoy did the spadework in Moscow. By that summer, they were gathering dirt on Putin's agriculture minister for the owners of Stolichnaya vodka as well as scoping a big contract with Gazprom for a London-based security firm and investigating several other powerful Russians who held sway over lucrative deals being sized up by British clients.

Initially they worked at arm's length, but then it occurred to Litvinenko that clients might be impressed by his man on the ground in Moscow. Lugovoy was a good talker and always seemed to win people over quickly, so perhaps bringing him to meetings would be a good way to get more business. He told Attew there was someone he should meet—"a friend and a source" from Russia—and arranged for them all to get together at Heathrow airport when Lugovoy flew through London in June.

On the day of the meeting, the defector led the private spy boss up the escalators to the raised dining area in terminal 1, where Lugovoy was waiting. Litvinenko couldn't help but notice that his partner had acquired very expensive tastes since he started showing up in London. He insisted on shopping at Harrods and had taken to sporting silk ties and patterned suits set off with an enormous gold watch.

As the three men shook hands and settled around a table, Attew's sharp eyes took in every micromovement of the new man's face. Lugovoy was as fluent as ever, explaining that there was nothing he couldn't find out about anyone in Russia—whether it meant intercepting calls, bugging buildings, or having targets tailed—but Attew felt a strong dislike forming. There was something scarily cold, he thought, about this cocksure character with his flashy watch and inscrutable gaze. By the time the meeting broke up, he had resolved to have nothing to do with Lugovoy.

The private spy boss wasn't the only person who thought Lugovoy was bad news. Nikolai Glushkov had finally been released from Lefortovo after serving time for his failed escape attempt, and he fled to Britain, where Boris and Badri put him up in a Berkshire mansion with servants and an eleven-acre pond. The former Aeroflot boss was enjoying a quiet home counties life quaffing fine wines and organizing pirate treasure hunts for the local children. But his face darkened as soon as he learned that Lugovoy was hanging around town. Glushkov insisted that the newcomer had set up the foiled escape to frame him on behalf of the FSB, and he implored Boris and Badri to eject their former security man from their circle. But nobody listened.

"Relax," Patarkatsishvili told him soothingly. Too much prison time had clearly made poor old Glushkov paranoid. Lugovoy was one of them, he said, and that was final.

Litvinenko agreed, so when Attew contacted him a few weeks later with a new commission, he didn't hesitate to turn to his regular partner for help. And this time, the job was red-hot.

Attew needed information on none other than Viktor Ivanov— the former KGB officer who, according to Litvinenko's information, had led Putin into business with the Tambov gang in the '90s as the mobsters smuggled drugs into the St. Petersburg seaport. Ivanov remained one of Putin's closest allies, and one of Attew's clients was on the brink of going into business with him. Litvinenko was tasked with carrying out the due diligence on the deal, and he asked Lugovoy to get him some fresh intelligence on Ivanov's latest activities to add to the information about his days in St. Petersburg. But when his partner's report arrived, Litvinenko was dismayed. It covered just a third of a sheet of paper and contained almost nothing that wasn't already in the public domain.

"I can't work with this," said Attew disdainfully when he saw the document. "There's nothing in here." Abashed, Litvinenko promised to get him something better. He found another Russian partner to work with and came back with an eight-page report containing the information he had assembled on Putin and Ivanov during his time in the FSB's organized crime squad, combined with fresh information supplied by other sources. This time, Attew was delighted. This was, he said, "exactly the type of report I would hope to expect," and its contents were so damaging for Ivanov that Titon's client immediately pulled the plug on the deal.

Litvinenko was thrilled with this outcome, but he was frustrated that Lugovoy had let him down. So the next time he saw his partner in London, he handed over a copy of the second report as an example of the sort of work they should aspire to. That was how Lugovoy returned to Moscow with all Litvinenko's incendiary evidence connecting Putin and Ivanov to the Tambov gang tucked safely inside his suitcase.

London and Moscow—October 2006

Something was wrong with Anna Politkovskaya. When Litvinenko met his friend at a Caffè Nero on one of her visits to London, he saw that her face was drawn with worry under her trademark steel-rimmed spectacles.

"Anna, what is it?" he asked, shocked to see the fearless journalist looking so shaken.

"Alexander," she said. "I'm very afraid."

Politkovskaya told him she had been receiving threats that she believed came directly from Putin. She had been threatened often enough before, but this time she felt a terrible foreboding. Every morning as she said goodbye to her son and daughter before leaving her flat, it was as if she were seeing them for the last time. And she couldn't say why, but she felt especially vulnerable in the elevator of her apartment building.

"Anna," he implored her. "Don't go back to Russia." But Politkovskaya's children were there, as well as her elderly parents. Besides, she was on the verge of publishing a new exposé about the systematic torture of prisoners by pro-Kremlin troops in Chechnya. She said goodbye to Litvinenko and flew home.

On the afternoon of October 7, Politkovskaya pulled up outside her apartment building in her Lada and began unloading her grocery bags. She was in a hurry—her story was scheduled to go out the next day—so she didn't see the thin man in the baseball cap watching as she hastened inside. Politkovskaya left the first load of bags upstairs and came back down in the elevator to collect the rest. When the doors slid open, the thin man was waiting. He fired two shots into her chest and a third into her shoulder. By the time the fourth bullet entered her skull, she was dead. The gunman dropped his pistol and its silencer next to her slumped body and disappeared.

The assassination of Anna Politkovskaya provoked an international outpouring of grief and anger. The US-based Committee to Protect Journalists declared her the thirteenth reporter to be assassinated since Putin came to power. Hundreds of protesters gathered in Moscow to decry the killing, and candlelight vigils were held in cities around the world. Even Tony Blair and George W. Bush were moved to condemn the murder, calling for a "thorough investigation into this terrible crime" in a joint statement. But Putin was laconic. He said the Russian authorities would get to the bottom of the shooting, but he dismissed Politkovskaya as a "very minor" figure who had "no influence on political life."

Litvinenko was devastated. He was outraged that his brave friend had been cut down and terrified that he would be next. But his fears were allayed somewhat the following week, when he received the long-awaited news that he and his family had been granted full British citizenship. Attew was working in his office, at the top of a smart town house in Mayfair, when Litvinenko burst in waving his passport.

"I'm British!" he yelled, literally jumping for joy. Now Anatoly would grow up an English gentleman, he joked, and maybe one day his son might even work for MI6.

The family attended their citizenship ceremony at Haringey Civic Centre on October 13. Afterward, Litvinenko took Anatoly to a memorial for Politkovskaya outside Westminster Abbey and spotted Felshtinsky in the crowd.

"I just received my citizenship!" he told the historian. "Now they will not be able to touch me." Felshtinsky smiled back at him kindly and kept his thoughts to himself.

Litvinenko told Anatoly they now belonged fully to this country where anyone could stand up and speak the truth without fear, and he resolved to use that freedom to stick up for Politkovskaya's memory. The next week, he and Zakayev attended an event honoring their friend at the Frontline Club, a gathering place for journalists near London's Paddington railway station. When the speeches were finished, Litvinenko got to his feet.

"My name is Alexander Litvinenko, and I am a former KGB and FSB officer," he said in faltering English, before the event's interpreter came to his aid. "I think that because I'm here, I should really speak up and say what I know," he went on in Russian, standing ramrod straight. "Who is guilty of Anna's death? I'll give you a straight answer: it is Mr. Putin, the president of the Russian Federation."

The declaration caused a small sensation inside the snug little club, with its wooden floors and exposed brick walls. Litvinenko was not a well-known face in London media circles, and the press pack was riveted by this intense blue-eyed man who spoke with palpable feeling about his friend Anna—a woman so brave, and so determined, that she had carried on reporting even under the specter of her own death. "Journalists of the stature of Anna Politkovskaya can only be killed by one person," he told the room. "That is Putin. No one else."

XI

London—October–November 2006

On a sunny early autumn day a week after Politkovskaya's murder, Lugovoy was back in London. This time he wasn't alone. His companion was Dmitri Kovtun, a childhood friend and classmate from Moscow's elite military academy who had just returned from a decade trying and failing to make it as a porn star in Germany. The pair had lost touch when Kovtun moved to Hamburg to look for his big break, but after years working as a pot washer, drinking, and drifting aimlessly through the city's red-light district, he had finally given up and come home. Kovtun was desperate by the time he ran into Lugovoy back in Moscow, and his old friend offered him a chance to transform his life. There was a job to do in London—and if they pulled it off, they would both be made men.

Lugovoy brought Kovtun to meet Litvinenko in mid-October, arriving laden with designer shopping bags and dressed in loud checks. He introduced his companion as one of his oldest friends, selling him as a master at digital surveillance who could help them dig up dirt on targets in Russia. Litvinenko took an immediate dislike to Kovtun. The newcomer was surly and brooding, with sallow skin and shadowed eyes, and he looked shifty in his shiny silver suit. But Lugovoy insisted that Kovtun could be trusted and announced that he was bringing him to a meeting they had planned that afternoon with an important client.

The appointment was with a British company called Erinys International, which wanted the men's help scoping a big security deal with the Kremlin-owned gas giant Gazprom. The Russians walked over on foot and were met at the door of the firm's smart Mayfair offices by Tim Reilly, its upper-crust energy director. Reilly shook their hands and ushered them into the boardroom, stifling a smile at their gaudy attire. As soon as they sat down, Lugovoy asked him to serve them some tea. It was an unseasonably warm day, and nobody really felt like a hot drink, but he was oddly insistent, so Reilly obligingly poured out three cups. When they got down to business, Lugovoy did most of the talking—rattling off bold claims about the strings he could pull in Russia's oil and gas industry—while Kovtun sat in morose silence and Litvinenko eyed him with growing distaste. The three cups of tea went cold without anyone taking a sip.

When the meeting broke up, Litvinenko departed hastily for the bus back to Osier Crescent, where Marina was cooking her spicy chicken soup. He felt strangely uneasy about the way the meeting had gone, he told her over dinner. He couldn't say why, exactly, but he found Lugovoy's friend from Moscow "very unpleasant." Later, he began to feel a little unwell. He threw up once and emerged from the bathroom looking worried.

"I feel so weak," he told Marina. But he turned in for an early night, and by the morning he was himself again.

Lugovoy and Kovtun flew back to Russia. But less than a fortnight later, Litvinenko's partner was back. He showed up first at Downside Manor to see Patarkatsishvili, and the pair spent a pleasant afternoon shooting the breeze in a gazebo out on the grounds. Then he swung by Down Street to see Berezovsky. The oligarch wanted some advice on providing security for a Russian journalist who had recently fled to Britain. The journalist's apartment building had been bombed after she published a book chronicling Putin's crackdown on democratic freedoms in Russia, and she had turned to Berezovsky for protection. While the two men were discussing her security, Glushkov burst into the oligarch's office brandishing two bottles of wine that he wanted

Berezovsky to order in bulk for his private jet. But the old Aeroflot director backed quickly out of the room as soon as he saw who was visiting.

At dusk, Lugovoy left Down Street and made his way over to the Sheraton on Park Lane, where he had arranged to see Litvinenko in the hotel's grand glass-ceilinged parlor. This was the real purpose of his trip—but when Litvinenko arrived, his plan quickly went off-kilter.

The defector had decided to let Lugovoy in on a major secret, and he was relieved to see his partner waiting for him without Kovtun when he entered the parlor. He sat down at the table, ordered a pot of tea, and produced two disposable SIM cards that he'd bought so the pair could communicate more securely. Then he leaned in and began telling Lugovoy all about his secret work for the Spanish intelligence services.

Litvinenko explained that had been working alongside the spies in Spain for years as they unraveled connections between the Tambov gang and the Kremlin, and now he was preparing to travel to Madrid to meet prosecutors on November 8 as a first step toward testifying openly about the group's links to Putin. He was excited, and he thought the spies in Madrid might have some work for Lugovoy, too, so he invited his partner to come with him. Lugovoy nodded and maintained his insouciant manner, slugging back three glasses of red wine and dragging on a cigar as Litvinenko spoke. But he was listening intently. It was clear that he was going to have to fly back to Moscow for one more debriefing before he could finish this job.

The sixth anniversary of Litvinenko's arrival in Britain fell a few days later, on November 1, 2006. He had promised to be home in time for a celebratory dinner with Marina, but the rest of the day was clear, so when Lugovoy called to say he was back in London, Litvinenko gladly agreed to see him that afternoon.

His phone rang a second time that morning. This time it was Mario

Scaramella, a security adviser to a committee that was conducting a public inquiry into Russia-linked corruption in Italy. The defector had met Scaramella several times to supply evidence of an FSB agent he believed was operating under deep cover in Naples, and now the consultant said he'd uncovered something Litvinenko needed to know. The two men arranged to meet at the "old place"—a code for their regular rendezvous point in central London—and Litvinenko threw on a quilted denim jacket before setting out into the crisp autumn weather. He boarded a red London bus and then the tube to Piccadilly Circus, where he made out Scaramella's pudgy figure waiting by the winged statue of Eros under the square's illuminated billboards. As he drew closer, he noticed the consultant was looking rough and unshaved.

As soon as the two men came face-to-face, Scaramella announced that they were both in danger. He said he'd explain as soon as they were somewhere quieter, leading Litvinenko down the road to a branch of Itsu, the popular sushi restaurant, where they grabbed some sashimi and found a table.

"I have material," the consultant said the moment they were settled, producing an envelope from his briefcase and pulling out four grubby sheets of folded paper, which he slipped under the table to Litvinenko. The defector quickly saw what was making Scaramella so jittery.

The bundle contained two emails from a Russian source claiming close links to the Russian intelligence services who had written to the consultant in early October with a tip-off. Scaramella's name had been placed on an FSB hit list, the source said, adding that his contacts in the agency spoke "more and more about the necessity to use force" to exterminate Russia's enemies. The list itself had been pasted into the email, and Litvinenko was unsurprised to see his own name alongside Scaramella's. Berezovsky and Zakayev were on there, too. Most chillingly, so was Politkovskaya: the email had been sent just a few days before she was shot dead.

Litvinenko looked up and met Scaramella's round-eyed gaze. "Calm down," he told the Italian, sliding the documents into his bag. He said he'd need more time to study the tip-off before reaching any conclusions about its credibility.

Litvinenko was playing it cool, but his investigative senses were tingling. The emails contained descriptions of a number of officers allegedly involved in the plot to kill those named on the list, including a judo master with a lame right leg said to be running a network of assassins out of St. Petersburg. Perhaps, he thought, they might help to identify Politkovskaya's killer. He wanted to show the documents to Zakayev and Berezovsky as soon as possible, but first he had to keep his appointment with Lugovoy. So he hastily wrapped up lunch with Scaramella and hurried off toward the Millennium Hotel in Mayfair.

Litvinenko was known for his caution. He used burner phones to communicate with sensitive sources and frequently performed countersurveillance drills to check that he wasn't being tailed. He knew full well he had a target on his back, and he'd warned his fellow exiles more than once to beware of the long-lost acquaintance who appears suddenly from the past. But he'd been out of the FSB for years, and his standards were slipping.

This was the first time Litvinenko had been to the Millennium Hotel. In the old days, when attending a meeting in an unfamiliar place, he would have been careful to perform reconnaissance. He would have arrived early to scan the area, locate the exits, and watch who came and went. Had he got there half an hour earlier, history might have been different. Litvinenko would have observed an agitated Lugovoy crossing the lobby clutching something inside his jacket and slipping into the men's room for several minutes. He would have watched his partner emerge from the restroom and head into the Pine Bar—a wood-paneled room with soft leather upholstery and warm side lamps that just happened to be one of the only places in the hotel not covered by CCTV. He'd have spotted that Kovtun was there, too, paying his own furtive trip to the loo before joining Lugovoy in the bar, where the two men ordered gin and Champagne before calling the waiter back for tea. And he would have seen them fussing with the spout of the ceramic teapot that was placed before them on the table.

But Litvinenko wasn't worried—Lugovoy was a friend. He walked into the lobby at 3:59 p.m. and called his partner to announce his arrival without pausing for breath. Lugovoy came straight out to meet him wearing clothes he'd bought in the Harrods men's department on a shopping trip with Litvinenko a few months earlier—a tight blue-and-orange cardigan over a pair of smart gray jeans.

"Let's go," he said, gesturing toward the Pine Bar. He led the defector over to his table. "There's already some tea left here," he said casually, gesturing at the pot. "If you want you can have some."

Litvinenko poured. The pot was almost empty, and the tea that trickled out was green. He took three or four gulps—but it was cold and unsweetened, with an unusually bitter taste. He pushed the cup aside.

Then, to Litvinenko's displeasure, Kovtun appeared and sat down at the table. He looked paler than ever in a black zippered sweater, and he seemed depressed, or maybe hungover. Litvinenko wondered if he was a drug addict or an alcoholic. And then, quite suddenly, it began to dawn on him that he hardly knew this man he was meeting here, in this unknown place. Who was Kovtun? Why had Lugovoy brought them here? Out of nowhere came a creeping sense of unease.

The three men talked a bit of business over the din of the crowded bar, but soon Lugovoy was staring at his big gold watch, saying it was time to go. He had brought his entire family with him to London on this trip, and they had tickets to watch CSKA Moscow play Arsenal at the Emirates Stadium that evening, courtesy of Berezovsky. Lugovoy had been insistent on seeing Litvinenko, but suddenly it seemed there was nothing to say. Now his wife was in the foyer, gesturing for him to leave. Lugovoy went over to her and returned with a small boy clutching a bag from Hamleys, the famous London toy store. It was his eight-year-old son, Igor.

"This is Uncle Sasha," Lugovoy said to Igor. "Shake his hand." The boy obeyed. And then the family was gone.

Twilight was settling over the city as Litvinenko left the hotel and headed south through Mayfair. The lanterns were on by the time he reached Down Street. Litvinenko had been visiting a little less lately, since Berezovsky cut his stipend, but the office was still a place of comfortable familiarity. He took the elevator up to the second floor and passed the security guards at the door, waving to a departing Glushkov as he padded across the plush cream carpet to the photo-copier at the back. He began running off clean copies of the scrappy documents Scaramella had handed him, folding the emails carefully at the top to conceal the identity of the source.

Litvinenko had called Berezovsky on his way over from the Mil-lennium Hotel to say he had documents that might point to Politkovskaya's killers, and the oligarch was impatient. He, too, was running late for the match at the Emirates Stadium that night.

"Be quick!" he shouted to Litvinenko. The defector handed over a set of copies and then grabbed his phone, which was ringing in his pocket. It was Zakayev, calling from outside in his Mercedes to offer a ride home to Muswell Hill.

In the car, the two men began figuring out how they'd run down the new leads in the emails. Litvinenko couldn't shake his unease about the meeting with Lugovoy and Kovtun, but he kept his concerns to himself and called home to tell Marina he was on his way.

"Please don't eat anything!" his wife blurted out when she learned he was with Zakayev. She was busy preparing chicken pancakes to mark the anniversary of their arrival in Britain—the first they'd ever celebrated as citizens. He promised to keep an empty stomach.

Anatoly was back from school when Litvinenko walked through the door. While Marina finished preparing dinner, he spent some time examining Scaramella's documents before hole-punching the clean copies and placing them carefully in his files. When the family sat down to celebrate, Litvinenko delighted his wife by wolfing down five whole pancakes. She thought her husband seemed happy. Life in England had been good to them.

It was a peaceful evening, and the couple turned in at 11:00 p.m. But ten minutes after the light went out, Litvinenko ran to the toilet and threw up everything he'd eaten. Even when his stomach was completely empty, he couldn't stop retching.

"Maybe it will pass," Marina said.

"I don't think it will," he told her.

She made him a mixture of manganese and warm water, an old Russian remedy for food poisoning, but it came straight back up. Anxious not to disturb his wife and son, he retired to his study and spent a miserable night being violently sick every twenty minutes.

At dawn, Marina came in to check on him and was alarmed by his pallor. Litvinenko told her he was now throwing up blood and foam. He said he felt like he couldn't breathe, so she threw open all the windows and let the cold November air stream in.

"I have been poisoned," he told her.

XII

―

London—November 2006

In the hospital, Litvinenko initially seemed to rally. Doctors put him on a drip, and he regained a little strength. But the medics were mystified by his condition. At first they assumed he was suffering from severe food poisoning, but then they observed that his white blood cell count was falling fast. That meant his immune system was collapsing, but no one had the first idea why.

The patient himself continued to insist that he had been poisoned, but there was no sign of any recognizable toxin in his system to support that seemingly far-fetched claim. Marina told the staff that there was good reason to believe her husband: he was a former FSB officer, after all, and he knew "dangerous people." But the medics waved away her concerns, and days went by without any improvement.

When Marina visited on November 13, she was shocked by a sudden decline in her husband's condition. Litvinenko looked jaundiced, gaunt, and exhausted. She stroked his head to soothe him, and a clump of his hair came away on her glove. Then she saw that it was all over his sheets and pillow, too.

"What's this?" she shouted. "What happened to my husband?"

It had been nearly a fortnight since Litvinenko fell ill, and the doctors were no closer to a diagnosis. But then a hematologist who was brought in to review his case made a striking observation. Litvinenko's symptoms were similar to those of cancer patients after intense bouts of chemotherapy. The blood doctor soon refined his diagnosis: it looked like he was suffering from radiation sickness.

Staff brought in a Geiger counter to scan the patient's body for gamma rays—the most common kind of radiation—but they found none. Doctors were, once again, stumped. The next clue arrived that afternoon in the form of a new batch of test results from the medical lab. Traces of a toxin that looked like the heavy metal thallium had been detected in Litvinenko's system. The levels were too faint to explain the severity of his condition, and further tests were needed, but the results finally shifted the diagnostic calculus. This was now officially being treated as a case of suspected poisoning.

Litvinenko was transferred to a specialist unit at University College Hospital, in Bloomsbury, where he was put on an emergency course of Prussian blue—an antidote to thallium. A squad of armed police officers was stationed outside his bedroom door, on the hospital's sixteenth floor. And just before midnight, a wiry figure appeared at his bedside.

The suited stranger addressed Litvinenko by his English name, Edwin. He was pale and rawboned, with silvering hair slicked aside from a deeply creased forehead, and he introduced himself as Detective Inspector Brent Hyatt from Scotland Yard.

"Edwin, we're here investigating an allegation that somebody has poisoned you," he said impassively. "Can I ask you to tell us what you think has happened to you and why?"

Litvinenko had lain powerless to fight back as his condition deteriorated for more than two weeks, but his mind had been hard at work on the case. He told Hyatt that he had been poisoned by Andrey Lugovoy and Dmitri Kovtun.

The defector had not said as much to anyone else—not even to Marina. If Lugovoy and Kovtun had no idea that he'd given them up, he reasoned, there was a good chance they'd return to London, where they could be arrested. But he was ready to tell Hyatt everything. "It's very important for my case," he said.

The whole story came tumbling out in broken English. He explained how he'd blown the whistle on the plot to kill Berezovsky and fled to Britain, where he'd carried on investigating the FSB's role in the Moscow apartment bombings and other atrocities bearing the fingerprints of the Russian state.

"I live here," he said. "I spoke. I fight." He explained that his friend Anna Politkovskaya had been killed the month before, and he had stood up at the Frontline Club and told journalists it was Putin who killed her.

"I lost a lot of my friends," he said. "My wife cry. My son don't understand this."

He talked for hours into the night, telling the detectives they would find all the evidence backing up his claims in the files he kept at home, on Osier Crescent.

The next day, Hyatt returned with a Russian interpreter. Now Litvinenko could communicate more fluently, and he was unequivocal about who had ordered his poisoning.

"The order about such a killing of a citizen of another country on its territory, especially if it is something to do with Great Britain, could have been given by only one person," he said.

Hyatt regarded him levelly. "Would you like to tell us who that person is, sir?"

"That person is the president of the Russian Federation, Vladimir Putin."

Litvinenko told the detectives he wasn't naive. "You won't be able to prosecute him," he acknowledged, "because he is the president of a huge country crammed with nuclear, chemical, and bacteriological weapons." But he begged them not to let the matter lie. "I understand that this case is going to be perceived by everyone as political," he said. "But this case is not political—this case is criminal."

Hyatt interviewed Litvinenko at his bedside for a total of nine hours over three days. The defector was suffering from severe di-arrhea and had to break off frequently to use the toilet. Nurses interrupted at regular intervals to administer medicine, change his drip, and check his levels. As the final interview drew to a close, Lit-vinenko seized his chance for a final declaration.

"I feel very upset that this criminal, Putin, sits at the G8 as its chairman at the same table as the British prime minister, Tony Blair," he said vehemently. "Having sat this murderer next to themselves at the same table, Western leaders have actually untied his hands to kill anyone anywhere."

Litvinenko's condition was now dire. His heart rate was irregular, his organs were failing fast, and his digestive tract was so inflamed that he could hardly talk. He was moved into intensive care.

Marina kept a near-constant vigil, sitting with him all day and bringing Anatoly to see his rapidly emaciating father after school. Berezovsky flew back from a trip to South Africa to be at his bedside. Zakayev, too, was there every day.

Doctors were now saying Litvinenko had a fifty-fifty chance of sur-vival, but they were none the wiser as to the cause of his illness. His symptoms weren't consistent with thallium poisoning, and the levels detected in his system were too low to explain his rapid decline. Ra-diation sickness didn't seem to make sense, either, since the Geiger counter had failed to detect any sign of gamma radiation.

At a loss, Litvinenko's medical team reached out to a poison spe-cialist at another hospital who made an obscure suggestion. What if he hadn't been poisoned by regular gamma rays but by another form of radiation too rare to be detected by standard hospital tests? It seemed far-fetched, but it was all they had to go on, so the hospital staff took further urine samples from Litvinenko and sent them off to the British government's Atomic Weapons Establishment, at Alder-maston, for testing.

Litvinenko, meanwhile, sensed he was dying and was determined that the world should know why. He wanted a statement drawn up to be released in the event of his death, directly accusing Putin of his murder. His lawyer got to work and brought Litvinenko a draft.

"This is exactly what I want to say," the defector rasped. He scrawled his signature in spidery lettering across the bottom of the page.

Next, he needed to capture the public's attention, and Berezovsky called on his publicity adviser, Lord Bell, for help. The PR man's advice was clear: a picture would tell this story far more powerfully than words. The defector agreed, and Bell summoned a photographer to the hospital. When she entered the room, Litvinenko pushed aside his hospital gown to reveal the mess of wires and sensors attached to his gaunt chest. The flashbulb flared, and the image was captured: his body jaundiced and shrunken; his fierce blue eyes staring defiantly down the lens.

The picture made the story. The next day, Litvinenko's agonized face was plastered all over the front pages of every British newspaper, and a growing throng of journalists and TV crews clamored at the hospital gates for news of the poisoned Russian spy.

There was one last matter to take care of. Litvinenko had pledged the last years of his life to championing the cause of the Chechen people, and he wanted to make a final gesture of solidarity. He told Zakayev he wished to die a Muslim. With Marina's permission, the rebel leader spoke the *shahada* and brought an imam to his friend's bedside to perform the rites of conversion.

Litvinenko spent the next day drifting in and out of consciousness. His father, Walter, had flown from Russia to keep watch overnight. When Marina rose to go home to Anatoly, Litvinenko awoke suddenly.

"Marina," he said, looking at her directly. "I love you so much."

Later that night, Litvinenko lost consciousness for the last time. Marina spent the following day by his side as he lay in a coma. When night fell, she returned to Osier Crescent to put Anatoly to bed. While at home, she received a call from the hospital telling her to come back immediately. When mother and son arrived on the ward, they were shown into a private room.

The body on the bed was gray, skeletal, and hairless. Litvinenko was dead.

Six hours before, Scotland Yard had received test results from the Atomic Weapons Establishment revealing that the defector's body was riddled with alpha radiation. He had been poisoned with a rare nuclear isotope originating in only one place: a government nuclear facility in the depths of Russia's Ural Mountains. Its name was polonium-210.

In the early hours of the following morning, soon after Marina and Anatoly returned to Osier Crescent, huddled together and numb with grief, swarms of police officers converged on their home wearing protective suits, rubber boots, and gas masks. Their lives were in danger, they were told, and they must vacate the house at once. The pair spent a desolate night across the road at the Zakayevs' home. When they woke, their house was sealed with plastic and surrounded by a police guard. The property was humming with polonium radiation.

The family was asked not to talk to anyone while officials assessed the risk to the wider public. But when Walter Litvinenko emerged, blinking, from the hospital to a blaze of flashbulbs, the grief-stricken father broke down in tears and let it slip.

"My son was killed by a tiny little nuclear bomb," he sobbed in front of the cameras.

The British government could wait no longer before confirming that Litvinenko had been killed with radioactive polonium, and its COBRA crisis committee met to plan an emergency response to the defector's death. It was only a year since Britain's top intelligence officials had gathered around the table for a private audience with Vladimir Putin. Now the spy chiefs were there to brief the government on intelligence connecting the Russian president to a targeted nuclear attack in the heart of the capital.

Outside the bunker, chaos was breaking loose. Squads of public health officers in protective gear were scouring the streets of London for alpha radiation while camera crews pursued them at every step. "This is an unprecedented event in the UK," the government's Health Protection Agency said in a statement. "It is the first time someone in the UK has apparently been deliberately poisoned with a radioactive agent." The story was running on every news channel, and an emergency government hotline was deluged with calls from thousands of people who feared they might have been exposed to the radiation.

Berezovsky's advisers had by now released Litvinenko's final statement. The document the defector signed on his deathbed was sent to every newsroom in the country—and his last words rang out around the world.

I would like to thank many people. My doctors, nurses and hospital staff who are doing all they can for me, the British police who are pursuing my case with vigor and professionalism and are watching over me and my family.

I would like to thank the British government for taking me under their care. I am honored to be a British citizen. I would like to thank the British public for their messages of support and for the interest they have shown in my plight. I thank my wife Marina, who has stood by me. My love for her and our son knows no bounds.

But as I lie here I can distinctly hear the beating of wings of the angel of death. I may be able to give him the slip but I have to say my legs do not run as fast as I would like. I think, therefore, that this may be the time to say one or two things to the person responsible for my present condition.

You may succeed in silencing me but that silence comes at a price. You have shown yourself to be as barbaric and ruthless as your most hostile critics have claimed. You have shown yourself to have no respect for life, liberty or any civilized value. You have shown yourself to be unworthy of your office, to be unworthy of the trust of civilized men and women.

You may succeed in silencing one man but the howl of protest from around the world will reverberate, Mr. Putin, in your ears for the rest of your life. May God forgive you for what you have done, not only to me but to beloved Russia and its people.

—*Alexander Litvinenko, 21 November 2006*

Putin dismissed Litvinenko's statement as a fake. "It is a pity that tragic events like death have been used for political provocations," he told journalists at a news conference in Helsinki. Meanwhile, back in Russia, the state propaganda machine sowed doubt and confusion. A loyal Duma deputy named Sergey Abeltsev declared the defector's death "a serious warning to traitors of all colors, wherever they are located," while the Kremlin's media outlets churned out an ever more baffling array of conspiracy theories about how Litvinenko had met his end. The defector poisoned himself. Or Berezovsky murdered him to frame Putin. Or the mafia was responsible. Or MI6 had him assassinated. Or Zakayev was the killer.

But the radioactive evidence was incontrovertible. Lugovoy and Kovtun had left a glaring polonium trail all over London, allowing police to reconstruct their every move in lurid detail. The polonium pathway led from the hotel rooms where they slept to the offices they visited and the bars, restaurants, and strip clubs they patronized after hours. It even traveled with them all the way back to Russia. After the pair were widely named in the media as Scotland Yard's prime suspects, they visited the British embassy in Moscow to proclaim their innocence, only to leave polonium traces all over the furniture. The chair Lugovoy sat on was so radioactive it had to be burned.

Back in London, the polonium evidence allowed police to piece together an astonishingly vivid picture of the fate that had befallen Litvinenko. The Pine Bar was a nuclear disaster zone. The toilet stall

Lugovoy and Kovtun had visited before Litvinenko's arrival was heavily contaminated, as were the chairs and tables where they had sat. The teapot the assassins tampered with gave off an astronomically high radioactive reading, with the most concentrated levels on the spout. It had been placed in a dishwasher after the poisoning, spreading the nuclear contamination across tableware, glassware, and cutlery that the hotel had unwittingly continued giving to other guests. Scientists examining the room where Kovtun had slept found a mangled clump of hair in the bathroom sink that was clogged with pure polonium. The assassin had poured the dregs of the poison down the drain.

Lugovoy and Kovtun had brought the polonium with them to the Pine Bar, but it was Litvinenko who carried the radioactive trail with him when he left the hotel. After drinking the poisoned tea, the defector had set off for Down Street emitting an invisible radioactive glow. He had trailed polonium into Berezovsky's offices, leaving traces all over the photocopier he used to scan Scaramella's documents as well as the back seat of Zakayev's car as he traveled home.

The trail revealed that the assassins had likely attempted to poison Litvinenko twice before they finally succeeded. The first time was at the meeting in Reilly's boardroom, where the polonium appeared to have been slipped into Litvinenko's cup after Lugovoy insisted that they all drink tea. The defector had not taken a sip—but tests showed the whole table had been left "heaving" with radiation. Lugovoy had returned to the Best Western after the meeting and thrown the remainder of the vial down his bathroom sink.

The second occasion was in the Sheraton parlor. Lugovoy brought another vial of polonium to the hotel where Litvinenko had opened up about his work for the Spanish investigators. When the defector left, Lugovoy again returned to his hotel room and chucked the polonium in the trash. This time he spilled some and mopped it up with a couple of towels that a hotel cleaner later picked up and threw down the laundry chute. When Scotland Yard examined the scene, it was so radioactive that two nuclear scientists wearing full protective gear had to withdraw for their own safety, and the entire hotel was sealed off. The towels were sent to Aldermaston and impounded.

By then, more than three thousand people had called the government help line to voice fears that they might have been contaminated, and Health Protection Agency officials were looking for around five hundred members of the public they considered to be at risk. The entire staff of the Pine Bar was found to have been exposed to polonium, and anyone who drank from the contaminated teapot needed to be tracked down for testing. Two policemen tested positive. Reilly, Scaramella, Berezovsky, and Zakayev had also been exposed. And Litvinenko's family was contaminated, too. The defector himself was the only person to have fallen seriously ill from exposure to the poison—he was, after all, the only one who had ingested it in undiluted form—but the long-term effects of polonium contamination remain unclear.

The pathologists who were brought in to perform Litvinenko's autopsy wore full protective clothing. It was, they agreed, "one of the most dangerous postmortems ever undertaken in the Western world." Litvinenko had 26.5 micrograms of polonium in his bloodstream. Less than one microgram would have been fatal. When the body was finally released to the family, it was in a sealed lead-lined casket, and they were told that if they wanted to have him cremated, they would have to wait more than twenty years for the radiation to subside before his remains could be safely removed.

On December 7, Marina and Anatoly stood in the pouring rain on a hill overlooking North London and watched as the casket descended into the ground at Highgate Cemetery. Berezovsky and Zakayev were among the pallbearers who carried Litvinenko's body to its final resting place, and the rebel leader had brought an imam to say prayers as the coffin was lowered into its muddy grave. Walter Litvinenko stepped forward from the huddled mourners to give his son's eulogy.

"Sasha was killed for telling the truth by those who are afraid of what he had to say," he said in a voice so choked that other mourners strained to hear his words. A police guard kept the press pack at bay. The night before the funeral, Scotland Yard had announced publicly that their inquiry was officially a murder investigation.

The Crown Prosecution Service went on to formally charge Lugovoy and Kovtun with Litvinenko's murder, and Britain demanded that the two suspects be extradited to stand trial in London, but no one was holding out much hope. Moscow initially suggested that the two men could be "exchanged" for Berezovsky and Zakayev, but when that proposal hit a brick wall, Russian prosecutors flatly refused to extradite them.

Britain could simply not afford a total collapse in its relationship with Moscow over the killing. The UK was by then the biggest foreign investor in Russian oil and gas, and BP was scoping a new joint venture with Gazprom after acquiring its stake in Rosneft. Moreover, the West was staring down the barrel of Iran's advancing nuclear program, and its leaders needed Putin's help to put pressure on Tehran to step back from the brink. The relationship with Russia was too strategically important to pick an open-ended fight with the Kremlin. The situation was a stalemate. The UK expelled four Russian diplomats, and Moscow sent four British officials packing in return.

Putin's government built a protective wall around the two wanted men. Lugovoy capitalized on his role in the saga to acquire a macabre kind of celebrity in Russia, holding press conferences, giving countless TV interviews, and parading himself around the talk-show circuit, all the while branding Litvinenko a "traitor" and denying any role in his killing.

"He was sticking his nose in places where a dog would not stick his tail," Lugovoy sneered in one radio interview. "And so what happened to him was most likely due to his imprudent choice of associates and general reckless way of life."

Lugovoy's career in the public eye went from strength to strength.

He was given a seat in the Duma, making him immune from prosecution in Russia, as well as a role hosting a show called *Traitors* on Russian TV. Kovtun kept a lower profile, outside of a few appearances at heavily stage-managed press conferences where he morosely protested his innocence, but he was soon doing big business as a consultant in Russia. The onetime pot washer and failed porn star was suddenly a wealthy man.

For the spies in the River House, the poisoning of Alexander Litvinenko marked the realization of a long-held fear. The first MI6 heard of it was when Litvinenko's handler received a call from Detective Inspector Hyatt, calling from the defector's bedside. Litvinenko had proved the most cooperative of witnesses, yet as they tracked back through all his activities in the days before he fell ill, there was one item on his schedule he flatly refused to discuss: a meeting in the basement café of Waterstones on Piccadilly with someone he wouldn't name.

"Edwin," Hyatt had said sternly. "It could be absolutely vital that you tell us who that person is."

Litvinenko wouldn't budge, but he gave Hyatt the number he used to contact Martin, and the detective placed the call. As soon as Hyatt explained whom he was interviewing, the handler rushed right over to the hospital to debrief his informant, returning to the River House with the nightmarish news that an MI6 asset appeared to have been poisoned on British soil without anyone noticing.

The spy agency cranked into crisis mode, tapping every source and listening post for intelligence about who was behind the plot to kill Litvinenko. The picture that emerged was horribly clear. The FSB had enlisted Lugovoy and Kovtun to infiltrate the community of Russian exiles living in Britain and eliminate the defector in an operation personally overseen by the agency's director, Nikolai Patrushev. And all the intelligence suggested that the instruction had come from the top: Vladimir Putin himself had ordered the killing.

None of that source material could ever be made public without blowing the cover of highly sensitive informants and listening posts in Russia, but it left no room for doubt inside the River House. And the Russia watchers were collecting intelligence about three more strange events that served to heighten fears about the threat Putin posed to the West.

First, they learned that Igor Ponomarev, Russia's representative on the United Nations' International Maritime Organization, had collapsed and died in London after a night at the opera just two days before Litvinenko was poisoned. The diplomat had complained of severe thirst and drunk three liters of water—a known symptom of thallium poisoning—before keeling over, and his body had been rushed back to Russia on a diplomatic plane before any tests could be carried out by British medics. Ponomarev had formed close relationships with US diplomats in the course of his work, and he had arranged to meet privately with Scaramella on the day after his death. That connection, and the proximity to Litvinenko's poisoning, was too much to ignore, so the Russia watchers sent a formal request to their counterparts at the CIA for information about Ponomarev. When the response came back, the US spies confirmed what MI6 feared: they had intelligence suggesting the diplomat may have been poisoned.

Then came the death of Daniel McGrory. The veteran journalist at the London *Times* died of a sudden hemorrhage five days before the airing of an NBC documentary in which he was interviewed about his reporting on Litvinenko's death. Soon after the broadcast, a second contributor was targeted: a US security expert named Paul Joyal, who had also been interviewed by NBC. Joyal was shot and seriously wounded by two gunmen in the driveway of his home, in Maryland, and his attackers were never caught. There was no tangible evidence connecting either McGrory's death or the attack on Joyal to Russia— no suspects, no forensic evidence, no glaring radioactive trail. And while Joyal declared publicly that he believed he had been targeted by Russian assassins, McGrory's family insisted the journalist's fatal hemorrhage had been caused by an enlarged heart, as his inquest found. But the proximity of the two incidents was alarming enough to prompt the spies in the River House to reach out again to the CIA—and again, the US spies confirmed they had intelligence connecting both cases to Russia.

In the aftermath of Litvinenko's killing, the Russia watchers were left grappling with the knowledge that Putin was prepared to hunt down and murder his adversaries wherever in the world they might seek safe haven. He had passed laws sanctioning the killing of enemies of the state on foreign soil, and he had wasted no time in putting those laws into action. The development of his arsenal of chemical and biological weapons for use in targeted assassinations was gathering pace, and he had shown his willingness to imperil countless members of the public in order to hit his mark. Most chillingly, the threat to Britain's community of Russian exiles only seemed to be rising.

Putin had learned that he could murder a British citizen on the streets of the capital with impunity—and Litvinenko had been only one name on the FSB's kill list. Who was next?

PART FIVE

IMPUNITY

XIII

━━━━

Home Office, London—November 2006

Rain was spreading like a fresh bruise across the London sky as the unmarked car rolled up Whitehall toward Big Ben. The Scotland Yard protection officer scanned the road with a well-trained eye, clocking potential hazards as the car passed the spiked iron gates of Downing Street, and swung right on Parliament Square. He had spent years guarding countless government ministers and visiting foreign dignitaries, and there wasn't an inch of this maze of power that he didn't know like the back of his hand.

Nothing looked amiss as the car sloshed to a stop outside a modern multicolored glass building. London's black-cab drivers were doing roaring business in the rain, and the pavements were gray and empty except for a smattering of pedestrians under dripping umbrellas. But the city was in crisis. The protection officer had been summoned as the government scrambled to respond to a nuclear attack in the heart of London.

The doors to the Home Office slid open and the officer strode into the command center of British state security. He was shown upstairs to a large boardroom where a host of grave-faced officials was waiting. A stale sort of mugginess in the air told him they had been cooped up together for some time.

"There were six people on the Kremlin's hit list," the woman at the head of the table said as soon as he sat, "and they have already killed Litvinenko." Officials from MI5, MI6, and GCHQ were seated around the table, the officer noted, alongside the Home Office security chiefs. "This is a direct policy of the Russian state: they are killing dissidents," the chair continued. "We have some here, and they are coming for them." She addressed him directly. "Make them safe," she commanded.

Boris Berezovsky and Akhmed Zakayev were judged to be under "severe" threat of assassination, the officials around the table explained, meaning an attack was considered "highly likely," while a Russian journalist living in Britain and the Cold War defector Oleg Gordievsky* had also been identified as Kremlin targets. Another political hit on British soil would be an "unimaginable" disaster for the government as it struggled to salvage relations with Moscow and restore public confidence in the wake of the Litvinenko imbroglio. So the Home Office wanted Scotland Yard's Specialist Protection Command to work alongside the security services to provide "defense in depth" for each of the exiles on the Kremlin's hit list.

Specialist Protection was usually tasked with guarding the prime minister and members of the cabinet, so its officers had the same level of security clearance as Scotland Yard's counterterrorism command. That meant they could be briefed on intelligence British spies had gathered about the threats to the Russians on their watch.

Over the week that followed, they learned about the FSB's poison factory outside Moscow, where armies of state scientists were developing an ever-expanding suite of chemical and biological weapons for use against individual targets. There were poisons designed to make death look natural by triggering fast-acting cancers, heart attacks, and other fatal illnesses. There were labs set up to study the biomolecular structure of prescription medicines and work out what

---

* The other name believed to be on the Kremlin's hit list was Umar Israilov, a former bodyguard to Chechnya's pro-Kremlin president, Ramzan Kadyrov. Israilov had fled to Austria to file court papers implicating his boss in torture, rape, and murder. He was shot dead in 2009 outside the apartment in Vienna where he lived with his pregnant wife and three children.

could be added to turn a common cure into a deadly cocktail. And the state had developed a whole arsenal of psychotropic drugs to destabilize its enemies—powerful mood-altering substances designed to plunge targets into enough mental anguish to take their own lives or to make staged suicides look believable.

That Russia had poured such unimaginable resources into providing its hit squads with the tools of undetectable murder made the brazenness of Litvinenko's killing even more perplexing. Polonium had the potential to be the perfect traceless poison: its alpha rays made it hard to detect, and with a smaller dose Litvinenko would probably have died quietly of cancer a few months later. Perhaps, the security officials thought, the two assassins had overdosed him accidentally in their desperation to get the job done. Or maybe his death was deliberately dramatic, designed to send a signal to Russia's dissident diaspora in Britain. Either way, there was one thing the protection officer learned for sure: even if it looked like the death of a Russian exile was the result of natural causes, accident, or suicide, that conclusion might well not be worth the autopsy paper it was written on.

To add to the complexity, the FSB was inextricably intertwined with Russian mafia groups, which in turn had deep links to powerful organized crime gangs in Britain, so Scotland Yard needed to be ready for anything from a sophisticated chemical, biological, or nuclear attack to a crude hit contracted out to a London gangster for cash.

The greatest threat, by far, was to Berezovsky. The oligarch had made himself Russia's public enemy number one through his relentless attacks on the Kremlin and his efforts to foment insurrection in Putin's backyard, and he had effectively appointed himself the *chef de mission* of the entire dissident community in the UK. He had already survived several assassination attempts, and the Russia watchers were getting a steady stream of intelligence about new plots to kill him. Russia's state security and organized crime complex had grown into a multiheaded hydra under Putin's auspices, and competing factions within the FSB, the mafia, and the country's military intelligence agency (GRU) were all vying for the chance to harpoon the president's white whale.

Shielding Berezovsky was now the protection officer's top priority. It was time to pay a visit to Down Street.

Down Street, London—November 2006

Berezovsky was in typically rambunctious spirits. The murder of Litvinenko was a sickening blow, but it was also a resounding vindication. The assassination had, as the defector said in his dying statement, shown Putin to be just as brutal as his critics claimed, and finally the world was listening. Down Street was abuzz as the oligarch and his acolytes made sense of what had happened and conspired to ram home the message of their friend's murder.

The exiles were still reeling from the revelation that Andrey Lugovoy had been an enemy in their midst, and opinion was divided as to how long he'd been working against them. Nikolai Glushkov insisted that Lugovoy had been working for the FSB all along, ever since staging his escape attempt at Lefortovo. But the others found that almost impossible to believe. Had Lugovoy already been in Putin's pocket when he first reached out to Badri Patarkatsishvili after getting out of prison? Was he working for the enemy already when he mingled at Berezovsky's birthday party? Or had he been recruited later? One theory was that Lugovoy had been stopped at the border on his way back from visiting Litvinenko in London and found to be in possession of the incendiary report on Viktor Ivanov that the defector had prepared for Dean Attew. Perhaps he had been threatened with more jail time for treason if he didn't start cooperating.

Only Patarkatsishvili flatly refused to believe that his former security chief had gone rogue. The Georgian oligarch had always preferred Lugovoy to Litvinenko, whom he'd regarded as a dangerous obsessive full of "crazy theories." He insisted that Lugovoy had been framed and horrified his friends by continuing to take the assassin's calls when he rang from Russia to protest his innocence.

For his own part, Berezovsky had no doubt about who had administered the polonium—but he did disbelieve that the poison had really been meant for Litvinenko. Hadn't he himself been warned, years before, of a radioactive plot to kill him on British soil? Wasn't he Putin's true nemesis? The oligarch was busy telling everyone that Lugovoy had really been sent to eliminate *him* but must have failed and seized the chance to poison Litvinenko instead. So when the protection officer showed up in his office with the news that he was at the top of the Kremlin's UK hit list, he was thrilled. Finally the state was endorsing what he had been saying all along: Vladimir Putin was trying to kill him.

The protection officer was a tall, elegant man with close-cropped silver hair and pale blue eyes. He was a shade more erudite than many of his Scotland Yard colleagues, and he formed an easy rapport with Berezovsky. It would be necessary, he explained, to scour every detail of the oligarch's lifestyle for weak spots that could be exploited by the Kremlin's assassins. The first step was to perform a full "ingestion audit"—cataloging everything Berezovsky consumed to assess his susceptibility to poisoning. During a series of interviews, officers filled their notebooks with an exhaustive list of anything the oligarch ate and drank, learning more than they ever thought they would about the finest wines and whiskys money could buy, as well as documenting all the creams and lotions he applied to his body and the medication he was taking. It did not take long to identify a major problem.

Berezovsky was heavily reliant on Viagra, and, worse, he was taking a penis-enlargement formula that he had specially shipped over from Moscow. Still more alarming was his appetite for teenage girls, which made him a sitting duck for honey traps. The oligarch was constantly being contacted by disturbingly young sex workers from the former USSR and he frequently ferried them over to Britain for sessions on his private plane.

I have the absurd responsibility of trying to persuade a sixty-year-old billionaire that he has to rein all this in, the protection officer reflected wearily as he reviewed the results of his lifestyle audit. But he was used to this sort of ethical dilemma from years of guarding the great and the good in London. When an ambassador did drugs in the back of the car, or a diplomat brought a hooker back to his hotel, it was part of the job to look away.

"I'm not going to sit here giving you a lecture on morals or ethics, but you're very vulnerable here," was all he said to his charge. "This is how they'll kill you."

The problem wasn't just the girls. Berezovsky was forever being approached over the transom by would-be business partners and political allies who wanted his funding for this new enterprise and that new opposition party, and he was all too free and easy about meeting anyone who asked to see him.

Then there was the challenge of separating the Kremlin-sanctioned threats from those arising from the oligarch's own risky business dealings. Berezovsky had tangled often enough with organized crime to acquire some nasty private adversaries who had tried to take him out before, but the officer's remit was limited to protecting him from government assassins. The problem was that Berezovsky's private enemies could easily hire a moonlighting FSB hit squad to go after him, and the state was equally capable of enlisting another oligarch or mafia boss to orchestrate his killing as a cutout, so it was all but impossible to be sure where any given threat really originated.

The officer reasoned that there was no point confronting Berezovsky about the darker side of his life. After all, he would never answer truthfully anyway. But he instructed the oligarch not to meet anyone who approached him out of the blue on any pretext—be it sexual, commercial, or political—without first passing on the details to Scotland Yard for vetting.

The intelligence flowing into Specialist Protection from Britain's spy agencies indicated an ever-shifting kaleidoscope of new threats against Berezovsky. The officers were deluged with the names and photographs of a rapidly changing cast of individuals linked to the Russian security services or organized crime who were believed to be involved in plans to kill the oligarch. When a fresh plot emerged, officers would track Berezovsky down and yank him out of whatever dinner or business meeting he was attending to warn him he was in imminent danger.

The protection officer began to feel he was living in a John le Carré novel, meeting Berezovsky furtively at night on misty street corners in Belgravia to show him mug shots of his latest would-be assassins under the lamplight and implore him, please, for God's sake, not to agree to meet them.

The others on the Kremlin's hit list had adapted well enough to their new security regimes. Zakayev accepted an armed guard at his house when the threat level was deemed high, and the rebel leader never met anyone new without careful vetting and counter-surveillance measures. Gordievsky and the Russian journalist were conscientious about their safety. But Berezovsky was impossibly unruly.

On more than one occasion, he called the protection officer to announce that he had just met someone he had been warned might be part of a plot to kill him. And he flatly refused to stop antagonizing the Kremlin. He kept traveling to Belarus and Georgia to stoke unrest right on Putin's doorstep—even after being told that Scotland Yard could do nothing to protect him when he was overseas. And every time he gave another interview in which he took a potshot at Putin, fresh intelligence would flood in from Britain's listening posts in Moscow indicating that new plans were being laid to silence him. It was almost, the protection officer thought, as if you could feel the chill wind blowing in from the east.

But the oligarch seemed to thrive on it. "I am what I am," he would say. "I am Boris Berezovsky, and I crave conflict." It was as if he had a strange sort of destructive energy, the officer thought, that made him want to run right into danger.

Berlin, Germany—2007

Scot Young was spinning out. He had spent months lying low in Miami before his Coconut Grove mansion was sold to pay his debts, and his extended spell in the land of the cocaine cowboys had only exacerbated an already spiraling addiction. He was drinking copiously, too—so much so that even Jonathan Brown was worried. Young still acted the wheeler-dealer, with his rolls of fifties and his flashbulb grin, but something was clearly very wrong. Was it all the booze and blow that made him so glassy-eyed and unreadable these days, his friend wondered. Or was that fear?

Brown had been deeply spooked by Litvinenko's murder, and he'd tried to bring it up in earnest, but Young was flippant.

"Can you imagine, drinking a cuppa tea and your hair falls out?" he'd quipped. "Fucking nuts, Jon!"

Brown was worried about the danger to Berezovsky, too, but Young didn't have much to say about that, either, and he still stubbornly refused to be drawn out on what had really caused his sudden financial collapse. After leaving Miami, he'd decamped to Berlin, where he was staying in high style at the Ritz-Carlton on a friend's tab, ostensibly to scout for new property investments—but when Brown called him he rambled incoherently about strange deals involving cars with trunks full of cash. Whatever he was really up to, Brown got the distinct impression that his friend was running from something.

By then, Michelle's ever-growing team of lawyers and investigators were crawling all over Young's affairs. He was scrambling to keep a lid on his Russian business dealings—moving boxes of documents to remote rural storage spaces, wiping his hard drives, deleting his emails, and destroying his phones—but his secrets had sprung a leak.

Alexander Perepilichnyy, a Russian financier who fled to the UK to blow the whistle on a massive Kremlin-linked fraud, collapsed and died suddenly while jogging near his home in Surrey, England, in November 2012. *(Public record)*

Dr. Matthew Puncher, the scientist who measured the fatal dose of radioactive polonium used by two Russian agents to poison Alexander Litvinenko in London, was found stabbed to death at his home in Oxford in 2016.

The high-rolling property dealer Robbie Curtis was part of the "dining club" who regularly met Berezovsky and Young at the exclusive Cipriani restaurant in Mayfair. He was the second of the group to die in an apparent suicide when he tumbled in front of a train in 2012.

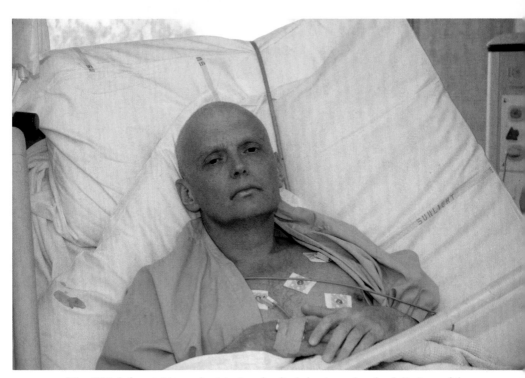

The FSB defector Alexander Litvinenko died slowly under the full glare of the world's media after being poisoned with radioactive polonium in 2006, allowing time for images of his gaunt and hairless frame to be beamed around the globe and for him to solve his own murder by accusing the Kremlin of ordering his killing. *(Getty Images)*

Vladimir Putin's former propaganda czar Mikhail Lesin arriving at the Dupont Circle hotel in Washington, DC, on November 4, 2015. The next morning, he would be found bludgeoned to death in the penthouse suite. *(FBI)*

Scot Young (left) met the organized crime boss Patrick Adams at a pub called the Barley Mow in Mayfair on a wintry afternoon in 2012, and afterward Young told his friends that "nothing would happen" because he was being "looked after." What the pair didn't know was that they were being watched.

Young (second from left) caught on film at Boujis nightclub with his girlfriend Noelle Reno (far left). By now he was telling friends, family, and the police that he was being tailed by a team of Russian hit men.

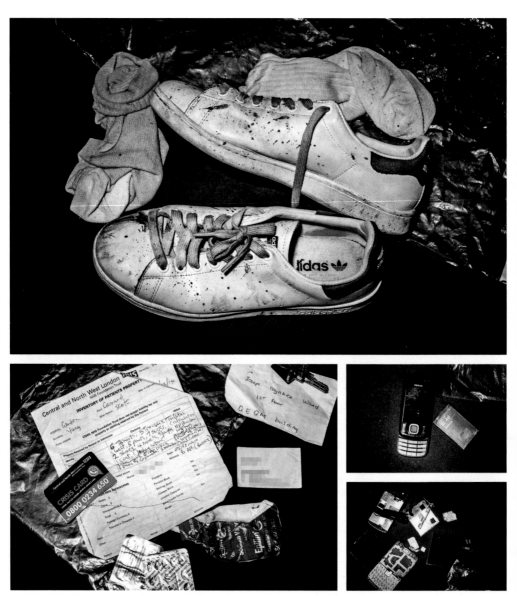

Evidence from the scene of Scot Young's death, including his bloodied shoes and socks, and the phones in his pocket when he fell. (*Laura Gallant, BuzzFeed News*)

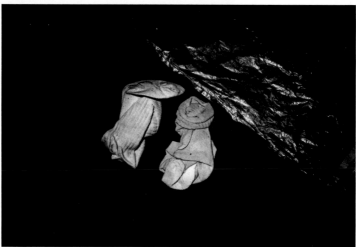

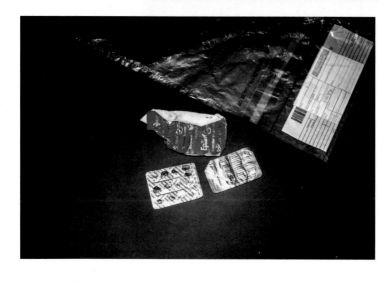

The view from the window from which Scot Young plunged to his death onto the wrought-iron spikes of the fence below.

On either side of the outside windowsill, Young's daughters, Sasha and Scarlet, found rows of faint scratch marks in the dirt—about as far apart as the fingers on a hand.

Michelle had swiped an old laptop that he'd given to his daughters, and she hired a computer forensics expert to restore its deleted files. The trove of evidence she uncovered included two asset schedules appearing to show that Young had been sitting on properties and investments worth hundreds of millions of pounds in the run-up to his apparent financial collapse.

Michelle had also uncovered files suggesting that Young had set up a network of opaque offshore vehicles to carry out a complex series of transactions code-named Project Marriage Walk before announcing his intention to leave his wife and had sent cryptic emails to friends suggesting he was secretly rearranging his affairs. "I am signing my life away at the moment," he wrote in one email a year before Project Moscow collapsed. The transactions were so complex that Michelle's lawyers, accountants, and investigators were stumped as to what it all meant, but they were using the files to pursue disclosure orders in the divorce courts that would force Young to come clean about where his money had gone.

Young begged his wife to desist, promising to find a way to pay her tens of millions of pounds if she stopped digging. People were trying to "crucify" him, he warned her in one legal meeting, and if she didn't leave well enough alone he wouldn't be alive to pay her a penny. But Michelle rejected every offer. She was convinced that her husband was hiding billions—and she wasn't going to stop until she got her fair share.

London—2007

Yuri Golubev had kept a low profile since arriving in London. He knew Berezovsky—everyone who was anyone did—but had stayed well away from his provocative antics. Golubev was the oligarch's antithesis: cautious, cool-tempered, and devoutly religious. He was one of the cofounders of Yukos, and though he had fought to save the oil giant after its owner, Mikhail Khodorkovsky, was thrown in prison, he had done so without much fuss. Golubev had worked alongside Stephen Curtis to fend off the Kremlin's attacks, and when the lawyer was killed he quietly continued the fight alone. But it had all been to no avail: Yukos had been crushed under the weight of the multibillion-dollar backdated tax bills the Kremlin had cooked up, and it had eventually been declared bankrupt the previous year.

Golubev was sixty-four, and life was winding down now that the battle was over. He lived quietly in a Mayfair apartment a stone's throw from Selfridges, read voraciously, prayed often, and recited W. H. Auden to his visitors. It was a pleasant enough life, but he never felt truly happy in London. As levelheaded as he was, he was sentimental about one thing, and that was mother Russia. Some days, the homesickness threatened to get the better of him, and he longed to return to Moscow for good—but that was a dangerous dream. Ever since Khodorkovsky had fallen afoul of Putin, Golubev had received a continual stream of threats, and he knew it wasn't safe to go back for good.

Back in Moscow, Golubev kept a prized collection of Eastern Orthodox icons—hundreds of brightly colored depictions of Jesus, Mary, and the apostles painted on canvas or sculpted from metal and wood. It was among the most significant collections in Moscow, and many of the icons were rare enough to be very valuable, so Golubev made sure it was well guarded with round-the-clock private security. But soon after Litvinenko's murder, he confided in friends that all the icons had been stolen in a break-in. Golubev was heartbroken at the loss of his collection, and he was frightened. The intruders had somehow penetrated every layer of security without leaving a trace, he said. In his mind there was only one entity capable of pulling off such a feat, and that was the state. He feared the break-in was part of a campaign of government intimidation.

In January, Golubev flew to China for surgery on his knee but started to feel unwell and returned to London earlier than planned. His flight was routed via Moscow. Nobody heard from him for a few days after he got home to Mayfair. On January 7, a friend gained entry to his apartment and found his body slumped in an armchair. Golubev was dead.

London was still on high alert after the killing of Litvinenko, and the death of another exile caused a small stir, but the police quickly shut down the case. Golubev wasn't one of the Russians under Scotland Yard's protection, there was no sign of foul play, and tests suggested he had died from a heart attack, so police released a statement declaring that the former Yukos executive had died of natural causes. But then Moscow countered with an unexpected move.

Russia's prosecutor general, Yuri Chaika, gave a statement declaring that there were "all grounds to suppose" that Golubev had suffered a "violent death," and he called on the UK authorities to investigate fully. Chaika deepened the intrigue by claiming that the Russian government had evidence of attempts to use mercury to poison several other people connected to Yukos. The situation did not sit well with the Russia watchers. They reached out to the CIA to request any information the US spies had gathered about the latest death on British soil—and, once again, their American counterparts sent back intelligence pointing to Russian involvement in Golubev's death.

Scotland Yard publicly dismissed the suggestion of foul play, and in the absence of any tangible evidence, the case remained closed. But the protection officer knew too much to draw any comfort from the notion of a death by natural causes, and he doubled down on his efforts to protect Berezovsky.

The oligarch had stayed relatively quiet immediately after Litvinenko's slaying, but by the spring he was ready to launch his next broadside. The protection officer woke one day in April to discover that his charge had given an interview to the *Guardian* renewing his declaration that he was plotting the violent overthrow of President Putin. Berezovsky claimed he had forged close relationships with members of Russia's ruling elite and was bankrolling secret plans to mount a palace coup.

"We need to use force," he told the newspaper. "It isn't possible to change this regime through democratic means."

The Kremlin immediately hit back, denouncing Berezovsky's call for revolution as a criminal offense that should void his refugee status in Britain. Scotland Yard said it would investigate those allegations, but the oligarch was unconcerned: Judge Workman had already ruled that he couldn't be sent back to Russia to stand trial.

The protection officer was horrified. Berezovsky's latest pronouncement was followed by yet another flood of intelligence indicating that the FSB was setting up a fresh plot to kill him. And this was no empty threat. Soon after the first reports came in, Specialist Protection received an urgent call: word had just come over the wire that an assassin was on his way to Britain.

XIV

—

Moscow, London, and Eilat—June 2007

The hit man was a fearsome figure in the Russian ganglands—and he was no stranger to the man he was coming to kill. Movladi Atlangeriev was the godfather of Moscow's Chechen mafia, known as Lord or, more reverently, Lenin throughout the underworld. He started out in the '70s as a smart young Chechen hoodlum with a taste for fast Western cars and a talent for burglary and rose to riches in the '80s running a gang of thieves targeting wealthy students across the capital. At the turn of the decade, as communism fell, he persuaded the heads of the city's most prosperous Chechen crime groups to band together and form a single supersyndicate under his leadership—and that was how he became one of the most powerful gang bosses in Moscow.

The new group was called the Lozanskaya, and it soon asserted its strength in a series of bloody skirmishes with the local mob, leaving the streets strewn with the mutilated bodies of rival gang bosses. Racketeering, extortion, robbery, and contract killings were its stock-in-trade. But Atlangeriev was a suave man with smoky good looks and an enterprising mind to match his wardrobe of well-cut suits, and he blended well with Russia's emerging business elite. The gang quickly branched out under his command, taking over swaths of the city's gas stations and car showrooms. That was how it established a lucrative relationship with Berezovsky.

The businessman made good money selling Ladas through dealerships under the gang's control, and then he paid the Lozanskaya to provide protection as his car businesses grew rapidly in the early '90s. When Berezovsky was attacked with a car bomb during his battle with the gang boss Sergei "Sylvester" Timofeev, some said it was Atlangeriev's mob who had struck back on his behalf. And when the oligarch fell out of favor with Putin and fled to Britain, the Chechen crime lord kept in touch.

Atlangeriev called from time to time to talk shop, and he had showed up before in London offering strange propositions to the oligarch and his associates. Several months before Alexander Litvinenko's death, the crime boss had reached out to Akhmed Zakayev.

"I know him!" Litvinenko exclaimed when his friend mentioned who had come calling. The defector remembered the Chechen gangster well from his time in the FSB's organized crime division. Part of his job had been recruiting moles to work undercover in the criminal underworld, and the Lozanskaya had grown so powerful by the mid-'90s that the FSB was desperate to get someone on the inside. The ever zealous Litvinenko decided to go straight to the top. Collaborating with the state came with many privileges—not least the ability to operate with impunity—and Atlangeriev proved receptive. Litvinenko had played a key role in his recruitment.

Helping cultivate the godfather of the Chechen mafia as an FSB collaborator had been a major coup, but that was back when he was still a true believer in the Russian security state. Since his defection, he had been following his recruit's activities from afar with dismay. Litvinenko learned that Atlangeriev had become a key asset in the FSB's efforts to destroy the separatist movement in Chechnya and prop up the pro-Kremlin regime. His gang had been linked to state-sponsored terror attacks and assassinations in the region, and he had played such an important role that he had reputedly been given several medals and an engraved pistol by the head of the FSB himself, General Nikolai Patrushev.

"He's 100 percent under FSB control," Litvinenko told Zakayev.

Meeting Atlangeriev would be fraught with danger, but the two men agreed that the rebel leader should go ahead and secretly record the encounter so that Litvinenko could supply his MI6 handlers with evidence of the FSB at work in London. The defector said he would oversee his friend's protection during the meeting.

Zakayev told Atlangeriev to meet him at the Westbury hotel, in Mayfair, arriving at the establishment's discreetly low-lit Polo Bar in advance to prepare the ground. Litvinenko brought in a team of security operatives who swept the room for hazards, slipped recording devices under the table where Zakayev was to sit and wait for the crime boss, and positioned a surveillance team around him. The rebel leader took up his post. He had seen plenty of action in his time, but even he felt like he was in a spy movie, with one member of the surveillance crew at the next table and another posing as an electrician in the corner. Litvinenko had been tight-lipped about where the security team came from, but Zakayev was sure they were from MI6.

The crime boss turned up looking as sharp as ever. He was still arrestingly handsome in his midfifties: swarthy and even featured, with a swimmer's shoulders under his crisp white shirt. *He looks like George Clooney,* Zakayev thought. The gangster laid his cards on the table right away. He said he worked for the FSB and came bearing a proposal directly from General Patrushev. If Zakayev dropped his campaign against Putin and came back home, the Russians would give him a senior government job.

"I am a Chechen man," Atlangeriev told the rebel leader. "You can trust me." Zakayev was thrown. In Chechen tradition, if one man invited another to travel, it was his solemn duty to ensure the guest's safe passage—but why would the FSB be trying to lure him back if not to kill or capture him? Then Atlangeriev's phone rang loudly, and the crime boss leaped to his feet.

"Yes, General," he said, standing ramrod straight and eyeing Zakayev. "He is here in front of me." *Look at him,* the rebel leader thought as Atlangeriev carried on the call with fawning deference.

He's so afraid he's standing to attention even when they can't see him. What kind of guarantees can he possibly give me if he's so scared?

"It's a trap," Litvinenko told his friend as soon as the meeting was over. "Don't trust him." But he was excited: they now had evidence of the FSB offering Zakayev a government job, while in public the Kremlin was still calling him Chechnya's answer to Osama bin Laden. Zakayev declined the offer to return to Russia, and he and Litvinenko passed their evidence to the British authorities.

Now, a little more than a year later, in June of 2007, Atlangeriev was on his way back to London. And this time, the Russia watchers knew he was coming with orders to kill Berezovsky. The intelligence pointing to his involvement in a live FSB plot to eliminate the oligarch had come through six weeks earlier, and the protection officer had been dispatched to instruct Berezovsky not to meet him under any circumstances. That hadn't been the only warning: Yuri Felshtinsky had also received a call from a Chechen source to alert him that the crime boss had been enlisted to dispatch Berezovsky, and then a separate source inside the FSB had tipped the oligarch off to the plot.

Atlangeriev's movements and communications were monitored, and when he bought flights to London via Vienna, the protection officer received an urgent call from MI5.

"He's arriving at Heathrow," the voice at the other end of the phone said. "Remove the target."

The officer raced over to Down Street to tell Berezovsky his assassin was on the way and he needed to get out of the country immediately. As always, the oligarch perked up at the prospect of an adventure and flung open his office door with a flourish.

"Warm up the aircraft!" he bellowed across the lobby to his secretary. "I need to leave today."

Berezovsky took off for Israel, accompanied by a young officer who had just joined Specialist Protection after a spell as a London beat cop and couldn't believe that this was his new world. The private jet landed at Ben Gurion Airport, and the party crossed the tarmac to a helicopter waiting to whisk them out to the coastal town of Eilat, where the oligarch's £200 million superyacht rose like a gleaming shark's fin from the turquoise waters of the Red Sea.

The rookie officer was shown aboard by an Amazonian hostess who took him to a private cabin, where a dinner suit was laid out on the bed in his exact size. There were deck clothes, too—shorts, sandals, polo shirts, shoes, and a cap—all branded with the yacht's name, *Thunder B*. The vessel had an onboard wardrobe department with clothes in every measurement so the oligarch could keep his guests appropriately dressed whatever the weather. The young cop looked around him in disbelief and decided that if he was doing this, he might as well do it properly. He donned the dinner jacket and bow tie and made his way up on deck.

Back in London, Scotland Yard's counterterrorism department had swung into high gear alongside the Specialist Protection unit to prepare a response plan for the assassin's arrival. The primary target of the hit was Berezovsky, but the intelligence suggested that Akhmed Zakayev was also at risk. Armed police officers were stationed at the rebel leader's home, on Osier Crescent, and the officers ran drills with the family to plan their escape if the house came under attack. Surveillance teams were positioned in the surrounding streets, backed up by heavy assault units poised to swoop in if Atlangeriev appeared. "You'd only have to sneeze and you'd have an armed response," the protection officer joked—but as far as he could tell the rebel leader never cracked a smile. It was Marina Litvinenko's birthday—the first she had celebrated since her husband's death—and armed officers were sent across the road to her house, too, to stand guard at the barbecue she was throwing for their friends.

Now that the targets were secure, Scotland Yard could afford to play cat and mouse with the assassin. Officers formed a "pursue and attack" plan: surveillance teams would follow Atlangeriev around London for as long as possible in order to gather intelligence about his activities before swooping in and arresting him when it looked like he was ready to strike.

The hit man was not coming alone: he was traveling with a young boy, which looked like the same modus operandi Andrey Lugovoy had employed in bringing his family to London as a cover for the hit on Litvinenko. Maybe, the officers hoped, if they stayed on his tail long enough the new assassin might even lead them to a secret polonium warehouse in the heart of the city.

"I need pursuit teams. Gunships. Three surveillance teams—sixty officers on the ground," the protection officer told Scotland Yard's counterterrorism commander. "We need chemical, biological, radiological, and nuclear teams in full protective gear sent in to swab all his luggage."

The police chiefs agreed on the strategy—but then they were summoned to the Cabinet Office, where a meeting had been convened to brief ministers and officials from the Home Office, Foreign Office, and Downing Street. By then, Atlangeriev was in the air and time was short, but the officers met with resistance as they laid out their plan. If Scotland Yard got caught tailing an FSB agent around London, there would be a major public fuss, and the diplomatic fallout with Russia would be another headache the government didn't need. Couldn't the hit man just be detained at the border? The officers pointed out that Atlangeriev hadn't yet committed any arrestable offenses in Britain, and the intelligence implicating him in a murder plot couldn't be revealed without exposing sensitive sources and listening posts in Moscow. It was essential to follow him in order to prove he really was here to kill Berezovsky before they could arrest him.

After some wrangling, the operation was approved—but the officers were instructed not to say a word to the media either before or afterward. If they were successful in apprehending Atlangeriev and journalists called with questions, their statement should be as short and uninformative as possible. "Police have arrested someone. End."

Berezovsky's threat level was moved from "severe" to "critical"—meaning an attack was considered imminent.

Atlangeriev would arrive in just a few hours. An operations room was hastily set up, where commanding officers could coordinate the activities of surveillance teams on the ground, with hazardous materials units sweeping behind the assassin for radiation traces and armed response teams at the ready.

In a nearby room was a cabal of security-cleared officers tasked with monitoring a live intelligence feed from MI5 and MI6 as well as reading Atlangeriev's text messages and listening to his phone calls in real time as soon as he landed. That classified information and intercepted material had to be kept out of the central evidence chain, otherwise it would have to be disclosed in court if Atlangeriev ever came to trial, which would reveal sensitive sources and methods. But when the officers in the intel cell picked up anything relevant, they were to bring it into the ops room and read it out to the senior commanding officer to help shape decision making.

Once the ops room and the intel cell were up and running, the surveillance teams were stationed around the airport, and the hazmat crews donned their protective gear. It was time for police chiefs to contact bosses at Heathrow to prepare the ground for the assassin's arrival.

The plane on which Atlangeriev landed was held on the airstrip for a little longer than usual. The hit man waited with the other passengers, unaware that his bag had been removed from the hold and was being searched and swabbed by officers in hazmat suits outside. When the passengers were allowed to disembark, Atlangeriev and his child accomplice breezed through passport control, collected their luggage from the carousel, and cleared customs with nothing to declare. The pair made their way out of the terminal building and approached the cab stand, where a black taxi was waiting. They climbed in.

London's iconic black cabs had long been the protection officer's secret weapon. Unbeknownst to most Londoners, Scotland Yard owned a secret squadron of such cabs for use in special operations, and the security and intelligence services also ran their own fleets of undercover taxis. The cars were so ubiquitous as to be invisible, so there was no more anonymous way to travel around the city. The protection officer had used them to move Tony Blair during an active assassination plot and to transport the British-Indian novelist Salman Rushdie around London during his decade in hiding following the publication of *The Satanic Verses*. It was possible to make anyone, no matter how high-profile, disappear inside the passenger compartment of a black cab—and a well-timed taxi ride was often the best way to get up close and personal with a surveillance target.

Atlangeriev directed his taxi driver to the Hilton on Park Lane and settled back in the leather seat, unaware that he had just revealed where he was staying to the officers tracking his every move at Scotland Yard. The driver dropped the hit man and his young accomplice outside the hotel, and the pair made their way through the revolving doors at the base of the glowing blue skyscraper. Then officers from the intel cell came running into the ops room. Atlangeriev had placed a call to Berezovsky.

By the time his phone rang on board *Thunder B,* the oligarch was well prepared. The morning after his hasty escape from Britain, three British security officers had arrived in Eilat and boarded the yacht to brief him. It was a baking hot day, and the officers looked disheveled in sweat-dampened shorts and T-shirts, but they waved away Berezovsky's largesse and made it clear they were there on serious business. Gathered around a table in the shade on the lower outside deck, they told him they needed his help to buy Scotland Yard some time. If Atlangeriev realized that Berezovsky was completely out of reach, he might just abort the mission and go back to Russia before the authorities had a chance to gather any intelligence. So when the would-be assassin called, they told him to act friendly and say he'd be available to meet in a few days' time.

Berezovsky wasn't ordinarily one to follow instructions, but he was relishing his leading role at the center of this live operation against an enemy agent, so he did as he was told when Atlangeriev called. Then he phoned Down Street and told his secretaries to be on high alert for the assassin's arrival and to tell anyone who called that he was busy. After that, all that remained was to wait. He passed an enjoyable few days on board *Thunder B,* sunning himself on deck, scuba diving, and zooming around on his Jet Ski while the British authorities tracked his assassin around London.

Scotland Yard's surveillance operatives found themselves on an unexpected sightseeing tour. They had hoped Atlangeriev might lead them to the heart of FSB activity in the capital, or possibly to a warehouse crammed with radiological weapons, but ever since his call to Berezovsky, the hit man had acted for all the world like a tourist showing a kid around the city. As he and his young companion traipsed through Trafalgar Square and past Buckingham Palace, the hazardous materials officers crept behind them swabbing and scanning for traces of toxins or radiation—but everything came up clean.

The officers judged that when Atlangeriev separated from the boy, that would be the indicator that he was gearing up to strike. They waited, but the sightseeing went on for days, and the protection officer began to get twitchy. Berezovsky was a busy man: he couldn't stay on his yacht forever. Then finally word came back from the surveillance team that the hit man had set out from the Hilton alone.

"This is the critical moment," the commanding officer shouted. Atlangeriev had dropped his easy touristic demeanor, and now he was visibly wary of being tailed. He performed textbook countersurveillance moves as he navigated the city—taking circuitous routes, doubling back on himself, and hopping on and off different modes of transportation to throw off anyone trying to follow. Between them, the surveillance teams just about managed to stay on his tail as he visited various addresses—but they couldn't follow him inside without blowing their cover. Then a readout from the intel cell suggested that the hit man was planning to buy a gun.

"We need to take him off the board," the commanding officer told the team. Scotland Yard called the officers guarding Berezovsky on *Thunder B* and told them to prepare him for his big moment. It was time to call his would-be assassin and propose a meeting.

That evening, three plainclothes police officers positioned themselves in the lobby at Down Street. The receptionists on the second floor had been asked to stay late to greet the assassin politely when he turned up, and they waited with trepidation as time ticked by without anyone appearing. After a while, they called downstairs to ask the elderly concierge at the front desk whether anyone had arrived to see Mr. Berezovsky. Yes, the old man said a little shakily, a gentleman had come in a few moments ago, and now there were three others with him in the lobby.

"What are the gentlemen doing now?" the receptionist asked.

"The gentlemen are talking," the concierge replied. "Three of them are lying down, and one is standing."

When Atlangeriev entered the lobby, two of the officers had swooped in and pinned him to the floor before he reached the elevator, while the third flashed the concierge his police badge. The hit man was arrested on suspicion of conspiracy to murder and taken into police custody, where he was interrogated for two days, while his child accomplice was taken into the care of social services.

But then the order came down to let him go without charge. It wouldn't be possible to make charges stick without disclosing intelligence that would give away far too much about British sources in Moscow, the officers were told, and the diplomatic fallout from publicly accusing the Kremlin of ordering another assassination in Britain so soon after Litvinenko's would have been catastrophic. So Atlangeriev was handed over to immigration officials who designated him a "persona non grata" and put him on a plane back to Russia.

That, the officers were assured by their superiors, amounted to a "really strong diplomatic poke in the eye."

There was a commotion in some quarters at Scotland Yard over the decision to send the assassin home, but others were more sanguine. The protection officer comforted himself with the thought that the FSB might have killed one exile on British soil, but now Scotland Yard had prevented the murder of another. The way he looked at it, that evened the score. He called Berezovsky and told him it was safe to come home.

By then journalists had gotten wind of the dramatic arrest in Mayfair and were inundating Scotland Yard with questions. The press bureau gave out the elliptical response the government had preordained, and when his jet landed, Berezovsky was told to say nothing. The one thing that would increase the threat to his life, he was told, would be to embarrass Russia over its failure to kill him.

"Just lie low and keep your head down," the protection officer said sternly.

Soon after, Berezovsky stood up in front of a packed press conference in central London and told journalists that Scotland Yard had just foiled a Kremlin plot to assassinate him.

"I think the same people behind this plot were behind the plot against Alexander Litvinenko," he said. "Not only people in general, but Putin personally."

Berezovsky held back the details of who had come for him and how the plot had been stopped, but he told his friends he had to go public with the attempt on his life in order to protect himself. Keeping state secrets was a dangerous game, he said: it was safest that the whole world know the truth. And, of course, he had never been one to pass up the chance for a dramatic press conference.

The protection officer was furious. "We've been fucked up the arse," he shouted at the MI5 liaison officer in charge of monitoring threats against Berezovsky. He couldn't shake the notion that he and his colleagues had unwittingly become pawns in Berezovsky's big game.

Six months after the press conference, Scotland Yard received a report of the fate that had awaited Atlangeriev upon his return to Moscow. As he walked out of a traditional city-center restaurant on a bitterly cold winter night, the crime lord had been assailed by two men and bundled into the back of a car, which sped off into the darkness. Berezovsky's failed assassin had been driven out into the woods and shot at point-blank range in the head.

London—October 2007

Berezovsky was hyperactive with glee in the wake of the foiled murder plot, and he was readying himself for a new battle. The oligarch had hit upon the idea of suing his old enemy Roman Abramovich in the British courts, claiming that he had been forced to surrender his interests in Sibneft and Channel One at a massive loss as the Kremlin moved to crush his business empire in 2001. He filed a multibillion-pound claim for damages at the Royal Courts of Justice, in London, but the proceedings couldn't get under way until Abramovich was served with a summons to attend trial, and Berezovsky spent months trying and failing to track down his old foe to deliver the documents. That October, he finally had a stroke of luck.

Abramovich was now the owner of the Premier League football club Chelsea FC, and he'd been spending more time in London since leaving his wife for a twenty-five-year-old supermodel earlier that year. The forty-year-old tycoon was out shopping on Sloane Street when Berezovsky spied him. The oligarch had been doing a spot of shopping himself and was emerging from the Dolce & Gabbana boutique when he caught sight of Abramovich entering the nearby Hermès store flanked by three bodyguards. He sent one of his own guards back to his armored Maybach to retrieve the court papers, which he had been carrying with him for months just in case such a moment arose, and then barreled toward Hermès clutching the documents. His path was blocked at the door of the boutique by

Abramovich's three security men, and a scuffle ensued between the two sets of bodyguards, during which Berezovsky seized his chance to force open the door and barge inside.

"I've got a present for you," he crowed before hurling the court papers at Abramovich and turning on his heel. Berezovsky proceeded to phone all the journalists in his Rolodex to brag about his triumph. "It was like a scene from *The Godfather,*" he told one reporter.

The CCTV from the shop proved that Abramovich had received the court summons, and so began an epic legal battle between the two billionaires that would rage for more than four years, flushing out eye-popping details about the pillage of Russia in the '90s and giving Berezovsky a platform from which to fire off a fresh volley of incendiary accusations at the Kremlin.

Berezovsky was manic with excitement after deceiving an FSB assassin and hitting Abramovich with a court summons in such quick succession. But unchastened as he was by the recent attempt on his life, it had put him in mind of a few administrative matters that would need to be resolved in the event of his death. As usual in such moments, he turned to Badri Patarkatsishvili for help.

"I'm not that much afraid," he told his partner. "But I think there are things we should discuss in case something happens to me."

Patarkatsishvili invited him to say more, and the oligarch began enumerating the outstanding obligations that would need to be taken care of should Scotland Yard's finest fail him. The list amounted to a string of favors owed to a dizzying number of girlfriends. This young woman was a student who needed her education paid for; that girl had nowhere to live in Moscow and needed help keeping a roof over her head. After the recital had gone on for half an hour, Patarkatsishvili threw back his head and laughed his belly laugh.

"Boris, do me a favor," he said. "Let me die before you."

___

XV

London, Surrey, and Tbilisi—November 2007

Badri Patarkatsishvili had never really settled into British life. He spent swaths of his year in Surrey to be close to Berezovsky, and though he could hardly have established himself in a grander setting than the magnificent Downside Manor, there was still something about Britain that made him feel small. It didn't help that he had never mastered the language, so he couldn't enjoy the culture in the same way Berezovsky did, and he had no way of communicating directly with their army of British lawyers, financiers, and fixers. But there was also the general sense that no one quite understood who he was here. Patarkatsishvili had never craved the limelight, and he was happy to let Berezovsky take center stage, but he did like to be treated with the basic reverence he felt a multibillionaire was due.

Things could not have been more different back in Georgia. The mustachioed oligarch was the country's richest man by lightyears, and his personal fortune dwarfed the entire government budget of the tiny poverty-stricken state so vastly that he could afford to treat Tbilisi as his own personal toy town. He'd snapped up the city's soccer club, its basketball team, its theme park, and its circus. He built a spanking new shopping mall in the city center as well as a massive holiday resort on the Black Sea, and he established a national TV and radio network called Imedi—meaning "hope" in Georgian.

If his people ran into trouble, he appeared like a fairy godfather in a fur hat and made their difficulties disappear with a wave of his checkbook. Twice, when the government defaulted on its energy payments, he'd stepped in to settle Tbilisi's entire gas and electricity bill himself. He funded charitable projects and schools—even a cash-strapped monastery. And when the Georgian National Olympic Committee ran out of money, in 2004, he took over as chair and paid for its athletes to compete in the Athens games out of his own purse.

Patarkatsishvili was a businessman in his bones, and he saw Berezovsky's war with the Kremlin as a threat to their investments in the West, so he did his best to steer clear of political drama and stay focused on managing their money. But there was one major exception. As equable as he was about most things, his passions ran high when it came to his homeland, and he liked being his country's Mr. Big. Perhaps that was why, when Georgia erupted with mass protests against its corrupt post-Soviet government in 2003, he'd broken his vow of political abstinence to help fund the opposition.

The unrest culminated in the Rose Revolution, which toppled the regime and brought the US-backed Mikheil Saakashvili to power on a platform of EU and NATO accession. It had started the wave of "color revolutions" that swept the former Soviet states, enraging Putin and cementing Patarkatsishvili's status as an enemy of the Kremlin. But his relations with Saakashvili soon turned sour. The president introduced a raft of economic reforms that threatened Patarkatsishvili's near monopoly on the country's private sector, and the oligarch retaliated by using his TV and radio stations to attack the new administration.

It didn't take long for the new government to become mired in its own allegations of corruption and human rights abuses, and by 2006 a new protest movement began mushrooming up across the country. By then, Patarkatsishvili had grown tired of struggling to do business amid a blizzard of arrest warrants and freeze orders as Moscow prosecutors put pressure on foreign banks and governments to clamp down on the money he and Berezovsky had expropriated. He was looking for a way to mend fences with the Kremlin—and that was when he hit upon his big idea.

Putin needed to be pacified, and it occurred to Patarkatsishvili that Georgia was the one place where their interests now aligned. If he poured enough money into the country's new protest movement, perhaps he could create a second uprising big enough to topple the US-backed president and undo the outcome of the Rose Revolution. Ridding Georgia of its pro-Western government would be a massive free gift for the Kremlin. Would that be enough to win him a reprieve?

He and Berezovsky had already announced their intention to "divorce" as a partnership—telling friends privately that the arrangement was a sham to protect their joint business interests and place a cordon sanitaire around Berezovsky's political activities—which meant that Patarkatsishvili could make overtures to the Kremlin with apparent independence. Perhaps he might be able to persuade Putin to ease off his attacks on their fortune in exchange for ousting Saakashvili, while Berezovsky could carry on kicking the Kremlin as he pleased from a respectable distance.

Berezovsky liked that idea, and he came up with his own brain wave. What if Patarkatsishvili toppled Saakashvili and then ran for president himself? If he succeeded, they would have an entire country under their control, right on Russia's doorstep. To his surprise, his partner didn't dismiss the idea out of hand, so on a late spring day in 2006, Boris and Badri sat down together with two of their closest advisers and penned a letter to Putin. The message was one of general goodwill, noting a mutual interest in the downfall of Saakashvili, and it was signed by Patarkatsishvili. The Georgian oligarch sent it to the Kremlin—and then he lit the fuse on his campaign to depose the government in Tbilisi.

It took eighteen months for the protest movement to erupt into an uprising. Patarkatsishvili had poured money into ten opposition groups that were mounting an escalating campaign against the Georgian administration, and he stepped up his own attacks on Saakashvili, branding him a "fascist" and using his TV station to raise hell for the regime. In November of 2007, tens of thousands of protesters took to the streets of Tbilisi to call for the removal of Saakashvili.

Riot police fought for five days to disperse the crowd with tear gas and water cannons, hospitalizing more than five hundred protesters, and then they raided Patarkatsishvili's TV station and took it off the air. Saakashvili declared a fifteen-day state of emergency and accused the Georgian oligarch of spearheading a Russian-backed plot to sow turmoil in Tbilisi, but he moved to quell the unrest by announcing an early election the following January. Prosecutors declared that Patarkatsishvili was wanted for plotting a coup, and the oligarch fled back to Downside Manor. Two days later, on November 10, he announced his intention to run in the presidential election from Britain.

Patarkatsishvili kicked off by pledging $1 billion of his own fortune to turn Georgia into a "shining country." The money would be spent on raising the minimum wage, boosting pensions, paying the utility bills for most Georgian households for the next eighteen months, and buying up the country's entire crop of citrus fruit and grapes.

American diplomats stationed in Georgia eyed Patarkatsishvili's bid with intense suspicion. They knew the Georgian opposition movement was crawling with Russian intelligence agents working to destabilize Saakashvili's US-backed administration, and they suspected Patarkatsishvili of having a "darker side" than the benevolent bon vivant most of his associates knew. In one confidential cable back to Washington, the US ambassador noted that although the Georgian oligarch had long worked as Berezovsky's "enforcer," he remained disturbingly close to some "extremely unsavory figures" in the FSB—including Andrey Lugovoy. "Despite his differences with the government of Russia, Patarkatsishvili is believed to be closely allied with Russian intelligence services," the cable stated.

It was true that Patarkatsishvili kept active links with people inside FSB. He made no secret of those associations, telling his friends it was best to keep his enemies close, but he never would say what he discussed at his frequent meetings with agents in both London and Tbilisi. The extent to which he was communicating with elements of the Russian state about his activities in Georgia remained a mystery. But the battle for Tbilisi turned ugly fast.

First the former Georgian defense minister came forward to accuse Saakashvili of ordering Patarkatsishvili's assassination, only to be arrested for corruption two days later. Then Akhmed Zakayev obtained a tape of a Georgian security official ordering a Chechen warlord to eliminate the oligarch—either by murdering him in London or by blowing his private jet out of the sky with a bazooka as it landed in Tbilisi. "Even if he had a hundred people guarding him, well, that's not a problem," the official said. "We'll destroy these guards."

The warlord had declined the commission, instead taping the conversation and passing the recording to Zakayev, and Lord Bell helped make hay out of the evidence of Saakashvili's brutality by passing the tape to the London *Times*. But then Patarkatsishvili's own campaign was engulfed in scandal when it emerged that he, too, had been contemplating an assassination plot to rig the election.

The oligarch had been approached in late December by a senior Georgian police official who had offered to help him overthrow the government, and the pair met in London to discuss murdering the country's minister of the interior as part of a complex ploy to trigger mass unrest ahead of the election. The problem was that the police chief had been sent by the Georgian government, and he was wearing a wire. It was a classic sting operation, and Patarkatsishvili was caught in the act. Saakashvili's people released the tape on Christmas Eve, and it blew the oligarch's campaign out of the water.

When election day came around, a fortnight later, Patarkatsishvili was trounced, with just 7 percent of the vote, and Saakashvili cruised to reelection. It was a sickening defeat—and the usually equanimous oligarch wasn't just humiliated, he was also terror-stricken. Now that his plot to oust Saakashvili had backfired, he could never return to Georgia, and he had nothing to barter when it came to dealing with Putin. He was trapped in Britain, and he told his friends his days were numbered. He surrounded himself with 120 bodyguards and lay low at Downside Manor for weeks.

By the following month, he was beginning to rally, and on February 12 he headed into London for a meeting with a lawyer he'd hired to advise him on salvaging his business interests in Georgia. As usual, the oligarch had gone for the very best money could buy, and the man who greeted him at a smart office in the City of London was no less a figure than Lord Goldsmith, Tony Blair's former attorney general. The meeting turned into quite a festive little gathering: Yuli Dubov and Nikolai Glushkov came to offer their support, along with Berezovsky and Lord Bell. The talks ran on for more than five hours.

Patarkatsishvili seemed energetic and engaged for most of the meeting, but he began to complain toward the end that he was feeling off-color and stepped outside for some fresh air. Afterward, as the exiles stood on the pavement waiting for their cars to be brought around, they joked that it was a pity no one from the FSB was there to witness such an all-star lineup of the Kremlin's worst enemies.

Patarkatsishvili and Berezovsky retired to Down Street for a private chat before the Georgian was driven back to Downside Manor in his $600,000 Maybach. He ate dinner with his wife, Inna, but soon after the meal he complained again that he was feeling unwell and went upstairs to lie down.

Berezovsky heard the news in the early hours of the morning. Badri Patarkatsishvili was dead.* He had been found slumped in the master bedroom at around 11:00 p.m. and could not be resuscitated. The oligarch drove at top speed across Surrey to Downside Manor, but by

---

* There is no suggestion that any of those present at the meeting in Lord Goldsmith's office were connected to Patarkatsishvili's death.

the time he arrived the mansion had already been cordoned off as officers scanned the whole property for radiation, and police refused to let him in. Lord Bell received a distraught call from Berezovsky around 3:00 a.m.

"They've done Badri," the oligarch sobbed.

Surrey police initially said they were treating the death as suspicious, but then they quickly reversed that position and announced that an autopsy had shown "no indication" that the demise of the rotund fifty-two-year-old was attributable to anything other than natural causes. Like Golubev, Patarkatsishvili appeared to have died naturally of a heart attack—a conclusion Surrey police said they had reached after "very extensive toxicological testing," which was later supported by the coroner's verdict.

But British spies were less certain. Sure, Patarkatsishvili was chronically unfit, ate fatty Georgian food, drank heavily, and lit one cigarette from the butt of another from morning until night. There was no disputing that he was a prime candidate for a heart attack. But he had also been the target of several previous assassination plots, and the Russia watchers knew well that his enemies had plenty of ways of making a death look natural.

When the British reached out to the CIA for assistance, the US spies replied by saying they strongly suspected Patarkatsishvili had been poisoned. They could not determine whether the job had been carried out by Georgian or Russian hit men or by organized crime hoodlums, but all their intelligence pointed strongly to another political assassination on British soil. Still, with no forensic evidence to support that conclusion, and no discernible poison in the dead oligarch's system, the police case remained firmly closed.

Berezovsky was beside himself. "Part of the blame lies with me," he howled. "I dragged him kicking and screaming into politics." He had a black-and-white photograph of Patarkatsishvili blown up and hung on the wall of his office at Down Street, and he sat beneath it raising tearful toasts with a one-hundred-year-old Armenian brandy that had been a gift from his dead friend and smoking Parliament 100's—Badri's favorite brand of cigarettes. For almost two decades, the men had spoken to each other every single day, and Boris told everyone the only person he had ever loved as much as Badri was his mother.

But in the wake of his death, Patarkatsishvili's friends and relatives began picking over his affairs—and they uncovered a world of secrets.

The first shocking revelation was that Patarkatsishvili had been living a double life for years. He had married his wife, Inna, in Tbilisi three decades earlier, and the pair had two daughters and three granddaughters—but after his death a second woman came forward to reveal that she, too, had wed the Georgian oligarch—in St. Petersburg in 1997—and that the pair had a fourteen-year-old son. Patarkatsishvili's second wife and child wanted a share of his riches.

The second shock was that the Georgian oligarch had died without leaving a will or any instructions as to how his massive fortune should be carved up among his survivors. Berezovsky claimed that he and Patarkatsishvili had always split everything down the middle, so he was entitled to half the estate, but the dead man's family said the two men had severed all relations in their economic divorce, so his partner wasn't due a penny. The oligarch insisted that the separation had been a sham and everything was still shared—but all that had been agreed on a handshake, and he had nothing to prove it.

For years, Patarkatsishvili had taken care of every practical aspect of Berezovsky's life, allowing him to continue his political posturing unencumbered by the everyday travails of business. Now that he was gone, chaos descended. As lawyers and advisers struggled to make sense of Patarkatsishvili's affairs, they uncovered layer upon layer of shell companies wrapped up in obscure trusts and tangled offshore funds. Vast tranches of the oligarch's supposed fortune were nowhere to be found, and almost nothing was in his name.

Berezovsky was appalled by the mess his partner left behind. He had never paid any attention to how their affairs were structured, where the money was stashed, or how Patarkatsishvili had organized contracts. Both men had come up in the Soviet era, when the ban on private business made it unwise to leave a paper trail, and agreements were held in place by the timeless laws of honor and violence. The suggestion that anything should be put in writing would have been a gross affront to their trust.

But now it was becoming clear that Patarkatsishvili had been putting certain things in writing—just without his partner's knowledge. He'd been signing vast swaths of what Berezovsky considered to be their shared fortune over to other people, registering the ownership of assets to childhood friends, casual acquaintances, and distant relatives. Hundreds of millions of pounds' worth of treasures had been placed under the control of a stepcousin of Patarkatsishvili from Tbilisi named Joseph Kay—including Fisher Island, the star-studded Miami islet where Oprah Winfrey and Julia Roberts had homes; the New York branch of Buddha-Bar; and luxury resorts in Spain and Morocco.

Then there was the money stashed in the New World Value Fund, which Boris and Badri had set up to take delivery of their payments from Abramovich, and the multiplicity of other offshore trusts and funds the pair had used to siphon their fortune out of Russia. Much of that had been handled by Ruslan Fomichev—a man Berezovsky had long described as the only person in the world who knew everything about their business affairs—but the oligarch was left flabbergasted when the financier sided with Patarkatsishvili's family.

Fomichev had been gradually backing away from Berezovsky for several years. He was still doing big business in Russia, and the association with the Kremlin's number one enemy was nothing but trouble. He had moved out of his office at Down Street around 2005, and Patarkatsishvili's death provided the opportunity he needed to cut ties for good.

What followed was one of the largest estate battles in legal history, as war broke out between Berezovsky, Kay, and the late tycoon's two wives over the fortune. And it left the onetime godfather of the oligarchs scrabbling to save himself from financial ruin. Berezovsky sued his partner's family for his share of the money, and he went after Fomichev, too, lodging a claim over interest payments on a $50 million loan he had made to his financier years before. His great remaining hope was the case against Abramovich, which, if he won, would yield billions of pounds in damages. But with Curtis and Moss long dead, and Fomichev now a foe, Patarkatsishvili had been the only person left to attest to the private deals the pair had done with Abramovich. With his partner's death Berezovsky had not only lost control of his fortune, he had also lost his star witness.

In the months after his last goodbye to Patarkatsishvili, Berezovsky was left wondering whether his partner had really been the friend he'd seemed. Wasn't it Badri who had reintroduced Lugovoy into their circle? Hadn't he kept taking the assassin's calls long after Litvinenko's death? His partner had always stayed uncomfortably close to the FSB, and he had been anxious to find a way back in with Putin. Now it turned out that, for years, he had been squirreling their shared fortune out of Berezovsky's reach.

A few months after Patarkatsishvili's death, Berezovsky called his assistant into the room and ordered him to take his partner's portrait down from the wall. He was alone now. But he wasn't about to stop fighting.

PART SIX

PEREGRUZKA

XVI

South Ossetia, Georgia—August 2008

The tanks came barreling through the Roki Tunnel, snaking beneath the snowcapped peaks of the Greater Caucasus mountains that form a forbidding natural barrier between Russia and Georgia. They were heading for the separatist stronghold of South Ossetia, where rebels had been fighting to break away from Georgia and rejoin their ethnic kin on the Russian side of the ridge ever since the territories were split by the fall of the Soviet Union. Now the Kremlin was sending in the cavalry.

Russia had been stoking separatism in South Ossetia for years, and it had been steadily turning up the heat since President Saakashvili's reelection in Georgia that January. At the start of August, Kremlin-backed fighters in South Ossetia started shelling nearby Georgian villages, and Saakashvili sent in the army to restore order. No one foresaw the ferocity of Russia's response.

The Kremlin ordered a full-scale invasion of Georgia on all fronts: land, air, sea, and cyber. Troops poured across the border to occupy South Ossetia and the separate rebel region of Abkhazia while fighter jets dropped bombs across the country, warships covered the coast, and hackers unleashed waves of attacks on Georgian government websites. It was the first time Russia had invaded a sovereign state since the fall of the USSR, sparking the first European conflict of the twenty-first century. And by attacking a US ally on its way to NATO membership, the Kremlin was drawing its sword on the entire Western military alliance.

America had been steadily upgrading the Georgian military since Saakashvili put the country on course to join NATO four years earlier, and it had sent a thousand US troops to stage a training exercise outside Tbilisi only weeks before the invasion. The US secretary of state at the time, Condoleezza Rice, had visited Georgia the previous month, standing up next to Saakashvili to pledge full support for the country's future membership of the alliance.

"We always fight for our friends," she declared.

But the invasion was a crisis for Washington. In the final year of the Bush administration, tensions with Moscow had already escalated over US plans to build an antiballistic-missile defense system in Poland and the Czech Republic, designed to shield the West from Iranian nuclear attacks. Putin had reacted furiously, warning that the new system would turn Europe into a "powder keg," and then he made a point of visiting Iran—glad-handing the country's president and championing its right to pursue its civilian nuclear program.

The US could not afford a full-scale conflagration with Moscow: the Kremlin's cooperation was considered vital to stopping Iran's pursuit of nuclear weapons, and the US army needed access to Russian supply lines to get equipment into Afghanistan. So when Russian troops took hold of South Ossetia and Abkhazia, occupying a fifth of Georgia's internationally recognized territory, America did not fight for its friend.

The Kremlin announced at the end of August that it had liberated South Ossetia and Abkhazia from Georgia and now recognized them as independent republics. Russia shut out UN and EU monitors and went on to sign treaties with the de facto governments of the two separatist regions, agreeing to integrate them into Russia. Putin had gambled on the West's unwillingness to fight—and won.

Geneva, Switzerland—March 2009

Hillary Clinton arrived in Geneva armed with a big red button. President Barack Obama had taken over the White House determined to thaw relations with the Kremlin, and he had dispatched his new secretary of state to meet her Russian counterpart on neutral Swiss territory. She was there to pull off a stunt designed to defuse tensions with Moscow.

There had been a changing of the guard in Russia, too, at least on the face of it. Putin had been constitutionally barred from running for a third consecutive term in the presidential elections the previous year, so he had stepped aside in order to allow his loyal lieutenant Dmitry Medvedev to take the reins. The West was yet to wake up fully to the fact that Putin was still running the country from his temporary perch as prime minister, and hopes abounded in Washington that the new man in the Kremlin might be someone with whom the White House could do business. So the previous month, the vice president, Joe Biden, had used the administration's first foreign policy speech to express America's intention to "press the Reset button" on its relationship with Russia, and now the secretary of state had been sent to Switzerland armed with a physical manifestation of that metaphor.

Repairing fraught relations with a rival nuclear superpower by performing a skit in front of the world's media wouldn't have been a comfortable commission, even with the most elegant of props. But Clinton gamely grabbed her chance at a press conference with the Russian foreign minister, Sergey Lavrov, producing a pale green box tied up in ribbon and pulling off the lid with a flourish.

"I wanted to present you with a little gift which represents what President Obama and Vice President Biden and I have been saying," Clinton said with a rictus grin, speaking very slowly and tweezing the button out of the box as if handling a grenade. "We want to *reset* our relationship."

Lavrov peered at the strange gift. The red button was mounted on a bright yellow plinth emblazoned with the English word *reset* and the Russian word перегрузка, or *peregruzka*. He turned it over in his hands, and a smile spread across his lips.

"You got it wrong," he said.

The officials in the State Department needed to brush up on their Cyrillic. The Russian word on the plinth did not say *reset,* as intended, but *overload.* Laughter erupted in the room. Lavrov pressed the button anyway.

America's big gesture may have misfired, but the two countries still released a shared statement promising a "fresh start" in Russo-American relations. Russia went on to announce that the US military could use its airspace to reach Afghanistan, and America shelved its planned missile shield. In May 2010, Russia finally agreed to international sanctions against Iran over its nuclear program, and in return the United States canceled sanctions in place against Russia for exporting arms to the Islamic republic. Spring had arrived, and all the frost seemed to have melted. But the next big freeze was on its way.

New York—June and July 2010

Anna Chapman was rattled. The glamorous young spy was living under deep cover in New York as part of a cell of ten Russian agents operating illegally in America, and she was starting to suspect that someone had sold them out.

Most of her coconspirators were posing as married couples—living in leafy suburbs, working vanilla jobs, and even starting families—but Chapman had taken a different tack. Before coming to America, she had married an unwitting young Englishman named Alex Chapman, acquiring a British surname and passport that provided the perfect new identity when she left him for her new assignment. At twenty-eight, she was the youngest in the spy ring, with flame-red hair, piercing green eyes, and an IQ of 162—all of which proved useful when getting close to power—and she was posing as a single businesswoman running a successful international property company in the heart of Manhattan.

The agents' goal was to build contact with influential figures and relay the intelligence they gleaned using classic spycraft tactics such as dead drops, brush passes, and ciphers. They had developed good relations with a former intelligence official and a scientist involved in developing bunker-buster bombs, and now they were on the cusp of cultivating a US cabinet official.

On a Saturday morning in June of 2010, Chapman received a summons from the handler she knew only as Roman. He contacted her using their special code and ordered her to meet him at a coffee shop in downtown Manhattan, which was odd because Roman was usually a stickler for two golden rules: they only communicated on Wednesdays and never face-to-face. The regular drill was for Chapman to bring her laptop to a public place such as Macy's or Barnes & Noble while Roman pulled up nearby in a white minivan so they could send each other messages over an encrypted wireless network. But this time, he arrived in person and gave her an assignment to hand off a fake passport to another agent the next morning.

Chapman smelled a rat. Not only did the rendezvous violate Roman's usual rules, the new assignment was also unlike any other he had previously given her. She called her father, a KGB veteran working at the Ministry of Foreign Affairs in Moscow, to tell him she feared her cover had been blown and she needed to get out of the country. But it was too late. FBI agents were listening in on her call, and they swooped in the very next day, arresting Chapman and nine other agents around Washington, New York, and Boston.

The FBI had been tracking the illegal spy network in an operation code-named Ghost Stories, after the agents' practice of assuming the identities of the dead. Chapman was right: someone had sold them out. Investigators had been reading their emails, decrypting their ciphers, intercepting their calls, and filming their brush passes, and the man she had met was not really Roman but an undercover US agent. Two weeks later, the spies pleaded guilty in a federal court in Manhattan, and preparations began to send them back to Russia in the biggest East-West spy swap since the Cold War.

The story of the illegal Russian spy cell went global—later spawning the hit TV show *The Americans*—and the media went to town on Chapman's looks. Tabloids plastered pictures of the young agent across front pages headlined THE SPY WHO LOVED US and RED HEAD.

"Do we have any spies that hot?" Jay Leno asked Joe Biden on late-night television.

"It was not my idea to send her back," the vice president quipped.

Back in Britain, Chapman's ex-husband cashed in on his cameo in the international drama, selling details of the couple's sex life and an album full of intimate photographs to a London newspaper. Five years later, the thirty-six-year-old Alex Chapman would be found dead in an empty house in the British port city of Southampton, apparently from a multiple-drug overdose.

The spy swap was carried out speedily to preserve the Obama administration's delicate efforts to reset relations with Russia. The ten illegal agents were flown to Vienna on July 9 and traded on the airstrip for four Russians caught spying for the West. The agents were given a heroes' welcome back in Moscow, receiving state honors from President Medvedev for their services to the motherland in a ceremony at the Kremlin. Chapman was greeted personally by Putin and won a job heading the government's youth council to add to a budding career as a model and television presenter.

Among the Western agents released in return was Sergei Skripal. The onetime military intelligence officer had been convicted of selling secrets to Britain and incarcerated in a high-security military detention facility in 2006, but now he was a free man. He was flown to the UK, where he made a new home in the sleepy cathedral city of Salisbury. The spy swap seemed to have gone smoothly for both sides.

But soon after the agents' return to Moscow, Putin announced that the traitor who had betrayed them to the FBI had been identified. "It was the result of treason," he thundered, foretelling an ignominious fate for the mole who had blown the illegal spy network. "It always ends badly for traitors: as a rule, their end comes from drink or drugs, lying in the gutter."

The culprit was Alexander Poteyev, a decorated colonel who had won the Red Star for his efforts during Russia's long and bloody war in Afghanistan and climbed the ranks of the Foreign Intelligence Service after the fall of the Soviet Union. Poteyev had been posted to the United States in the 1990s, and when he returned to Moscow, he was named the deputy head of the ultrasecret department known as Directorate S, set up to oversee the sleeper cell in America.

A military court put Poteyev on trial for treason, and Chapman testified that he must have provided the US authorities with the information that led to her arrest; the FBI agent who contacted her posing as Roman had used a code that only he and her handler could have known. The court handed down a sentence of twenty-five years in prison—but there was no one there to lead away in handcuffs. Poteyev had skipped the country.

As the FBI was plotting the arrests of Chapman and the other illegals, the deputy head of Directorate S asked his bosses for an impromptu vacation. He boarded a train to Minsk, and from there he traveled to Ukraine, where he acquired a fake passport. Poteyev had made it to a CIA safe house in Frankfurt before being picked up and whisked away to America.

"Try to take it calmly," he wrote to his wife in a text message that prosecutors read out at his trial. "I am leaving not for some time but forever. I didn't want to, but I had to. I am starting a new life and I will try to help the children."

Putin bemoaned the turncoat's escape in a television interview. "The man betrayed his friends, comrades in arms, and the people who sacrificed their lives for the motherland," he raged. "How can he look into the eyes of his children? Pig!"

Now the Obama administration had a new headache as it struggled to smooth over relations with Moscow. The master spy who had just arrived on US soil was a priceless intelligence asset—and he was squarely in the Kremlin's crosshairs.

Langley, Virginia

In a verdant stretch of Virginia's Fairfax County, buried in the thickly forested backwater of Langley, lies the CIA's headquarters. Inside the sprawling complex, America's intelligence chiefs were reckoning with a brand-new threat. The United States was harboring scores of defectors under its government resettlement program, many of them Russian, and while the runaways were provided with new identities, the working assumption had always been that the Kremlin would never dare come after them in America. But intelligence was now flooding into Langley indicating a slew of threats against Russian defectors living in the United States. Chief among them was Colonel Poteyev.

The Russians suspected that the man accused of blowing the lid off Anna Chapman's spy ring had been recruited as a double agent during his stint in the United States in the 1990s, and had been supplying an astonishing stream of top-secret intelligence ever since. Poteyev had to be protected. But he was proving a hard man to look after.

Under the US government's defector resettlement program, it was standard practice for the CIA to provide Poteyev and his relatives with new names and passports to protect their identities. It was also standard for the agency to encrypt the defectors' communications, help them find jobs and schools for their children, arrange psychiatric treatment to deal with the depression that frequently accompanies exile, and even offer plastic surgery to make their faces unrecognizable. But Poteyev didn't want to hide. He told his CIA handlers he wanted to live in the open under his own name. They beseeched him to think better of it, but Poteyev was implacable. He wasn't going to skulk away in the shadows. If his former colleagues came for him, then so be it.

It didn't take long. That November, the Russian media reported that a contract killer had been dispatched to kill the mole who had sold out the illegals. "We know who he is and where he is," a high-ranking Kremlin source told one newspaper. "You can have no doubt—a Mercader has already been sent after him." That was a reference to Ramón Mercader, the Spanish hit man sent to Mexico in 1940 by the KGB to kill Leon Trotsky with an ice pick.

Poteyev had moved to Florida, where he settled into a new life fishing and passing his days quietly on the sunny coast, albeit under twenty-four-hour watch. Sure enough, sometime after his defection, a Russian hit man did make it to his address with orders to kill him— but his surveillance team raised the alarm before he was harmed. For a while, the threat seemed to have fizzled. And then suddenly the Moscow media lit up with the news that the traitor who betrayed Russia's spies to America was dead.

The Kremlin-controlled television channel Rossiya-1 led with the parable of Poteyev, an intelligence officer of "impeccable lineage" who had met a "sorry end" after selling out to the United States—yet another example of how "life punishes traitors." Poteyev's name was added to the growing list of enemies of Putin's government who had died in recent years, and the New York Times cited him in a front-page article as one of many examples of the dark trend.

But three months after his chilling obituary was broadcast, the dead man ambled into a Florida Walmart and purchased a saltwater fishing license. He filled out the form using his own name and gave as his address an apartment in a gleaming nearby high-rise. Soon after that, he registered to vote as a Republican. Poteyev was, in fact, very much alive—and he still wasn't hiding.

The CIA had seen these sorts of fake stories about the deaths of defectors before. Russia sometimes used them as a way to smoke out its enemies, prompting them to reach out to relatives or friends under watch in Russia to provide reassurance that the reports were false, thereby giving the FSB an email address or phone number to hack. But Poteyev was living in the open under his own name. Had Russia resorted to spreading the fake reports of his death in order to maintain the message that traitors would be crushed, having tried and failed to kill him?

Whatever lay behind it, America's spy chiefs handed down orders that the story must not be debunked. It was safest for everyone that the world was allowed to think Poteyev was dead. If Russia was embarrassed by the revelation that the traitor lived on, its assassins might come back to get him for real. The CIA was now working with the FBI to plan a coordinated response to future assassination attempts on other Russian exiles in the United States, and the targets were under round-the-clock protection. This was a considerable logistical challenge. America sheltered up to a hundred defectors at a time under its resettlement program, and the States had always been a place where Russian runaways could be assured of safety. Not anymore.

CIA Moscow Station

The CIA's man in Moscow was a husky white-haired veteran nearing the end of his career, and he'd spent long enough in Russia to get a little jaded about death. "Yes, Putin has been known to commit assassinations—first of all, news flash; second of all, big deal" was his stock response to the idea of spending time gathering string on Russian hits. "I'm trying to get plans and intentions on what the Kremlin is trying to do on a much bigger scale than somebody getting murdered."

He preferred to use his time gathering intelligence on what he saw as the big strategic questions—Russia's intentions toward NATO, its activities in Syria, and its nuclear plans. But the Moscow station had a standing requirement to assess the capacity of the Russian state to stage hostile operations in the United States, and now the matter had become more pressing. The CIA's spies in Moscow had been tasked with figuring out how much harm Russia could do if it came after its enemies in America the same way it had elsewhere in the West.

As they studied the body count of Russia's antagonists overseas, they were struck by a glaring trend. The rate at which Russian exiles in the United Kingdom met untimely deaths clearly defied natural explanation—particularly those exiles in Boris Berezovsky's immediate circle. They knew the oligarch was Putin's most bitter foe, so it came as no surprise that his associates would be targeted, and they weren't expecting Berezovsky to die peacefully, either. What did raise eyebrows among the spies in Moscow was the ease with which Russia seemed to be cutting down its adversaries in Britain.

If Russian runaways died in the United States with the same regularity they did in the UK, it would surely not go unnoticed. Government oversight committees would be asking questions. The intelligence agencies would take a greater interest than MI6 seemed to be showing, and the FBI would put a stop to it. Then again, they reasoned, London was a notorious hub for Russian money, so perhaps that changed the equation.

When the CIA man in Moscow met his MI6 counterparts over beers, he quizzed them over what was going on in Britain.

"Look," he said gruffly, "how's it possible for Russians to kill regularly without having to worry about it too much? Basically get to the UK and kill?"

The British spies readily acknowledged the problem. "We know the Russians have an active program of killing people in the UK," he was told. "But it's not our responsibility. That would be Scotland Yard."

The spies in Moscow weren't alone in marveling at the death toll in Britain. Back in Langley, the rising body count of the Kremlin's enemies in the UK was being reviewed with growing concern. America's intelligence staff had been tracking the deaths since Berezovsky and his entourage first fled Russia and many had long since concluded that the British government was woefully incapable of protecting its own inhabitants from the long arm of the Russian state. But until now, that had not been a cause of undue concern. Picking off the odd exile in Britain was one thing, but it had seemed inconceivable that Putin would dare to pull that kind of stunt on a rival superpower. That calculus had now shifted.

As threats to defectors in the United States spiked following Poteyev's defection, the spies at Langley were left asking themselves an uncomfortable question. By failing to stand up to Russian aggression in Britain, had America's closest ally unwittingly emboldened Putin to believe he could kill with impunity wherever in the West he chose?

XVII

Down Street and Downing Street, London—May to July 2010

The slight blue-eyed man who arrived at Down Street on a warm summer day in 2010 approached the reception desk and explained, with a lisp, that he had come bearing a gift for Mr. Berezovsky. It was Rafael Filinov, a deceptively mousy Russian telecom tycoon with whom Boris and Badri had once done good business, and he was shown upstairs to the oligarch's private office. Berezovsky knew perfectly well that Filinov kept close links to the FSB, but he was rarely one to turn away an old acquaintance, despite his protection officer's best efforts, so he ushered the visitor ebulliently inside and closed the door. Filinov handed over the package. It came, he said, from a mutual friend in Moscow. Andrey Lugovoy sent his regards.

The oligarch eyed the delivery and decided this was the sort of moment that required an audience. He called his secretary and the old Logovaz director Yuli Dubov into the room before unwrapping the gift. Inside was a black T-shirt emblazoned with the logo for CSKA Moscow—the team he and Lugovoy had watched at Emirates Stadium on the night of Litvinenko's poisoning. It might have been mistaken for a regular soccer shirt had it not been for the fact that the soccer ball at the center of the team emblem had been replaced with the international sign for radiation danger. POLONIUM-210, the lettering around the symbol read. TO BE CONTINUED. The message on the other side was no more subtle. Printed across the back were the words: NUCLEAR DEATH IS KNOCKING ON YOUR DOOR.

Berezovsky didn't blanch. It was nice to know he hadn't been forgotten in Moscow. He had already survived at least two assassination attempts in Britain, and he was fairly certain he was indestructible. He said goodbye to Filinov and dispatched his secretary to Scotland Yard to hand the incriminating garment to the police.

Lugovoy could well afford to be so bold. He knew the Kremlin would never give him up, and the UK was sure to drop its push to extradite him before the diplomatic toll got too high. "The more the British dig in their heels over this problem, the worse it will be for our relations with them," he crowed to the Interfax news agency in one interview. And his calculations were correct.

Britain's new Conservative prime minister, David Cameron, had arrived at Downing Street on May 11 eager to put all the unpleasantness of radioactive poison plots in the past. Promoting British energy interests in Moscow and pulling more Russian money into London were central parts of his plan to revive the country's recession-stricken economy, so he was determined to restore friendly relations with the Kremlin. But on his very first day in office, the government had been confronted with fresh intelligence pointing to a new Russian assassination plot.

This time, the target was Akhmed Zakayev, and the would-be hit man was another friend turned foe: a onetime Chechen separatist soldier who lived near the rebel leader in Muswell Hill and paid regular visits to Osier Crescent. Spies suspected that the soldier had switched sides and was now working for the region's pro-Russian regime as an assassin. He was believed to be responsible for the recent murder of another ex-soldier who was shot dead in Vienna after implicating the Russian government in torture. The assassin posed a "serious threat" to Zakayev's life, the spies said. Immediate action was required.

The government did act quickly—but quietly. The home secretary moved to expel the soldier from the country as discreetly as possible, canceling his leave to remain while he was abroad on other business. But as soon as that fire was put out, another flare had gone up.

Lugovoy's flagrant threat to Berezovsky was a further headache the authorities could have done without.

When Cameron and Medvedev met at the G8 in Canada at the end of June, the encounter was followed by warm pronouncements from both leaders—and no one mentioned Litvinenko's murder or the subsequent threats to Berezovsky and Zakayev. Cameron declared that the two countries shared "a lot of common ground" and called for a "stronger bilateral relationship," dripping charm as he told the press pack he had promised to start following Medvedev on Twitter and was looking forward to regular phone calls with Moscow. The love-in continued when the two leaders met again in South Korea months later, and Cameron announced delightedly that he had accepted an invitation to visit Russia the following year.

From then on ministers fought with all their strength to keep a lid on the messy business of Russian murder. Citing the need to prioritize "international relations," the government blocked efforts by Marina Litvinenko to secure a judge-led public inquiry into her husband's death after attempts to extradite Lugovoy and Kovtun fizzled. And when other Kremlin adversaries died in Britain, the government used national security orders to prevent inquests from hearing all the evidence—starting that very summer, with the strange case of the spy in the bag.

Pimlico, London—August 2010

The heating was on full blast when police broke down the door of the British spy's grace-and-favor apartment in Pimlico, just over the bridge from the River House. Detective Chief Inspector Colin Sutton wrinkled his nose and pushed inside. It was a sweltering day in August, and the temperature in the flat was unbearable—but otherwise the place was in perfect order. *Too perfect,* thought Sutton.

The apartment had been locked from the outside, and there was no sign of a break-in. Nothing was out of place, except a mobile phone, laptop, and several SIM cards laid out neatly on the table and a large red North Face sports bag that had been placed carefully inside the bathtub. Padlocked inside was the body of Gareth Williams.

The thirty-one-year-old spy had been dead for ten days. His body had decomposed so badly in the heat that it would prove impossible to determine how he had perished. There were no fingerprints or DNA traces on the rim of the bathtub, the bag's zipper, or the padlock, which had been fastened from the outside. The key was underneath his body, inside the bag.

Williams was an elite code breaker from Britain's Government Communication Headquarters (GCHQ), a mathematical genius who had been sent up to the River House to help the spies at MI6 crack a difficult international case. He hadn't shown up to work for more than a week, but his colleagues at MI6 had failed to raise the alarm. It was only after his sister called GCHQ to ask why he wasn't answering the phone that the spies notified the police, who went to the secret service flat where he was staying in Pimlico and found his body.

Sutton, a senior homicide detective at Scotland Yard, had received a call from his commanding officer that afternoon to tell him that a British code breaker had been found murdered. The link to British intelligence would mean that the force's counterterrorism team would be crawling all over the case, his boss said, but it belonged to homicide. So he'd better get down to the scene and show them who was in charge.

Sutton was a murder cop to his core, the sort who read whodunits on his breaks from solving real-life murders, and he shared his commanding officer's suspicion of Britain's shadowy security and intelligence agencies. In his view, his security-cleared colleagues in the counterterrorism unit were too close to the spies who gave them the top-secret briefings that couldn't be shared with the rest of the force. He didn't want them hanging around trying to find out what the homicide cops knew—and what they didn't.

When Sutton got to the scene, sure enough, there was Detective

Inspector Brent Hyatt from counterterrorism. Hyatt had been a minor celebrity in police circles ever since catching the job of interviewing Litvinenko on his deathbed, but Sutton didn't have much time for that sort of fanfare.

"We're taking this on," Sutton told him brusquely. "It's a murder."

His hackles went up as soon as he got inside the flat. It looked to him like someone had staged the crime scene—wiping the place down to eradicate DNA and fingerprints, removing incriminating evidence, and leaving out the phones, laptop, and SIM cards as decoys for the police to find easily. Why, he wanted to know, had the spies delayed telling the police that Williams had gone missing? Even after Williams's sister raised concerns, his employers waited five hours before they notified Scotland Yard. Had someone been in to sweep the apartment for anything that would compromise national security before calling the police? Sutton didn't have the bandwidth to take the case himself, but he handed it over to a younger colleague, DCI Jackie Sebire, and told her not to let the spies push her around.

Sebire was a shrewd detective, but Williams's highly secretive work created obstacles for her investigation from the outset. MI6 was pushing the theory that Williams had not in fact been murdered but rather had been asphyxiated by accident in a sex game gone wrong, and the media was briefed that the spy had been visiting bondage websites and drag clubs, had a wig collection, and kept a £15,000 collection of women's designer clothing.

The murder detectives pressed on, but they were barred from speaking to Williams's colleagues at MI6 and from reviewing key evidence, instead being forced to rely on counterterrorism officers to conduct the inquiries and pass along anonymized notes. An iPhone found in the spy's apartment had been restored to factory settings, and the discovery of nine computer memory sticks in Williams's MI6 locker was kept secret—Sebire only learned about the find more than eighteen months later when it emerged in questioning at the coroner's inquest into the spy's cause of death. But by then, homicide had already given up and shut down its case.

The coroner went on to deliver a devastating verdict for MI6 and Scotland Yard's counterterrorism command. Dr. Fiona Wilcox dismissed the theory that the spy had suffocated in a sex game and condemned the leaks to the media about his private life as a possible attempt "by some third party to manipulate a section of the evidence." She ruled that Williams's death was "unnatural and likely to have been criminally mediated," blaming the spies and counterterrorism cops for obfuscation and failures in the handling of the evidence that made it impossible to determine exactly how he had been killed.

Throughout the inquest, Williams's work remained a closely guarded secret. Britain's foreign secretary at the time, William Hague, had signed a public-interest immunity order preventing any information about his MI6 duties from being disclosed on national security grounds. But locked away inside those sealed files were the keys to the code breaker's last puzzle.

Williams had been working on Russia. He had just qualified for operational deployment, and in the months before his death he had been traveling regularly to the Fort Meade headquarters of the US National Security Agency (NSA), in Maryland, where he was helping to crack complex financial webs used by Kremlin-linked mafia groups to move illicit money around the globe. His work was so sensitive that he had been given security clearance to visit the NSA's facility in the Utah desert, which is classified as "above top secret."

The US State Department demanded that nothing about Williams's joint operations with American intelligence agencies be made public, so the British government intervened to keep the details of his work out of the police file, which was handed over to the inquest. Publicly, at least, the code breaker's death would remain an enigma. But while MI6 was standing in the way of Scotland Yard's investigation, spreading the theory that Williams had died as a result of what the men in gray called his "unusual sexual proclivities," the Americans sent a file of deeply alarming information to the River House. Intelligence coming in from US sources and listening posts suggested Williams was the victim of another Russian hit on British soil.

London—2010–12

Berezovsky was pouring his energies into a brand-new passion. The legal battles he was waging on many fronts had kindled a sudden fixation on the virtues of British justice, and he had taken to waxing lyrical about the rule of law and the place of courts in a civilized country. So rhapsodic had he become that, even when his estranged wife extracted a record divorce settlement of up to £220 million in the London courts, thus demolishing the lion's share of his remaining wealth, he hailed the outcome as further evidence of the unflinching rigor of Lady Justice.

For all the high-flung rhetoric, the truth was that Berezovsky had nowhere else to turn. With Patarkatsishvili gone and his fortune in tatters, all that remained was to go through the British legal system to try to claw back every penny he could from his partner's family as well as from former friends he felt had betrayed him. He was firing off lawsuits in all directions, and his litigious zeal was fueled by two big early wins.

First, the oligarch took on the Russian government by proxy. He went after a man named Vladimir Terluk, who had appeared in a Kremlin-controlled TV broadcast accusing Berezovsky of Litvinenko's murder. The motive, Terluk said, was to stop Litvinenko from revealing that he had helped Berezovsky obtain political asylum in Britain through fraud. He claimed the pair had conspired to fabricate the plot to kill the oligarch with a poison-tipped pen, which had finally persuaded the authorities to grant him safe haven, and he claimed to know this because Litvinenko had tried to enlist him—

Terluk—to help them. Berezovsky was sure Terluk was an FSB stooge, and he issued a claim for libel at Britain's Royal Courts of Justice.

The proceedings were chaotic. Terluk represented himself, but in a twist of events described by one high court judge as "extraordinary," a team of Russian state prosecutors turned up en masse during the trial, in February of 2010, and came to his aid. The four officials from the prosecutor general's office in Moscow positioned themselves around Terluk in the courtroom, requested a set of earphones so they could follow the simultaneous translation of the hearing, and repeatedly intervened despite not being party to the proceedings. They passed Terluk notes and documents, prepared applications for him, and tried to submit papers privately to the judge. At one point, one of their mobile phones rang loudly in court.

"That must be Mr. Putin on the line," Berezovsky's QC quipped.

When the Russian prosecutors asked to cross-examine Berezovsky, the judge told them that was a step too far. He ruled that Terluk's claims were false and "calculated to put at risk Berezovsky's refugee status and leave to remain in the United Kingdom," awarding the oligarch £150,000 in damages.

Terluk appealed that judgment and tried to introduce new evidence from Andrey Lugovoy implicating Berezovsky in Litvinenko's murder. The assassin's testimony was supported by a statement from a senior Moscow prosecutor, Vadim Yalovitsky. The judge threw out the appeal, describing Lugovoy's evidence as "not sensibly capable of belief" and lambasting the Russian prosecutors for their attempts to meddle in the British legal system.

The oligarch's next victory came in his lawsuit against Ruslan Fomichev over interest the financier refused to pay on a $50 million loan that had been frozen by Swiss prosecutors as soon as it entered his accounts. Fomichev fought hard to avoid disclosing details of his dealings with his former boss, and his lawyers argued that testifying could expose him to danger. "Those who cooperated with Mr.

Berezovsky and even his former and remaining friends are actively prosecuted in different jurisdictions," they wrote in one submission. "Some of them died, and not all by a natural death." But the judge gave Fomichev short shrift, ordering him to pay up in a stinging ruling that described him as an "untruthful" witness.

Those victories had not yielded anything close to the sort of windfalls Berezovsky needed to restore his fortune, but they provided vindication and whetted his appetite for the bigger fights to come. He was gearing up for a major battle with Roman Abramovich, and his war with Patarkatsishvili's family raged on.

Disputes had also broken out over the New World Value Fund, the trust originally used by Stephen Curtis to hold the payments from Abramovich to Boris and Badri. Berezovsky was battling Patarkatsishvili's family over the spoils, while Fomichev was determined to get his cut, and efforts were being made to chisel Curtis's family out of his share. Scot Young had sniffed the chance to make a quick buck. The fixer was back in town, and he stepped in to broker a peace deal that involved carving up parts of the fund among some of the warring parties, making sure to line up a healthy commission for his labors.

Young had done everything he could to claw his way out of the swamp since getting back from Berlin. He had resumed scouting deals for Berezovsky as well as working for a shadowy group of Monaco-based Russians funneling money into Britain through London properties, foreign exchange trades, priceless works of art, and glitzy Mayfair restaurants. He could no longer front for the deals himself now that he was bankrupt, but he could still set them up and cream off a tidy cash commission. The superfixer was getting back into business—but the mystery of his missing fortune was no closer to being solved. And he was more terrified than ever.

Sasha and Scarlet had grown into smart young women in their late teens with all the cut-glass polish of the finest private schooling, and they were starting to ask difficult questions. They remembered a time when they owned fifteen ponies and the tooth fairy never left less than a crisp £50 note, but now they'd been yanked out of the exclusive all-girls Francis Holland School with more than £30,000 in unpaid fees and were living in straitened circumstances with their mother in a poky flat in Pimlico.

The divorce courts had decreed that their father should pay Michelle £27,500 a month for their maintenance, but the money never materialized. Meanwhile, he seemed able to maintain an extraordinary lifestyle for himself, turning up to see them in an array of fast cars and hopping between breathtakingly beautiful apartments in the most exclusive enclaves of London. But he insisted he was living on the largesse of his friends, and when they asked him about where all his money had really gone, all he would tell them was: "It's complicated."

The girls were furious with their father for tangling their family up in his web of lies, and they told him they couldn't take much more humiliation after his bankruptcy forced them out of school. Still, they couldn't help but carry on loving him. Sasha was fifteen now and the spitting image of her father: the same wide puppy-dog eyes; the same impish grin. Even if her dad *had* let them all down, he was somehow still the person who made her feel safest. She could tell him anything that went through her head, and he never judged her. She thought he was invincible.

Scarlet was two years older and a little less wide-eyed. She was tall and slender, with long black hair, china-white skin, and intense green eyes, and she'd taken to modeling to supplement the family's finances as well as shooting for top marks in her final exams. But she still found time to text her dad several times a day, and he showered her with affectionate messages in return. "Love u v much," he would text her. "Dont let anything or anybody get u down! U r to good for that. U daBEST."

Young wooed his daughters with eye-popping treats to make it all feel temporarily better, including VIP concert tickets, or the time he showed up with £5,000 worth of Topshop gift certificates from his friend the retail tycoon Sir Philip Green. He regularly took them out for pizza at a beloved Italian restaurant in South Kensington, and he was always there when he said he'd be to give them bear hugs and make them laugh by goofing around. When he wasn't with them he called every day to ask how they were, what was happening at school, and how they were getting on with their homework.

But in the past couple of years, the calls had started to get darker. The girls had been home alone one evening in 2008 when their father phoned breathlessly to tell them he was being followed and he thought they were all in danger. He begged them to get to a safe place immediately but warned them that people might be watching their house. The next time the girls saw him, he told them everything was fine and shrugged off their questions, distracting them with his usual tomfoolery.

The following year, Young called the police at 3:00 a.m. to beg for protection. The officers who came to his flat noted in their report that he "believed he was going to be assassinated by gangsters and the Russian mafia." They said he hadn't slept in three days and "had not eaten or had anything to drink all day except for a Scotch egg" because "he was concerned he was going to be poisoned." He requested armed protection and asked that MI5 and MI6 be informed. Instead, police determined "there was no information to corroborate his allegations of his life being in danger" and referred him for psychiatric tests.

Doctors concluded that Young was "paranoid, with a manic flavor" and had a "complex delusional belief system." They committed him under the Mental Health Act and moved him to St. Charles Hospital, where the medical team noted that he appeared "sweaty, suspicious, and restless"—attempting at times to kiss other patients and expose himself. He accused nurses of being "in the league of the KGB" and tried to kick down the ward doors to escape.

Young had been scheduled to attend a divorce hearing with

Michelle a few days later, facing jail if he failed to disclose documentary evidence of his losses. But doctors at St. Charles Hospital wrote to the judge that he was mentally unfit to attend. Michelle was furious, asking that Young be jailed for his recalcitrance, but the judge granted his wish and delayed the hearing. The next day, doctors noted a "significant improvement": Young was exhibiting "no psychotic features," though he still maintained—calmly now—that his fears had been justified. While he was there, Sasha got another call from her father to say that someone had been following him and to beg her again to get herself and her sister to safety. He confided that he had deliberately engineered his committal because he believed the hospital was the safest place for him to hide.

Young's fears multiplied when two of his friends died in rapid succession. Paul Castle and Robbie Curtis were an inseparable pair of roguish, high-rolling property dealers who dined with Young and Berezovsky often at Cipriani, their favorite Italian restaurant in London. Castle played polo with Prince Charles and was known by friends for "spending more money than God" on Champagne, while Curtis had made a fortune on luxury rentals in the early 2000s and liked to boast that he had once dated the model Caprice. Like Young, the two tycoons had recently suffered a dramatic financial collapse, and their friends had heard they'd run into trouble doing risky deals with gangsters linked to the Russian mafia.

Castle was the first to go. One morning in November of 2010, the fifty-four-year-old took tea at the Grosvenor Hotel, as was his habit, before turning up at his Mayfair offices in apparently good spirits. But then, friends heard, enforcers for a Russian-linked crime gang burst in, threatened him, and forced him to hand over a valuable collection of luxury watches. Castle walked straight out of his office and into the Bond Street tube station, where he was captured on CCTV diving with his arms outstretched into the path of an oncoming train. After his death, his friends told the press anonymously that he had been driven over the edge by "very, very nasty people" connected to the

Russian mafia who had threatened to kill him slowly and painfully if he did not end his own life. The coroner deemed his death a suicide.

Curtis was devastated by Castle's death—and scared out of his wits. He told friends that he had gotten himself into trouble with the same Russian-linked organized crime gang that Castle was said to have crossed. Criminals had already thrown him out a window once before, he said, and he was so petrified that he sought protection from a London-based crime group just before his death.

"I need to make sure nothing happens to me," he said he'd told the gangsters. "Sorry, but it's too late," came the reply. "A hit has already been taken out on you."

Almost exactly two years after Castle's death, Curtis walked onto the platform at the Kingsbury tube station and tumbled in front of a train.

Young was in no doubt that both his friends had been deliberately driven to suicide, and he was so rattled that he refused to discuss them on the phone because he was convinced that his calls were being monitored. Two years later, another member of the Cipriani dining club—the British entrepreneur and former Tears for Fears manager Johnny Elichaoff—would throw himself to his death from the roof of a London shopping center after losing all his money in a catastrophic oil deal.

The police treated all three cases as straightforward suicides and did nothing to investigate evidence of mafia intimidation. But the spies in the River House had suspicions that the deaths could be linked to Russia and secretly asked the United States for information. Word came back from Langley that Castle, Curtis, and Elichaoff were all named in American intelligence files documenting suspected Russian assassinations in Britain. The US spies believed the deaths could be evidence of a "suicide cluster" engineered through manipulation, intimidation, or mind-altering drugs. And there were concerns on both sides of the Atlantic about another attempted hit in London that year.

German Gorbuntsov was a Russian banker who fled to London in 2010 after accusing businessmen linked to the Kremlin and the Russian mafia of ordering a botched assassination attempt in Moscow. By March of 2012, the forty-five-year-old was on the cusp of applying for political asylum in Britain, and he had arranged to meet Russian investigators in London to provide evidence backing up his allegations the same month. Gorbuntsov arrived home at his apartment in London's Canary Wharf one night in a black cab and stepped out into the darkness without seeing the thin, hooded figure waiting in the shadows. The hit man opened fire, shooting the banker four times using a pistol with a silencer before fleeing into a maze of alleyways.

Gorbuntsov narrowly survived. He lay in a coma, guarded by twenty armed police officers, for several weeks before regaining consciousness and accusing his enemies of ordering his killing. The shooting was viewed as a watershed moment for the Russian mafia in London. There had been an explosion of Russian organized crime in the capital over the previous decade, and the country's gangs were known for their violence, but until then the mobsters had largely refrained from opening fire in plain sight on the streets of the city. Scotland Yard had been lashed by crippling budget cuts as the recession set in, and its resources for tackling organized crime at the top level were dangerously depleted. If the Moscow mafia was sufficiently emboldened to conduct its "wet work" right out in the open, the police had nothing like the capacity they would need to respond.

By then Young had given up on asking the police for protection and instead turned to an old associate in the London underworld for help. It had been twenty years since he'd started out doing odd jobs for London's most feared organized crime family, but he'd stayed close enough to Patrick Adams for the gang boss to send Scarlet and Sasha presents on their birthdays. The pair met for a long drink at a pub called the Barley Mow in Mayfair on a wintry afternoon in 2012, and afterward Young told his friends that "nothing would happen" because he was being "looked after." But what he didn't know, as the pair stood outside the pub saying their goodbyes in the dying evening light, was that they were being watched.

Determined to find her ex-husband's missing money, Michelle had hired a team of private eyes to track his every move, and a surveillance crew was tailing him around London on foot, in vans, and on motorcycles. The spies had already filmed Young doing deals in an array of exclusive West End bars and restaurants, visiting London's finest five-star hotels, and partying at Boujis with his new girlfriend, the model and reality TV star Noelle Reno. On another wintry day in 2012, they followed him to a meeting at the five-star Dorchester Hotel, a favorite haunt, where he disappeared upstairs and then came back down shaking and looking deathly pale. Later, Young would tell his friends that he'd been dangled out a high window in a room at the hotel by "heavies" working for the Russian mafia.

He hightailed it back to his flat only to be photographed reemerging with arms full of bags, suits, and shirts. Then he decamped to the nearby Columbia Hotel—a tired two-star establishment far out of keeping with his expensive tastes—where he checked in with cash using an alias. Michelle's spies followed him there and eavesdropped on his room by slipping a microphone under his door on a wire. In one phone call taped by the surveillance team, Young discussed handing over "the paperwork" to an individual in Russia and told an unknown caller that Berezovsky was "keeping his head down." He called Sasha, too, telling her again that he was scared and begging her to get herself, her sister, and their mother somewhere safe.

And that was when, out of the blue, Michelle was approached by a man with a message from Moscow. The Russian government wanted to see her.

Moscow—February 2012

The snow was lying twenty inches thick on the ground when the Aeroflot jet touched down at Sheremetyevo Airport on a bitter February morning. Michelle and her lawyer swept through arrivals and climbed into a car sent by the man who had arranged their visit: Howard Hill, a London-based private investigator who boasted of a direct line to the Russian government.

Hill had approached Michelle to suggest a trade: she would give evidence of Young's business dealings with Berezovsky to prosecutors gunning for the oligarch in Moscow, and they in turn would tell her what they knew about her ex-husband's missing fortune.

Right off the bat, the private detective provided what he said was FSB intelligence connecting Young and Berezovsky to a variety of lucrative sports deals in Brazil, Ukraine, and Britain, including a stadium development for the 2014 Winter Olympics, to be held in Sochi, Russia. And he set up a call with attorneys for Aeroflot, who told Michelle's lawyer that Young was believed to have helped hide hundreds of millions of dollars that the oligarch had siphoned off from the state airline while it was under his control. If she wanted to know more, Hill told Michelle, then she would have to come up with something to trade.

By then, Young had been forced to answer questions in court about Project Moscow, and files relating to the deal had been found on a hard drive seized by order of the judge. The ruse to funnel Berezovsky's money into the development had been unearthed, and Michelle's lawyer instructed an assistant to copy the documents for the trip to Russia. Then the two women got on the plane to Moscow.

Their car pulled up alongside a nondescript gray building close to the Kremlin, and they were ushered through a side entrance. Inside, they were greeted by a huge snaggletoothed man with a bristling black mustache who introduced himself as Vadim Yalovitsky.

Russia's deputy prosecutor general was a loyal and trusted servant of the Kremlin. He had been given the important task of thwarting the Scotland Yard detectives who flew to Moscow to investigate Litvinenko's death in 2007 by restricting their access to Dmitri Kovtun, and he had led the team that rushed to the aid of Vladimir Terluk in

Berezovsky's lawsuit, as well as providing a written statement in support of Andrey Lugovoy's evidence. Now he was looking for a new way to come after Russia's most hated oligarch.

Yalovitsky told Michelle straight up that the prosecutor general's office had information about her ex-husband that it would be prepared to trade. There was, however, a hitch: the investigator who had those files had been taken to the hospital, so they wouldn't be able to see them that day. But he said that shouldn't prevent her from turning over the hard drives she had brought with her. She declined, telling him she would only hand over her own evidence when she saw what the Russian state had to offer in return.

The next day, after the group enjoyed an extravagant dinner with prosecutors and government officials, Hill emailed Michelle's lawyer to say he'd met a senior member of the FSB who said the security agency had "substantial files" on Young. Discussions continued after the party returned to London about arranging a second meeting with Yalovitsky.

Hill circled back periodically, conveying requests from the prosecutor for evidence linking Young to Berezovsky and for the fixer's photo and passport details so the authorities could check his visits to the country. Michelle's lawyer obliged by supplying Young's date of birth and a selection of pictures. And then, all of a sudden, the door slammed shut. Hill reported that the prosecutor's office was no longer prepared to cooperate.

Michelle was no closer to finding the missing billions she was hunting, but what she did now know was that her ex-husband had somehow found his way into the sights of the Russian state. And by 2012, the FSB wasn't the only intelligence agency taking an interest in Young.

The fixer's activities had by then attracted such concern that his communications were being tapped by spies at the NSA's Fort Meade headquarters. The intelligence gleaned from listening in on his calls was so sensitive that some of it was marked top secret—the highest classification level, reserved only for information that would cause "exceptionally grave damage" to national security if it became public.

US spies were monitoring individuals connected to Britain's rapidly shrinking community of Russian runaways—and Young was central to that web. As the men around Berezovsky and his fixer dropped dead, the challenge was to determine whether they had been targeted by the Kremlin, murdered by Russian mafia figures, or deliberately driven to suicide—and the spies couldn't rule out the possibility that some of the deaths on their radar were entirely unconnected to Russia. But as 2012 drew to a close, US intelligence systems lit up with evidence of another high-profile death on British soil. And this time, there was no such ambiguity about who was behind the hit.

XVIII

St. George's Hill, Surrey—November 2012

The slumped body was caught in the headlights of a car nearing the brow of the hill through the dusk and drizzle. The driver leaped out, and a passing chef in full whites rushed to help. The man on the ground was large, dark, and deathly pale. He threw up repeatedly as the chef tried to administer mouth-to-mouth, and by the time the ambulance arrived he was completely unresponsive. Soon his heart stopped beating.

The dead man was Alexander Perepilichnyy, a mysterious multi-millionaire who had moved into a rented mansion in the exclusive Surrey enclave of St. George's Hill two years earlier and was rarely seen by neighbors except on his occasional jogs around the gated estate. The forty-four-year-old had returned home that morning, November 10, 2012, from a secret assignation in France. No one knew whom he'd been meeting, but he told his wife and eight-year-old daughter that Paris had been "really gray" and "gloomy" as he tucked into a bowl of Russian sorrel soup they'd cooked for his lunch. Then he went out for a jog and never came home.

To officers who attended the scene where Perepilichnyy collapsed at the roadside that damp afternoon, his death looked like a simple heart attack. They didn't think to check his name in the database used by Britain's spies to share intelligence with the police. If they had, they would have seen that the man on the ground had a target on his back.

Back in Moscow, Perepilichnyy had been a master money launderer for Russian government officials who conspired in a massive fraud with an organized crime network run by a mobster named Dmitri Klyuev. The criminals would seize control of companies in Russia. Then they would forge documents to make it look like they had sustained massive losses and apply for huge tax rebates that were approved by corrupt officials, who took a cut. Perepilichnyy was one of the financiers who helped funnel the proceeds out of the companies and into a sprawling network of offshore slush funds controlled by Klyuev and his government conspirators. The scam had run smoothly for several years, allowing the gang to embezzle the equivalent of $800 million from the state.

But trouble arose when a British-American hedge-funder named Bill Browder noticed that a group of companies he owned in Russia suddenly appeared to have racked up huge losses. Browder hired a tax attorney in Moscow named Sergei Magnitsky to investigate. The lawyer discovered that the companies had been fraudulently seized by the Klyuev gang and used to apply for the biggest tax rebate in Russian history—$230 million—which had been hurriedly approved on Christmas Eve and siphoned off as soon as it hit their accounts. He dug deeper and identified the corrupt tax officials who had sanctioned the rebate as well as a lieutenant colonel from the country's interior ministry who had also conspired with the Klyuevs, and he reported the whole scam to the authorities.

It was a brave move and a naive one. The authorities did nothing to investigate the officials and mobsters Magnitsky had identified. Instead, they arrested the lawyer and accused him of perpetrating the fraud himself. The thirty-seven-year-old spent almost a year behind bars, where he refused to change his testimony despite being severely beaten. He was isolated in windowless, sewage-flooded cells; deprived of food, water, sleep, and toilet access; and denied medical care. In November of 2009, after 358 days of extreme mistreatment, he died in prison.

Brandishing Magnitsky's death, Browder sparked an international outcry, mounting a campaign for sanctions against the Kremlin officials responsible for both the fraud and his lawyer's murder. That was when Perepilichnyy finally turned against his paymasters. In 2010, shortly after Magnitsky's death, he fled to Britain and approached Browder with an explosive cache of evidence documenting the fraud in lurid detail.

The financier's files revealed how the money stolen from the Russian purse had been split up and funneled into a complex offshore network through thousands of transactions in more than a dozen Western countries—including the United States and the UK. It had fueled an orgy of spending on yachts, private jets, London mansions, couture clothes, and exclusive private-school fees. Perepilichnyy himself had bought a luxury beachfront mansion on Dubai's Palm Jumeirah island for the husband of one of the government officials involved in the fraud and funneled millions more into his accounts. And buried within the documents was a clue to an even darker reality.

Perepilichnyy had signed agreements on behalf of his government clients to transfer millions to a shadowy company at the center of a secret network of slush funds often used by criminals to funnel money in and out of Russia. Its owner, obscured behind opaque corporate filings, was a man named Issa al-Zeydi. He would go on to be outed by the US government as a front man for the Syrian chemical weapons program. It would take time for the authorities to piece all that together. But the financier had not just blown the whistle on a Russian crime: he had also exposed a network of slush funds with all the hallmarks of a Kremlin black-money conduit. And it was funding the development of internationally outlawed weapons that the Syrian despot Bashar al-Assad would soon unleash on his own people.

Browder passed Perepilichnyy's information to the authorities in every country through which the embezzled money had been routed, sparking criminal investigations in more than a dozen jurisdictions. The Swiss froze the Klyuev gang's accounts, and the fraud prompted the United States to issue sanctions against forty-nine people, including a network of senior Kremlin officials. But the UK refused to open an investigation, despite evidence that £30 million of the stolen money had ended up in London. Years later, a high-ranking detective at the country's National Crime Agency would come forward to claim that he had attempted to open a case but had been ordered to shut it down by a senior official with links to the Foreign Office.

The British government had no appetite for a fight with the Kremlin over the fraud, nor was there any interest in stemming the flow of Russian money into the country's recession-hit economy. When Putin returned to the Kremlin in the spring of 2012, having retaken control from Dmitry Medvedev in an election tainted by allegations of vote rigging, the British prime minister launched a charm offensive. David Cameron welcomed the resurrected Russian president to London to watch the judo competition during the 2012 Olympics, and later that year BP merged with Rosneft, the state-owned Russian giant, to create the world's largest oil company. Then plans got under way for a visit to Sochi the following spring.

A new flash point had emerged between the Kremlin and the West over Russia's support for the Syrian regime as it cracked down brutally on civilians, and Cameron fancied himself the global statesman who could bridge the divide. He and Putin went on to discuss the bloodshed in Damascus over a ten-course lunch in Sochi, including burnt caramel pudding in the shape of Big Ben. Cameron agreed during the meeting that British intelligence would resume cooperation with the FSB for the first time since the death of Alexander Litvinenko.

Despite the unwillingness of central government to act on Perepilichnyy's evidence, the spies in the River House had taken a keen interest. The financier had set up home in Surrey and become a prized source for several Western intelligence agencies investigating the flow of dark money out of Russia. He knew he was taking his life in his hands. Three other conspirators in the fraud he had exposed had already met untimely ends—one died suddenly of liver disease, another succumbed to heart failure, and a third plunged to his death from a balcony. And the first harbingers of his own demise had followed soon after he made it to Britain.

Contacts in Russia had told Perepilichnyy his name was on a hit list, and he'd started receiving a stream of threatening messages over Skype. Then a company founded by Dmitri Kovtun attacked him with a series of lawsuits over money he allegedly owed Litvinenko's assassin. The financier had taken out a multimillion-pound life insurance policy with Legal & General for "family protection purposes" in the event of his "premature" death. Medical checks required by the policy had given him a clean bill of health—but when he dropped dead at the roadside months later, Surrey police were happy to assume he died of a heart attack.

When Browder learned of the whistle-blower's demise and wrote to ask the force to launch a murder inquiry, police chiefs intervened to tell investigators to play down suspicions about Perepilichnyy. At a meeting a month after the financier's death, Assistant Chief Constable Olivia Pinkney ordered the officer leading the investigation to "make it a nonissue," remarking gnomically that though there was "ambient interest" in the case at a senior level, a Home Office official was "helping to keep a sense of perspective within central government." The officer in charge of the case, Detective Superintendent Ian Pollard, proposed to keep his statements to the media "bland and simple," and police went on to announce that there was "no evidence to suggest that there was any third-party involvement" in Perepilichnyy's death. A "full and detailed range of toxicology tests" had, they said, found nothing suspicious in the whistle-blower's system. The case was closed.

But then came another astonishing revelation. Perepilichnyy's life insurance company had ordered its own tests on the dead man's stomach contents, and its lawyers told the coroner overseeing a routine inquest hearing that a plant expert at Kew Gardens had identified what appeared to be traces of a deadly poison in his stomach. The toxin, the expert said, bore striking structural similarities to a rare Chinese flowering plant of the genus *Gelsemium*—nicknamed "heartbreak grass" because its leaves trigger cardiac arrest if ingested. The same expert later told the inquest she couldn't definitively identify the substance because the sample sent to the lab was too small. Further tests were impossible, because most of the contents of Perepilichnyy's stomach had been thrown away by the police toxicologist.

The revelation was enough to persuade the French police to open an inquiry of their own in light of Perepilichnyy's mysterious trip to Paris immediately before his collapse. Detectives opened an official file, noting that the financier was "clearly threatened with death in Russia" and that he told Swiss prosecutors he was "on a list of future victims of the Russian mafia." They designated the case a suspected "organized assassination."

The Paris visit was shrouded in mystery. None of Perepilichnyy's family, friends, or business associates knew what he had been doing in the French capital. The only clues were that the financier had taken a Eurostar train on November 6, booked himself into two hotels simultaneously, and returned on the tenth with a €1,200 receipt from the Prada store on the Champs-Élysées and nothing to show for the purchase.

The French investigation quickly turned up a red-hot lead. Detectives seized records showing that Perepilichnyy had been joined at the five-star Le Bristol hotel by a Ukrainian woman for two nights, during which time they had ordered the "romance pack" before checking out on November 10—the day he returned to the UK and died.

French detectives reached out to their British counterparts following the find, but the authorities stonewalled their inquiries, maintaining that the death was unsuspicious and that no further investigation was necessary. The Paris police were urged to await the British coroner's findings on Perepilichnyy's cause of death before taking the matter further. So the French sat on the discovery, making no further inquiries for years, while over in London, the financier's inquest remained snarled up in government red tape. And all the while, the woman with whom Perepilichnyy shared his clandestine assignation was living in an opulent penthouse apartment on the glitzy Avenue Victor Hugo, holding all the secrets of his last night alive.

Paris—November 2012

Elmira Medynska sashayed up the Champs-Élysées turning heads at every step. Even on the most glamorous avenue in Paris, she was a striking vision: towering over her male companion at well over six feet, with her white-blonde hair, sharp-angled features, and penetratingly dark eyes. The twenty-two-year-old had arrived from Ukraine that morning for her third tryst with Alexander Perepilichnyy.

Their first encounter had been earlier that year at an exclusive nightspot in Kiev, after which she'd traveled to join him for a short holiday in Nice, on the French Riviera. Perepilichnyy never told her anything about his life, his family, or his work. He was handsome in a homey way, with tousled hair and gentle eyes, and he liked to take her shopping and send her roses. But the danger signs were already showing.

At a bistro lunch during their summer stay in the south of France, he'd taken a phone call, walked out into the street, and started screaming into the receiver. And as soon as she arrived in Paris it had been clear that his nerves were frayed. He'd taken her for lunch at the Four Seasons but kept going outside to take mysterious phone calls that seemed to spook him, and his hands were trembling so much that he spilled his wine all down his front. Medynska was incensed. She was not used to anything less than the undivided attention of the men she entertained, and she told Perepilichnyy as much. He proposed to take her shopping to make it up to her.

That was how they ended up on the Champs-Élysées, where he

bought her a handbag from Prada and a pair of black Louboutins. But while she was trying on her shoes, he kept pacing up and down and checking his email, and he was so distracted that he bought them in the wrong size. After that, even with the aid of the romance pack back at Le Bristol, the mood was frosty.

The next evening Perepilichnyy tried to salvage the occasion by taking Medynska for dinner at Buddha-Bar in Paris, having made reservations at a series of other restaurants as a decoy, but he remained tense as they tucked into their sushi and tempura. He refused to sit with his back to the rest of the customers, demanding the seat on the banquette facing outward, and he sent his food back twice before taking a bite. His mood seemed to turn even more sour when he started eating, and she couldn't help but notice that his eyes kept wandering to the stairs. As soon as they finished, he said he needed to get outside for some fresh air.

Out on the street, he felt better. They held hands as they made the short walk back to the hotel. But when they got to their room, he went straight to the toilet, where he stayed for an hour. He started running the water, but it didn't obscure the sound of vomiting. When he finally emerged, his eyes and face were red and his skin was clammy, but he declined to call for a doctor.

In the morning, it seemed as if nothing was amiss as they enjoyed a breakfast of eggs and hot chocolate, and Perepilichnyy asked Medynska to see him again before they parted, but she was disenchanted. She felt a pang of guilt when she got home and sent him a message apologizing for being cold—but she never received a reply.

Shortly after Perepilichnyy's death, Medynska set up a fashion business in Paris and rebranded herself Elmira Medins, moving into a palatial apartment on the Avenue Victor Hugo. Her Instagram feed features glamorous selfies snapped at five-star hotels and exclusive restaurants in Paris, Dubai, and Milan. She has held couture shows at Le Bristol, where she stayed with Perepilichnyy, and posted photographs taken at the Four Seasons, where they dined.

Several months after the financier's body was found in Surrey, she received an email from a British investigator who said her messages had been found on the dead man's phone and asked if she had met him in Paris. She replied that she had, and she received a second email asking if she knew four other women with whom Perepilichnyy had been connected. She didn't, but replied giving her mobile number and offering to travel to England to help with any investigation if he could get her a visa. She never heard from him again.

Years went by before Medynska heard any more from law enforcement. When she did, it was after she had been tracked down by journalists at BuzzFeed News and revealed her story in an interview. Only then was she called to testify at the inquest into the financier's death, which had been delayed for more than five years. Medynska told the coroner that she was "very scared" when she read about her paramour's demise on the internet, "because the last person to see him in Paris was me."

By that point, a staggering series of police failures had ensured that the full truth about the financier's death could never be known. Not only had Surrey police thrown away the contents of Perepilichnyy's stomach, they had also lost a vital cache of digital evidence shedding light on his last months alive. Files from the financier's computer had revealed a stream of threatening Skype messages, as well as details of a mysterious $500 million payment he had received shortly before he died. But both the primary police evidence disk containing those files and the backup somehow got accidentally wiped, and then officers discovered that the files had also disappeared from the server of the region's counterterrorism unit, meaning they could never be recovered.

Meanwhile, as had become its habit, the British government was fighting tooth and nail to keep the full truth about the dead man from his inquest. The home secretary initially used a public-interest immunity certificate to prevent the disclosure of a cache of government documents relating to Perepilichnyy on national security grounds.

And when further questions arose about the financier's work for MI6, the government obtained a second secrecy order banning the disclosure of any contact between Perepilichnyy and British intelligence.

In the years after the financier's death, the human casualties of the fraud he exposed continued to rise. A lawyer representing the family of Sergei Magnitsky in Russia nearly died in a fall from a fourth-floor balcony. A campaigner who pushed for sanctions against the Kremlin conspirators narrowly survived two poisoning attempts. And the director of a play about Magnitsky's killing died of a sudden heart attack. Six weeks later, so did his wife—who happened to be the playwright. But through it all, the British government remained unflinching in its insistence that there was nothing to suggest that the death of Alexander Perepilichnyy was anything other than natural.

The spies at Langley were infuriated. They had warned their colleagues in England that the Kremlin was aggressively stepping up its assassination program on UK soil. Now, they agreed among themselves that the "incompetent" British authorities needed to be held accountable for failing to put a stop to the disturbing trend. America's top intelligence official prepared a highly classified report for Congress "on the use of political assassinations as a form of statecraft by the Russian Federation," which listed multiple deaths in Britain. The report asserted with "high confidence" that Perepilichnyy had been assassinated on direct orders from Putin or people close to him, and the intelligence it outlined was passed to MI6. But the British government ignored that and other evidence connecting the Kremlin to another brazen hit on British soil. So Russia grew yet more emboldened.

Royal Courts of Justice, London—August 2012

Roman Abramovich was not in the packed courtroom to hear the verdict, but his opponent would have died rather than miss his big moment. At the end of a months-long trial that crackled with drama at every turn, Lady Justice Gloster was finally ready to deliver judgment, and Boris Berezovsky arrived at the Royal Courts of Justice bright and early to soak up the atmosphere.

The oligarch was by now down to his bottom dollar, but if his £3 billion claim against his former protégé went his way, it would restore him to riches at a single stroke. Sure, defeat would ruin him completely, but he wasn't one to waste time pondering the abyss. Asked by the swarming press pack outside the turreted court building whether he expected to win, he replied: "I'm confident," adding with a note of grandeur, "I believe in the system."

Berezovsky's claim was that he and Patarkatsishvili had been strong-armed into selling Sibneft to Abramovich at a "gross undervalue" as part of a Kremlin "black-op" to strip them of their business interests in Russia, and he was demanding billions in compensation. But Abramovich denied it all, claiming that Boris and Badri never owned any stake in the oil giant and that he had paid them $1.3 billion not to buy them out but in recompense for the *krysha* they provided while he was building up his businesses in the '90s.

Neither man had any paperwork to back up his claim because all their deals had been done on a handshake—"It's just how business was organized," Berezovsky explained, describing the Russia of the '90s as the "Wild East." More troubling, as the judge noted, was that "a number of witnesses, who would, or might, have been able to have given key evidence, were dead." So the verdict would have to swing on whose version of events Lady Justice Gloster happened to believe.

Berezovsky had been typically florid in the witness box, using his testimony to fire volleys at the Kremlin and burnish his own role in the invention of post-Communist Russia.

"I don't want to present me as a hero, but unfortunately you push me again," he said at one point, as he explained under cross-examination how he had single-handedly run off the Communists to secure Boris Yeltsin's reelection in 1996. Abramovich, on the other hand, had been quiet, measured, and respectful. He had given evidence in Russian and kept his answers short.

The trial riveted audiences in Britain and Russia, shining a searing spotlight on the smash-and-grab chaos of post-Soviet Russia, and the public gallery was so packed on the final day that the clerks had to open up a second courtroom to contain the overspill. At 10:30 a.m. Lady Justice Gloster entered in her wig and gown and settled on the bench as the court fell silent. Berezovsky, sitting near the back, looked fit to burst as she shuffled her papers. Then, with icy poise, she looked straight out into the gallery and demolished his case.

"On my analysis of the entirety of the evidence, I found Mr. Berezovsky an unimpressive, and inherently unreliable, witness, who regarded truth as a transitory, flexible concept, which could be molded to suit his current purposes," the judge declared. The oligarch's hands flew to his face. "At times the evidence which he gave was deliberately dishonest; sometimes he was clearly making his evidence up as he went along," she continued.

"At other times, I gained the impression that he was not necessarily being deliberately dishonest, but had deluded himself into believing his own version of events."

Abramovich, by contrast, had been a "truthful and on the whole reliable witness," the judge said, and she accepted his evidence.

Berezovsky walked out of the courtroom in a daze. Instead of emerging with his fortune restored, he was now saddled with his own crippling legal bill and would have to pay tens of millions more to cover Abramovich's costs. That was money he simply didn't have. The court had just heard that he'd already sold the mansion at Wentworth Estate and was shedding assets as fast as he could to pay his spiraling debts. But what hurt more than anything were the harsh words of the judge still hammering inside his head. Berezovsky had fought the fiercest information war imaginable against all the organs of the Russian propaganda state. Now, in a few short sentences, Lady Justice Gloster had ruined his reputation forever.

"I'm absolutely amazed what happened today," he told journalists in the street, shaking his head in a haze of bewilderment. "Sometimes

I had the impression Putin himself wrote this judgment." He shrank into the back of a black Mercedes and sped away from the crowd.

The oligarch decamped to a more modest mansion owned by his ex-wife in Ascot and struggled to come to terms with his fate. British justice had been his last love, and now, in his eyes, the system had betrayed him. He shed more valuable possessions, including a prized Andy Warhol painting of Lenin, and laid off all but one of his bodyguards.

The Scotland Yard protection officer was worried. There had been several more suspected plots to kill Berezovsky since Atlangeriev's assassination attempt, and the threats showed no sign of abating. The most alarming intelligence had come from Mossad, the Israeli spy agency, whose agents had picked up on an FSB plot to blow Berezovsky up the next time he visited Belarus—by planting fifteen land mines on the road to his dacha outside the city. The protection officer had been dispatched to Down Street to warn the oligarch that he would be "vaporized" if he went back to Belarus—but no sooner had that threat been neutralized than others emerged. The Russia watchers had detected a spike in the number of plots against Berezovsky since Putin's reelection earlier that year, and Scotland Yard had always relied on the oligarch to foot the bill for his own security. Police resources were seriously depleted by the government's austerity program, and there was no way Scotland Yard could afford to pick up the tab for the vast teams of bodyguards, surveillance units, and armored vehicles required to keep him safe around the clock. But without that level of protection, Berezovsky was a sitting duck.

The protection officer went to see his charge at Down Street and grew still more alarmed. Berezovsky had always exuded wealth and power, but now he looked disheveled and exhausted, as if he'd slept in his suit. The officer tried to venture some thoughts about boosting his personal security detail, but Berezovsky shut him down. There had been a time, he said, when he was so rich he barely knew the value of a million bucks. Now his pockets were empty.

"I am broken," he said before they parted ways.

Berezovsky could no longer sustain his fight with Patarkatsishvili's family and the other shareholders in the New World Value Fund, and he was forced to settle out of court for an undisclosed sum. The deal was partially brokered by Scot Young, who visited Down Street appearing unkempt and hollow-eyed in a baseball cap and jeans. *He looks like a bum,* the oligarch's secretary thought as the fixer walked by. It was the last deal Young would ever do for Berezovsky. The proceeds sank straight into the swell of debt and legal bills.

The oligarch descended so deep into his misery that he began taking antidepressants and opened a Facebook account to post rambling messages bemoaning his hubris. "I repent and ask for forgiveness for greed. I longed for riches, not thinking that this was to the detriment of others," he wrote. "I repent and ask for forgiveness for what led to the power of Vladimir Putin." His plight was heavily publicized in Russia—to the fiendish delight of an old adversary.

Andrey Lugovoy took to the floor of the Russian parliament in December of 2012 to crow over the oligarch's demise. "He takes antidepressants," the assassin jeered, and "flies to Israel from London economy rather than in his private jet." But he said he had learned that the "infamous tycoon and villain" was plotting to spend the payout he received from the New World Value Fund to finance new anti-Kremlin activities and accused those involved in the carve-up of "sheer cynicism, villainy, shamelessness of the highest degree." Lugovoy said he had passed a file of evidence to Russian prosecutors and the FSB and called for a crackdown on all those found to be providing financial assistance to Berezovsky.

Soon after Lugovoy's speech, Michelle Young received a call from another private investigator who had approached her claiming a connection to the FSB. "Boris Berezovsky is being dealt with," the man said. He thought she ought to know that her ex-husband's boss was about to end up "in a body bag."

PART SEVEN

THE FALL

XIX

The mansion was strangely silent when Boris Berezovsky's only re-maining bodyguard let himself in. It was the early afternoon of a bitingly cold day in March, and Avi Navama had been out running errands for several hours. The former Mossad agent had guarded Berezovsky for six years, long enough to start thinking of him as a second father, and he would once have refused to leave his charge un-attended for even a moment. But now that the rest of the guards had been disbanded and the servants were gone, he had to be all things to his master—cook, babysitter, errand boy—as well as single-handedly trying to keep the man safe.

Berezovsky was nowhere to be seen inside the château-style man-sion where he had been living for months on his ex-wife's charity, and Navama noticed that calls and texts were backing up on his mobile phone. Bounding up the stairs, the bodyguard found the bath-room door locked. There was no answer when he knocked. When no amount of hammering raised a response, he kicked down the door.

The oligarch was splayed on his back on the bathroom floor, his face a deep shade of purple. A length of his favorite black cashmere scarf was tied tight around his neck, torn from another length dan-gling from the metal shower rail overhead. Navama knelt and pressed his ear to his master's lips, but they were silent. The Kremlin's arch-nemesis was dead.

Berezovsky had seemed like a man on his way to the gallows in his last miserable months, and when officers arrived from the Thames Valley Police, both his bodyguard and his eldest daughter, Elizaveta, told them he had talked about ending his life. The bathroom door had been locked, and there was no sign of a struggle. A brief panic arose when a radiation detector sounded an alarm and hazardous materials specialists swooped in to check for traces of radioactivity, but none could be found. The police announced quickly that Berezovsky's death was not suspicious and closed the case.

The news that Russia's most defiant oligarch had finally fallen on his own sword drove a split through his friends. Some who had witnessed Berezovsky's descent into depression believed he was capable of suicide, but most were convinced that he had finally fallen victim to the Russian assassins who had been hunting him for years.

"Boris was fucking whacked," said Jonathan Brown. Lord Bell, the oligarch's PR guru, told everyone there was no doubt about who was responsible for his death.

"If you upset Putin, you disappear."

When the Scotland Yard protection officer heard of Berezovsky's death, he felt crushed. He thought back over everything that had gone into guarding the unruly oligarch—the panicked phone calls when new threats emerged; the heated COBRA meetings; the whispered warnings on lamplit street corners in Mayfair.

After all of that, he thought, *it comes to this.* He went to Down Street to offer his condolences to the oligarch's staff, but the fixtures were already being ripped out of the office on the second floor.

The downfall of Russia's public enemy number one was a prime propaganda opportunity for Putin. He capitalized on it by claiming publicly that the oligarch had recently written two letters throwing himself on the Kremlin's mercy.

"He wrote that he had made many mistakes and asked to be forgiven and allowed to return to his homeland," Putin said, adding that the letters were "fairly personal" and that he would not publish them because God would not approve of such a display. The Russian press was told that Abramovich, having received an apology himself, had delivered one of the missives to Putin personally.

The reaction to Berezovsky's death in the largely Kremlin-controlled Russian media was vitriolic. Channel One, the broadcaster Boris and Badri had once controlled, labeled him an "evil genius," while another Moscow daily branded him a "master of chaos," and a popular tabloid described him as a "giant spider who managed to entangle so many top officials in his web." The independent newspaper *Novaya Gazeta,* for which Anna Politkovskaya had once worked, gave Berezovsky the most balanced send-off, noting in an editorial that the oligarch had "viewed Russia as a chessboard, but one on which only he would be allowed to move the pieces."

Berezovsky's family was convinced he had been murdered. They were about to fly to Israel for a family holiday, and his beloved mother had just been diagnosed with terminal cancer—they couldn't believe he would have abandoned her when she had only a few months left to live.

It had been Elizaveta who first told the police that her father had expressed a wish to die, and that was true, but it by no means ruled out foul play in her mind. Berezovsky's sudden mental collapse had seemed to her too swift and powerful to be believed. He had confided to her one day, pale and shaking, that he felt as if "some chemical reaction inside" was causing him to feel such deep despair. She wondered whether her father had been poisoned with some mysterious mind-altering substance in his last months, and she set about investigating his death on her own.

When officers from the Thames Valley Police arrived at the oligarch's inquest to make the case for suicide the following year, Elizaveta was ready to square up to them. The coroner heard first from the Home Office pathologist who conducted the official postmortem and concluded that Berezovsky's injuries were consistent with hanging. But Elizaveta had enlisted an eminent German asphyxiation expert named Dr. Bernd Brinkmann to examine photographs of her father's body—and his testimony blew a hole in the police case.

Brinkmann announced there was "no way" that Berezovsky's injuries were consistent with hanging, positing instead that the oligarch had been attacked from behind and throttled before being strung up from the shower rail. The marks on the oligarch's neck were "completely different to the strangulation mark in hanging"—circular instead of V-shaped—and Brinkmann noted that his face was deeply discolored, whereas victims of hanging are usually pale. There was also a fresh wound on the back of Berezovsky's head and a fractured rib as well as the presence of an unidentified fingerprint on the shower rail.

The police position was that Berezovsky had sustained his additional injuries when the scarf snapped and his body fell, and they told the coroner they were "content" that Berezovsky had taken his own life. But Elizaveta offered the inquest a very different perspective.

"I can think of many people interested in my father's death," she said. Asked if she knew who these people were, she replied: "I think we all know."

The Kremlin had been trying for years to silence Berezovsky, and his daughter believed it had finally succeeded. "He was saying that Putin was a danger to the whole world," she told the coroner, "and you can see that now."

With such conflicting testimony, the coroner, Dr. Peter Bedford, said he could not determine beyond all reasonable doubt how Berezovsky had died, and the inquest recorded an open verdict.

The official police position did not sit easily in all quarters at Scotland Yard. Several officers in the Specialist Protection and counterterrorism units, who had spent years monitoring the threats to Berezovsky, would always suspect that he had, finally, been murdered. They knew Russia was perfectly capable of faking a person's suicide, having slipped the victim mind-altering drugs beforehand to make it look believable.

Behind the scenes, as had become traditional when Russian exiles died on British soil, the spies in the River House reached out to their

US counterparts to ask for intelligence about the oligarch's demise. The answer from Langley was no surprise. The Americans suspected Berezovsky had been assassinated. They did not have proof that the killing was carried out on direct orders from the Kremlin, but the evidence linking the oligarch's death to Russia was considered compelling. Berezovsky had made many enemies in his long-distance war with Russia, and he had given them many reasons to wish him dead. But US spies suspected it was a single maneuver that had sealed his fate.

Berezovsky had been living on borrowed time ever since stoking the Orange Revolution, which had toppled the pro-Kremlin regime in Kiev in 2004. And now, with his archnemesis dead, Putin was gearing up to assert his authority in Ukraine once and for all.

Crimea and London—February 2014

The masked men who surrounded the Crimean parliament under cover of darkness in February of 2014 carried Russian army-issue AK-47s and rocket-propelled grenades. They wore unmarked green flak jackets to obscure their allegiance, but they were acting under the aegis of the Kremlin. In the early hours of the morning, the Russian-backed troops stormed the seat of government in Ukraine's turbulent separatist region before seizing control of its airport and blockading its military bases. By the time the sun came up, the Russian flag was fluttering from the rooftop of the parliament building, and Crimea had been occupied.

The stage thus set by the masked soldiers he referred to fondly as his "little green men," Vladimir Putin ordered a full-scale Russian invasion of Ukraine's breakaway region, and within a month, he had announced the annexation of Crimea as a federal subject of Russia. The men in green pressed on to occupy the turbulent Donetsk and Luhansk regions of eastern Ukraine, armed and backed all the way by the Kremlin. They declared the two regions independent, sparking a full-blown armed conflict with the Ukrainian government in which thousands were killed, while Kiev was hit by waves of crippling cyberattacks emanating straight from Moscow.

The annexation of Crimea marked the end of any serious hope that Putin could be brought in from the cold, and Russia's expulsion from the institutions and alliances of the liberal world order was swift when it finally came. The NATO countries ceased all political and military cooperation with Moscow, and Russia was thrown out of the G8. President Obama signed a series of executive orders enacting sweeping economic sanctions, and the EU followed suit, crippling the Russian economy further as it reeled from a sudden slump in global oil prices. Major bilateral trade talks were suspended. And the United States went on to revive plans for its missile defense system by the Russian border.

In the first days of the invasion, the British prime minister hoped the trouble might blow over without damage to his dealings with Putin, and a top aide was photographed outside Downing Street holding a document stating that the UK would not back sanctions "or close London's financial center to Russians." But Putin's wholesale annexation of a sovereign European territory was too much.

"It makes it impossible to do business with him," one cabinet minister reflected privately as the government reckoned with the fallout.

David Cameron had no choice but to come out fighting. He made a statement directed at the Kremlin, and for once, he did not mince his words. "This is an incursion into a sovereign state, and a land grab of part of its territory, with no respect for the law," he said. Britain followed the rest of the NATO countries by suspending all military cooperation with Moscow and backing the EU sanctions.

Russia's next move was arguably its most brazen yet. In July, Kremlin-backed forces in Donetsk shot down a Malaysia Airlines passenger jet on its way from Amsterdam to Kuala Lumpur, killing all 298 people on board. Satellite footage and other digital evidence showed that the military-grade missile had been transported from

Russia on the day of the crash and fired from a field in an area controlled by Kremlin-backed rebels before the launcher was rushed back over the border. Ten Britons were among the dead.

Cameron demanded a phone call with Putin to express his anger about the attack and was further enraged when the Russian president snubbed him by taking three days to respond. That, it turned out, was the last straw.

Two days later, the home secretary, Theresa May, announced that the government would, finally, launch a full public inquiry into the murder of Alexander Litvinenko.

It was a stunning about-face. Until then, the government had stood in the way of every effort by Marina Litvinenko to get to the truth about who had ordered her husband's killing. An inquest was opened after attempts to extradite the two prime suspects failed, and the presiding judge promised an "open and fearless" investigation—but his path was blocked when the foreign secretary obtained a public-interest immunity order to stop the disclosure of critical classified information. The judge, Sir Robert Owen, asked the home secretary to establish a public inquiry with the power to consider the secret material in closed hearings, but even that was rebuffed. Theresa May acknowledged in her written explanation that "international relations have been a factor."

The defector's widow had filed for a judicial review of that decision, pressing on even after ministers rejected her application for legal aid to cover her costs.

"I really want to get the truth," she tearfully told reporters on the steps of the High Court. Three judges had ruled in her favor that February, describing May's refusal to hold an inquiry as "irrational" and "legally erroneous."

Since then, the government had remained silent. But six days after the downing of the MH17 flight, May announced that Marina Litvinenko could finally have her day in court.

Owen was brought in to lead the proceedings, and the hearings got under way. Over the course of the following eighteen months, the inquiry would hear public testimony from a cast of Putin's most savage critics, while in private the judge pored over a cache of top-secret intelligence documenting the murderous truth about the Russian leader the West had courted for so long.

If the government thought its dilatory move toward justice might serve as a deterrent, it had badly miscalculated. Putin thumbed his nose at the inquiry by personally decorating Andrey Lugovoy with a medal "for services to the motherland" during the hearings. And Russia's killing campaign was only going to escalate.

XX

Marylebone, London—December 2014

The London square was still and cold when the body fell, dropping silently through the moonlight and landing with a thud. Impaled through the chest on the spikes of a wrought-iron fence, it dangled under the streetlamps as blood spilled onto the pavement. Overhead, a fourth-floor window stood open, the lights inside burning.

The dead man was Scot Young. The onetime superfixer was by then the ninth in Berezovsky's circle of friends and business associates to die under suspicious circumstances in Britain. But when the police entered his penthouse on the night of December 8, 2014, they didn't even dust for fingerprints. They declared his death a suicide on the spot and closed the case.

Young had become a shadow of his former self before his fatal fall: ever more terrified in the wake of Berezovsky's death, hounded day and night by angry creditors, and still fighting tooth and nail to suppress the secrets of his Russian business dealings.

After seven years, sixty-five divorce hearings, and three months in prison for contempt, he had still failed to provide a satisfactory explanation for the sudden disappearance of his fortune, and the High Court had been forced to make its final ruling blind.

"Doing the best I can, I find that he still has £45 million hidden from this court," the judge had ventured. Young was ordered to give Michelle half of that and several million more to cover her legal costs, telling Young "this debt will exist for all time."

The money had not materialized, so Michelle continued her investigation into the whereabouts of the missing fortune. But shortly before his death, she received a frantic phone call from her ex-husband.

"I fucked it up in the end completely," he said. "I put my hands up, and I actually apologize to you. You were a very good wife. You used to run me a bath, make me tea." He made her an offer: if she stopped digging, he would find £30 million to give her the following day. But Michelle had told him that was nothing like enough "after billions of pounds being hidden," and their call ended angrily.

"Okay, Michelle," he said before hanging up. "I've tried to be nice. You're going to end up with sweet fuck-all."

When she heard the news of her ex-husband's fatal fall weeks later, Michelle came into her younger daughter's bedroom shaking all over.

"Your father has jumped off a building," she said in a daze.

Sasha didn't believe it. A few days before, her father had called to tell her he was checking himself into a psychiatric unit to stay out of danger. He was not supposed to be released for several more days.

Sasha called her sister, Scarlet, and the two of them set off to check on their dad in the hospital. But Young wasn't there. Staff brought them tissues while they phoned the police in tears and begged in vain for facts. Then, googling on their mobiles, they found articles reporting their father's death: he had fallen four stories from his bedroom window and been impaled on the iron spikes below—so deeply that a large section of the fence had to be cut away in order to remove his body. The two young women stumbled out of the hospital and threw up outside.

It wasn't until around 8:00 p.m. that the police finally showed up at their door—two days after Young's fall. Their father had killed himself, the officers said, and the death was not being investigated.

But Sasha and Scarlet had "zero belief" that their father had taken his own life. They knew he had been terrified of dying right until the end, and he had a crippling fear of heights. He had, they now realized, called them both sounding calm and cheerful just minutes before his body was found impaled on the spikes.

They phoned Jonathan Brown. The smoked-salmon mogul had been a favorite among their father's friends ever since they were kids in Miami, and they told him through sobs that their dad was dead. Brown's reaction was unambiguous. His friend had obviously been "fucking whacked," he said, "like everyone else." He had two questions: first, who was responsible? And second, "Am I next?"

Brown got on the first plane to London and the three of them made a pact: if the police weren't going to investigate this, they would.

First, they went to speak to Young's fiancée, Noelle Reno. She told them what she had told the police—that she and Young had split up right before he went into the hospital, and he had returned home unexpectedly at around 3:30 p.m. on December 8, just as she was waiting for a locksmith. They had a blazing row, Reno said, and Young refused to leave. In the altercation, one of her two phones had accidentally been dropped in the toilet, so after the locks had been changed she left Young inside the flat and set off to buy a new one. On her way, she said, Young called her on her second phone and said: "I'm going to jump. Stay on the phone and you will hear me." She hung up, and minutes later he had fallen—at around 5:15 p.m.

Sasha and Scarlet couldn't square that account with the calm, cheerful calls they received from their father during the same period. A call to Scarlet at 5:08 p.m. had gone to voice mail, and she still had the recording. "Hi, Scarlet, just wanted to say I love you loads, miss you terribly, and I'm all okay, don't worry about me. Love you! Bye," the message said. She would listen to that message what felt like a thousand times, trying to make sense of it.

A minute later—just five minutes before he fell—he called Sasha to tell her he loved her, too, and would ring her again in the morning. It isn't uncommon for those on the verge of suicide to leave messages for their loved ones that don't betray their intentions, but Young's daughters simply couldn't believe either of those calls had been meant as a final goodbye—so they carried on investigating.

Next, they went with Brown to examine the scene of their father's fall. The three of them had driven by the flat the night before, while it was still sealed off with police tape, and they were spooked to see a light on in the upstairs window. Now they walked through the door that the police had smashed open and took in the place where Young had spent his last moments.

The flat was immaculate, with pristine white walls and cream carpet. They made their way into the bedroom and went over to the sash window from which Young had fallen. Pulling it up, the two young women found that it only opened around fifty centimeters, about the same as the distance from their dad's elbow to his fingertips. As soon as they saw the window, they agreed it was hard to imagine how their father could have propelled himself out.

"That window was so small, and he was so tall," Sasha said. "It would take a few minutes just to maneuver out of it."

Stranger still, there was a can of Diet Coke, a packet of Marlboro menthols, and a cigarette lighter lined up neatly in a row on the narrow window ledge. Their father would have had to jump clean over them to hurl himself through the tight opening without knocking any of the items over. That scarcely seemed possible.

Leaning out the window, they looked down at the last sight their father's eyes took in and saw the sharp iron fence looming up below. It was unfathomable to them that he would have flung himself onto those spikes—especially with his almost debilitating fear of heights. And then they spotted something that gave them chills.

On either side of the outside windowsill, there were rows of faint scratch marks in the dirt, about as far apart as the fingers on a hand.

"I guess it's him fighting for his life," Sasha said.

They took photographs of the inside of the flat, the narrow window opening, and the marks on the sill. That, already, was more than the police had done. The two young women opened the wardrobe and each put on one of their dad's big snuggly sweaters, which still had his scent. Then they set off to confront the police.

They met with Detective Sergeant Christopher Page, the senior officer who had determined that Young's death was not suspicious. The two daughters told Page that their father had called them the Saturday before his death to say he was in danger. Scarlet explained that he knew "unsavory characters," including "a lot of Russian oligarchs," and warned them "constantly" that "we had to be careful, he had to be careful, everyone had to be careful." Several of their father's friends and associates had died under suspicious circumstances, they pointed out, including Boris Berezovsky and Robbie Curtis.

Page was unmoved. Reno's account of Young's last-minute call threatening to jump was enough to preclude any investigation.

"From our point of view it was a clear case," the detective told them. "He's threatened to commit suicide."

"Have we reviewed the CCTV to find out who went into and out of that flat?" Brown asked.

"The answer is I don't know," said Page. "I would suspect probably not."

"If you could just have a look," Brown implored. "Because the girls, it's on their heart, and they're going to live with this for the rest of their lives."

"We can only go on the information and the evidence that we have," Page said tartly. "I know that may not satisfy your questions or your theories on the matter."

"We want the CCTV," Scarlet insisted. "This is a really big thing for us. And has the apartment been properly inspected? Did you take recent fingerprints? Did you do *anything*?"

"We wouldn't have need, given the circumstances," Page said.

Eventually, the detective did agree to check the CCTV cameras in the area, though the police would later admit that they never watched the footage until they were ordered to do so by the coroner six months later. At the moment Young fell, every single camera in the square happened to be pointing away from the window.

Michelle was convinced that her ex-husband had faked his own death to get out of paying her divorce settlement, and Brown secretly hoped she was right. He wanted to see for himself, so he headed down to the morgue to inspect the body. *If it's not him, what a fucking amazing cover-up he's done,* he thought, resolving to do his friend one last favor by keeping quiet. But there was no such luck.

Two hundred people attended Young's funeral. The sisters were approached in the crowd by a man they didn't know who warned them to "stop asking questions" about how their father died—and things got stranger when Brown stood to give his eulogy and the vicar introduced him as "one of the last surviving members of Project Moscow." The coffin was accompanied by a display of white roses spelling DADDY. Brown walked alongside Sasha and Scarlet to their father's grave, and stood by them as his body was lowered into the ground.

Young's inquest came in July of 2015. The coroner heard first from the psychiatrist who had discharged him from the hospital on the afternoon of his death. She said Young appeared to be in the grip of a "manic episode" when he admitted himself, saying he was "hearing voices and feeling unsafe, as people wanted to kill him," and telling her he had momentarily contemplated jumping off a balcony, but thoughts of his daughters had stopped him. After four days in the hospital, Young was "stable and well," denying any thoughts of self-harm. Surmising that the manic episode had been caused by cocaine use, she deemed him well enough to go home, and he left the hospital around 2:30 p.m.

The psychiatrist told the inquest that it would be highly unlikely for Young to have become manic again straight after leaving the hospital unless he had used a lot of drugs. But toxicology tests showed he was clean and sober when he fell. Jaqueline Julyan, a barrister working for Young's daughters, played the voice mail Young had left for

Scarlet and asked the psychiatrist to comment on what it revealed about his state of mind.

"All I can deduce is that the signs of a manic stage are not there," she replied. "It is normal and matches his state when I discharged him earlier that day."

Next, Dr. Nathaniel Cary, the Home Office pathologist who conducted the postmortem, testified that in addition to injuries "consistent with impalement," Young had a "severe head injury," scratches on his arms, wrist, and thumb, and a cut on the tip of his middle finger. Julyan wanted to know how he had picked up these additional injuries. It was likely that Young "hit something as he fell," Cary said, adding that "sometimes people hit awnings." But there weren't any awnings on the house in Montagu Square, and no one had bothered to check whether it was possible for him to have hit anything else on the way down.

As for the wounds on Young's arms and hands, the pathologist said these were "typical of falls" because "people can grip to stay in." Except, of course, that Young was supposed to have thrown himself out the window deliberately. The barrister asked if the pathologist had performed any checks on the windowsill to establish whether there were any marks that could account for the injuries.

"That would be the responsibility of scene-of-crime officers," he said.

Detective Sergeant Page took the stand. Julyan showed him a picture of the scratches on the windowsill and asked if they had been examined by officers at the scene.

"I didn't see them," he said. "It was dark."

The lawyer asked if he had seen them when he went back in daylight.

"I didn't go back," he replied.

The detective acknowledged that the window was so small as to be "difficult to climb through," and he posited, stretching his arms forward like Superman, that Young had dived out "front first with hands out." But that wouldn't explain how he had hit his head. Why, Julyan wanted to know, had officers closed the window before photographing the scene rather than leaving it open to document the narrow gap through which Young was meant to have jumped?

"This was as the weather could change and we didn't want to lose the forensics," Page replied. But the officers had not carried out any forensic work.

The barrister asked how it was that Young had landed on the fence—a meter out from the wall.

"I've got no idea. These things would have been followed if it had been a suspicious death, but it was not suspicious," the officer replied.

At the end of the hearing, the coroner said that while she believed the police were "entirely correct" that there were "no suspicious circumstances," she could not ignore the evidence from Young's daughters and several of his friends that he had sounded calm on the phone in the minutes before his death—and she noted that the police had not explained either the marks on the windowsill or the trajectory of Young's body from the window onto the fence.

"I have concluded that there is inconclusive evidence to determine his state of mind and intention when he came out of the window," she said. The inquest recorded an open verdict.

It was a victory for Sasha and Scarlet, who hadn't wanted their father's death to go down as a suicide. Still, they had no real answers about how he had met his end. But while the police shut down the case, dismissed the Russian connection, and rebuffed their concerns, the spies in the River House were secretly asking their American counterparts if the fixer's risky dealings in Moscow had finally caught up with him.

The spies at Langley replied that yes, they did indeed suspect another assassination had slipped through Scotland Yard's dragnet. Young's death was yet another reason why US intelligence officials believed the Kremlin's killing campaign was accelerating. And their fears that the tide of Russian death might spread to American shores would soon be realized. One of Putin's top henchmen was on his way to Washington.

Before dawn one November morning in 2015, the mastermind of Vladimir Putin's global propaganda machine strolled into the lobby of the Dupont Circle hotel, in Washington, DC, and paid $1,200 in cash for a penthouse suite. Mikhail Lesin was the advertising Svengali who had worked with Berezovsky to propel Putin to power in 2000 before leading the new president's crackdown on independent journalism as media minister—a burly man with a bulbous head who had earned the nickname the Bulldozer as he systematically drove Russia's newspapers and TV stations under Kremlin control. His crowning achievement was the invention of Russia Today—the propaganda network he had built for Putin to "promote Russia internationally"—and it had grown into a sprawling global giant under his watch.

The spreading influence of RT had become a major source of concern for the US government: its widely shared disinformation about the occupation of eastern Ukraine and the downing of MH17 had prompted the US secretary of state at the time, John Kerry, to denounce the network as a "propaganda bullhorn" for Moscow. But now Lesin was ready to betray his own brainchild. He had joined the cast of Russian runaways hiding out in the West after falling out of favor in Moscow, and he was in Washington for a meeting with the US government.

The media mogul's glory days had ended in 2009, when Dmitry Medvedev took over the Russian presidency. Over the course of the following three years, Lesin traveled the world, spending lavishly and partying hard on a $40 million yacht named *Serenity*. He had spent more and more time in the United States, splashing $28 million on luxury California real estate for himself, his daughter—Ekaterina Lesina, an RT bureau chief—and his son, Anton Lessine, a Hollywood producer. Lesin had always been florid and fast-living, but his time away from Russia took the brakes off an already pernicious drinking problem. By 2012, when Putin returned to the Kremlin and invited him back into the corridors of power, he was unraveling.

Lesin returned to Moscow to take over Gazprom-Media and started by subsuming one of Russia's few remaining major independent outlets into the state-owned conglomerate. But his habit of disappearing on binges for days at a time soured his relationship with the Kremlin, and then his time in the United States started to catch up with him. Senator Roger Wicker had caught wind of Lesin's California spending spree and wrote to the Department of Justice in 2014 demanding an investigation on suspicion of corruption and money laundering. The case was referred to the DOJ's criminal division, and that was when Lesin abruptly quit Gazprom-Media and disappeared.

By the summer of 2015, US spies learned that Putin's propaganda chief was hiding out in Europe, terrified for his life. The word in Moscow was that the Russian president had finally cut him loose once he attracted the scrutiny of the US government, and without the *krysha* of the Kremlin, his many enemies had started to come after him. Lesin was holed up in the Swiss Alps, the spies heard, and he wanted protection.

Such rare schisms, when they do open up in the tightly controlled orbit of the Kremlin, offer golden opportunities for intelligence gathering—and the DOJ had prime leverage over Lesin in the form of the investigation into his wealth. Officials began communicating with the runaway through a third party, and he indicated that he was prepared to cooperate.

So it was that Lesin found his way to the Dupont Circle hotel under cover of darkness on November 4, 2015, on the eve of his planned meeting with the DOJ. Officials were eagerly expecting him to give up the goods on the inner workings of RT and its relationship with the Kremlin the following day. But before that, their potential informant had twenty-four hours to kill.

Lesin holed up inside the penthouse suite with two bottles of red wine, a six-pack of Guinness, and a bottle of Johnnie Walker scotch, and before long he was staggering drunkenly through the hotel corridors. After he had been shooed back to his room, a security guard checked in on him in the early afternoon and found him falling-down drunk. The guard asked if he needed any help, but Lesin put an arm around his shoulder and slurred "nyet."

Another guard popped his head around the door just after 8:00 p.m. and saw Lesin passed out on the floor. He was breathing but didn't wake, and the guard slipped away. The following morning, another member of the staff entered the penthouse to tell its disorderly occupant it was time to check out. The room was scattered with empty liquor bottles, and there was Lesin lying facedown in the midst of the mess. This time, he wasn't breathing.

The officials at the Justice Department received the disappointing news that their eagerly awaited meeting with the architect of Putin's global media empire would no longer be going ahead. Lesin was dead. He had been killed by blunt-force injuries to the head—and his neck, torso, arms, and legs had also been battered. The medical examiner further noted that the hyoid bone in the dead man's neck was fractured—an injury commonly associated with strangulation.

The FBI was brought in to help the local police with their investigation, but after an eleven-month inquiry, a federal prosecutor made an announcement that was viewed with disbelief by agents who knew the case. Lesin's death was nothing more than a sad accident, the prosecutor said. The media czar had bludgeoned *himself* to death by repeatedly falling down drunk alone in his room "after days of excessive consumption of alcohol." The case was closed.

Inside the FBI, agents who glimpsed what lay inside the sealed investigative file on Lesin's death whispered angrily about a cover-up. The file contained critical evidence ranging from surveillance tapes to witness interviews, the contents of which would thenceforth remain secret, and the authorities had also locked away more than 150 pages of evidence that had been gathered by a grand jury investigating the mogul's death behind closed doors. Even more explosively, the agents close to the case knew the FBI was sitting on a secret report containing high-level intelligence from Moscow—and it directly contradicted the official finding that Lesin had died by accident.

The report had been authored by Christopher Steele, the former head of the Russia desk at MI6, who now ran a private intelligence outfit that often did work for the FBI. Steele would later shoot to international fame as the author of a dossier alleging that Russia had been "cultivating, supporting, and assisting" Donald Trump in the run-up to the US election, and he was all too familiar with the Kremlin's killing program from his time in the top echelons of British intelligence. He had pumped his network of high-level Russian sources for intel on Lesin's gruesome demise and handed his final report to the FBI.

Steele's report said Lesin was bludgeoned to death by moonlighting state security agents working for an oligarch close to Putin whom the media czar had crossed. The thugs had been instructed to beat Lesin, not kill him, Steele said, but they had gone too far. That chimed with the whispers that US spies had picked up in Moscow. They had gathered intelligence indicating that Putin's former propaganda chief had been beaten to death with a baseball bat by enforcers for the same oligarch Steele had named.

US officials feared that the threat of Russian assassination had finally hit home—one senior national security official privately raised concerns that the Kremlin had started "doing here what they do with some regularity in London."

The East-West relationship hadn't been so badly fractured since the Cold War. The year before Lesin's death, hackers in Moscow had penetrated the computer systems of the White House and State Department in Russia's first cyberattack against the United States. And that September, Russia defied America and its allies by launching a full-blown military intervention in support of the Syrian despot

Bashar al-Assad as he continued his bloody suppression of the country's Western-backed rebels.

Still, antagonizing Russia further was a dangerous option. That same year, Iran had finally agreed to a long-term deal to limit its nuclear program and allow international weapons inspectors into the country in return for the easing of sanctions—and Russia had been a key party in the negotiations. Crucial work still needed to be done to bring the deal to fruition, and Moscow's ongoing cooperation was essential.

In the end, when Langley's long-held fears were realized and a prominent Kremlin enemy finally perished on American soil, the US authorities took a leaf out of the British playbook. They shut the investigation down.

XXI

___

Royal Courts of Justice, London—January 2016

Marina Litvinenko sat expectantly in the front row of court 73. At her side was her son Anatoly, now a young man of twenty-two with a neat side parting to match his flawless British accent, and behind them were two of her husband's few surviving friends: Yuli Dubov, looking scholarly in his wire-rimmed spectacles, and Akhmed Za- kayev, who arrived in a splendid fur hat. The Litvinenko inquiry had finally reached its verdict, and the public gallery was crammed with spectators eagerly awaiting the judge's findings.

There was general agreement that the judge would surely have to hold Lugovoy and Kovtun culpable in light of the glaring radioac- tive trail they'd left all over London. The big question was whether he would go further. The inquiry was supposed to be entirely impartial and free of political and diplomatic pressures, but many of those in the room had long since lost their trust in the British system. Would the judge be so bold as to direct the blame at the Russian state? Or would this be another very British fudge?

Sir Robert Owen arrived and took his seat with a nod at the packed courtroom. The judge had presided over lengthy public hearings and sifted mounds of secret intelligence in private before withdrawing to write his judgment. Owen was a pillar of the establishment—a seasoned snowy-haired justice recently retired from the High Court—and he had based the findings he was about to make on a coolheaded, lawyerly review of the evidence. But he embarked upon the oral summary of his conclusions with discernible trepidation.

"There can be *no doubt*," he began, speaking slowly and deliberately, as if laying land mines with every syllable, "that Alexander Litvinenko was poisoned by Mr. Lugovoy and Mr. Kovtun." Relief washed across the upturned faces in the front row, and the news began to flash across TV screens up and down the country. The judge hunched his shoulders as if bracing for his next declaration.

"I have concluded that there is a strong probability that when Mr. Lugovoy poisoned Mr. Litvinenko, he did so under the direction of the FSB," he continued. "I have further concluded that Mr. Kovtun was also acting under FSB direction."

It was an astonishing moment, and the silence in the courtroom was electric. Owen had laid the blame for Litvinenko's killing squarely at the door of the Russian state security agency. The judge's words were now running on every news channel, and editors were already clearing the next day's front pages. Owen, whose cheeks were visibly flushed, took a long pause before straightening his back and pressing on. His next statement went way beyond what anyone had expected.

"I have *further* concluded that the FSB operation to kill Mr. Litvinenko was probably approved by Mr. Patrushev, then the head of the FSB," he said. "And, also," he went on, his head a little bowed, gazing fixedly ahead, "by President *Putin*." Cries of "Yes!" rang out from the public gallery. After years of denials and secrecy orders and diplomatic discretion, this was an unimaginable watershed: a British judge had pointed an accusing finger straight at the Kremlin.

Owen had not limited himself to a narrow judgment on Litvinenko's cause of death; he considered it his calling to assess what motive lay behind the murder. He had heard evidence from more than sixty witnesses, including Litvinenko's collaborators in Britain and Russia, officials at MI6, the police officers who had investigated his death, and the scientists who uncovered the polonium trail that led straight back to Moscow. Akhmed Zakayev gave evidence. So did Yuli Dubov, Nikolai Glushkov, and Yuri Felshtinsky. Some—like Boris Berezovsky and Badri Patarkatsishvili—had testified from beyond the grave in the form of statements they had given to the police at the time of the defector's murder. And Litvinenko's own work had informed the inquiry. Owen's 328-page judgment was a high-explosive bomb packed full of the incendiary evidence the defector had spent his last years amassing against the Kremlin—all wrapped up in the decorous language of the British judiciary.

The judge laid out Litvinenko's theory that the apartment bombings that killed almost three hundred people in Russia had been "the work of the FSB, designed to provide a justification for war in Chechnya and, ultimately, to boost Mr. Putin's political prospects," noting that the book the defector had authored on the subject had been "more than a political tract" and was "the product of careful research." He also set out Litvinenko's suspicions that the Moscow theater siege was another FSB false-flag operation and that Anna Politkovskaya had been one of several people in Russia to be murdered for investigating the state's connection to the atrocities. And he noted that Litvinenko had gathered evidence pointing to "widespread collusion between the Tambov group and KGB officials, including both Vladimir Putin and Nikolai Patrushev" during his time inside Russia's state security agency.

The evidence that had been heard in open court amounted to a "strong circumstantial case" that the Russian state was behind Litvinenko's assassination, Owen found—but it had been the totality of the material before him, including a "considerable quantity" of secret intelligence, that sealed his final verdict. And he didn't view Litvinenko's murder in isolation: he noted that "leading opponents of President Putin, including those living outside Russia, were at risk of assassination." Owen's extraordinary judgment was published on the inquiry's website, along with transcripts from the public hearings and thousands of pages of evidence.

After the verdict, Marina Litvinenko stood on the steps of the High Court, her chin aloft. "I am of course very pleased that the words my husband spoke on his deathbed when he accused Mr. Putin have been proved true in an English court with the highest standards of independence and fairness," she told the TV cameras. The home secretary had already written to her "promising action," she said, adding that it would be "unthinkable that the prime minister would do nothing." And then she walked down the steps; her ten-year struggle to wrest the truth about her husband's death from the government's grip finally at an end.

But when Theresa May addressed the House of Commons soon after, she quickly played down the prospect of any real retaliation against Russia. The home secretary denounced the assassination as "a blatant and unacceptable breach of international law" but explained that it wasn't in Britain's interests to alienate Putin when the West needed his help resolving the crisis in Syria and tackling the threat from ISIS. Over at the World Economic Forum in Davos, David Cameron echoed that sentiment when asked what action he planned to take against Russia in light of Owen's findings.

"Do we at some level have to go on having some sort of relationship with them because we need a solution to the Syria crisis—yes we do," the prime minister said. "But we do it with clear eyes and a very cold heart."

Russia's reaction to the inquiry's verdict was one of unalloyed contempt. "There was one goal from the beginning: slander Russia and slander its officials," a foreign ministry spokeswoman said, warning that the outcome had "darkened the general atmosphere of our bilateral relations." Lugovoy was typically vituperative, describing the inquiry as a "pathetic attempt by London to use a 'skeleton in the cupboard' to support their political ambitions," and Putin's spokesman derided the judge's findings as an example of "subtle British humor."

In the end, the British government made the token gesture of or-

dering a freeze on any UK assets belonging to Lugovoy and Kovtun—
not that it was at all clear either man had any. As far as Britain
was concerned, that was the end of that. The thousands of pages of
evidence gathered by the Litvinenko inquiry were moved to the National Archives, the police files were shut away, and the teams of
detectives and government scientists who built the case upon which
the explosive verdict rested went back to their workaday lives. But the
sore was still running in Russia.

Russia—February 2016

The Mayak nuclear facility is a place so secretive that for many
decades it was not even on the map. Buried in the forests of Russia's
Ural Mountains and surrounded by a 250-kilometer exclusion zone,
it is home to the country's most closely guarded nuclear secrets. This
was the birthplace of the Soviet atomic bomb project and the site
of a series of devastating nuclear disasters that were covered up for
decades until the fall of the USSR. It is one of the world's most contaminated places, known by some as "the graveyard of the earth." And
at the start of 2016, it had just acquired a new claim to notoriety.

The reactor at Mayak had been outed in evidence presented at
Owen's inquiry as the likely source of the polonium used to murder
Alexander Litvinenko. That deduction had been based in part on
measurements taken by a respected government scientist named Dr.
Matthew Puncher, one of the team of public health officials brought
in after the defector's death to analyze the radioactive contamination in his system. Puncher's job had been to determine the precise
amount of polonium administered to Litvinenko, and his discovery
had incendiary implications. The dead man had ingested twenty-
six times the dose that would have been needed to kill him, and
there was only one place on the planet where the rare nuclear isotope originated in those quantities: the state-controlled reactor at
Mayak.

Back in 2006, Puncher had been an unassuming nuclear scientist in his midthirties with bushy hair and a bashful smile, unaware that his calculations would help put Vladimir Putin squarely in the frame for the most shocking assassination in memory. Now, almost ten years later—and just a month after Owen's inquiry finally reached its damning verdict—he was heading back to Russia to complete a highly sensitive project studying contamination levels in a notorious radioactive danger zone: none other than the Kremlin's polonium-producing nuclear site deep in the Ural Mountains.

The Mayak facility had been forced to accept foreign help to improve safety after a series of nuclear spills caused widespread sickness, mutations, and cancer in the local population, and Puncher had been put in charge of an Anglo-American government project to measure the effects of plutonium exposure on its workers. It was a prestigious assignment—code-named Project 2.4—but as he traveled back to Russia to complete his work in the wake of Owen's verdict, he was petrified.

Puncher and his colleagues had visited Russia several times as they built software systems to measure radiation at Mayak, and they had noticed something disquieting as they went about their work. They were being followed and, they suspected, bugged by men they feared came from the FSB. But something else had happened to Puncher out there in the Ural Mountains on his penultimate visit, the previous December.

The forty-six-year-old had returned from that research trip forever changed. He had always been a steadily sanguine man, but he had plunged suddenly into a howling depression that nobody who knew him could begin to fathom. He seemed to have lost all interest in his children, and his wife had to beg him just to get dressed and keep clean.

Nevertheless, he remained determined to finish his research, so he summoned the courage to return to Russia in February for what was to be his final trip. To his colleagues, it seemed that the visit went well. But when Puncher came home this time, he was in a state of even more excruciating distress. He told his family and colleagues that he had made a serious mathematical "mistake" on Project 2.4 that was so bad he was worried he might end up in prison.

His coworkers were baffled. The "coding error" Puncher insisted he'd made seemed to them to be no big deal—as far as they could tell he'd just used an alternative route to get to the same outcome, and it didn't affect the accuracy of his measurements. His colleague George Etherington assured him his fears of prosecution were "groundless" and that "he would look back and wonder why he worried so much." But Puncher remained inexplicably inconsolable. He was so distressed about this mysterious mistake that his mother felt compelled to ask him if anyone was going to die.

Her son reassured her there was no risk of that happening.

Oxfordshire, England—May 2016

When police entered the red-brick house, they found the scientist's body sprawled across the kitchen floor. Blood pooled around him from gaping wounds in his neck, arms, and stomach. There was no sign of a struggle—all the furniture was perfectly in place—and a large kitchen knife lay in Dr. Puncher's lifeless hand. A second, smaller blade was in the sink.

Detective Constable Rachel Carter, the local officer from the Thames Valley Police who inspected the kitchen, noted that the scene was "very unusual." She had rarely seen so much blood or such devastating stab wounds. But Puncher's wife told the police her husband's death made terrible sense. He had become so crippled with anxiety about his work, she said, that he had tried to hang himself with a computer cable the week before. And so, despite Puncher's role in solving Litvinenko's murder and the risks attached to his research trips to Russia, detectives decided there was nothing more to investigate. The police concluded that the scientist must have managed to stab and slash himself repeatedly with two separate knives before succumbing to his wounds. And they shut down the case.

DC Carter acknowledged in the evidence she gave at the inquest into Puncher's death that his injuries had been "so extensive," and he had lost so much blood, that she struggled to believe he had turned two knives upon himself. "It caused me some unease initially," she told the coroner. "I didn't know how he could have inflicted all those injuries on himself without losing consciousness." But despite her early doubts, the detective said she was ultimately "satisfied" that Puncher had committed suicide. "All the information told us he was very depressed," she said.

Suicides by multiple stab wounds are exceedingly rare—but the Home Office pathologist, Dr. Nicholas Hunt, testified that though he could not "entirely exclude" murder, it *was* possible for Puncher to have knifed himself that many times while still remaining conscious. He noted that the scientist had small wounds on his hands, which could have been sustained in defending himself from "a third-party assault with a blade," but it was also possible that the knife became "wetted with blood" and slipped in his fingers.

Puncher's wife told the coroner that when her husband returned from Russia, his disposition had "changed completely." A man who had loved doing homework with his children and cooking, who generally had a positive attitude, suddenly "just lost interest," she said.

Puncher's colleagues were equally baffled, and his employers at Public Health England told the coroner there had never been any reason to doubt the quality of his work. The mystery of what had happened in Russia to cause the scientist's sudden fit of mental anguish was never solved. But the coroner, Nicholas Graham, agreed with the police and ruled that Puncher's cause of death was suicide.

Behind the scenes, though the police investigation was shut down, US spy agencies provided MI6 with intelligence suggesting that Puncher's death was yet another Russian hit to add to the spiraling body count. It was possible, they said, that Russia could have driven the scientist to suicide. But their assessment was that he had likely been assassinated.

"Our intelligence reporting makes it clear that the Kremlin has aggressively stepped up its efforts to eliminate and silence its enemies abroad over the past couple of years," one US official noted after Puncher's body was found. "Particularly in Britain."

After the inquest verdict, the Kremlin made sure no one missed the political significance of the scientist's demise. The state-controlled Channel One aired a segment calling his death a "very strange suicide" and asking, "What was Matthew Puncher afraid of?"

"Could he have made a mistake in the case of Litvinenko?" the presenter hypothesized. "According to the British authorities, this question is not relevant."

London—March 2018

Nikolai Glushkov was the last of the exiles to die. The old Aeroflot director had been living a small life since Berezovsky's demise, growing old in a dingy suburban town house in South West London with a decrepit old dog and a cat called Braveheart. He was sixty-eight years old, and the blood disease that had threatened his health during his incarceration in Lefortovo had reduced him to walking with a cane. But he had one last fight left in him.

Aeroflot had launched a lawsuit against Glushkov in Britain's High Court, claiming that he and Berezovsky had looted $120 million from the airline while it was under their control, and the impoverished exile had no option but to represent himself. He pored over books about law and accounting as he prepared his defense, and he told everyone that the case would exonerate him and prove what he had claimed all along: that Aeroflot had operated for years as a front for Russian spying all over the world. But he was not blind to the danger he faced.

After Berezovsky died, Glushkov told the *Guardian* that Putin was working his way through a hit list of enemies in the UK, adding grimly: "I don't see anyone left on it apart from me." Nine months later, he collapsed after drinking Champagne with two Russians in the bar of a hotel in Bristol. When he came to, he told paramedics he believed he'd been poisoned. He was determined to make it to trial, where he planned to grill several senior Russian intelligence officials about their involvement with Aeroflot, but he confided in friends that he feared his days were numbered.

The exile was due in court for a preliminary hearing in the Aeroflot case one morning in March 2018, but the defense bench was empty. "I was expecting to see Mr. Glushkov, but I do not see him," a barrister for the state airline told the judge. A court clerk went out into the corridor to call the defendant's name, but there was no response.

When Glushkov's daughter drove to his house to check on him, she found her father dead. He had been strangled with his dog's leash.

The Russian media painted Glushkov's death as a gay tryst gone wrong, and one radio station claimed the exile could have died of AIDS. But this time, there was no suggestion from the British authorities that Glushkov's death might have been merely a salacious accident or a suicide.

The same night his body was found, dozens of counterterrorism officers cordoned off the house and erected police tents across his front garden. Scotland Yard confirmed quickly that the cause of death was compression to the neck—indicating strangulation either by hand or with the dog leash—and announced that the counterterrorism command would lead the investigation "because of the associations Mr. Glushkov is believed to have had." Later, they released video footage of a black van captured near his home the night he was strangled, asking anyone with information to contact them.

The proactive police response to the discovery of Glushkov's body contrasted starkly with the stubborn refusal to investigate the deaths of any of his friends in the years before. But in March of 2018, the world had just changed dramatically.

Glushkov was found strangled a week after Russia unleashed a chemical weapons attack on the streets of Salisbury, and the government had, finally, been forced into a combative posture. So this time, it treated the murky death of another Russian exile as exactly what it was: the murder of a Kremlin enemy on British soil.

The Novichok attack on Sergei and Yulia Skripal on a rainy Sunday in Salisbury was the latest dramatic salvo in a series of increasingly warlike moves by the Kremlin. Putin's security state had helped propel Donald Trump to the White House through a concerted campaign of meddling in the 2016 US election. Its hacking labs, internet troll factories, and fake news farms had sown disunity, disruption, and disinformation in democracies across Europe, while its financing of extremist fringe groups had stirred up race hate and violence around the world. It had sponsored an attempted coup against the government of Montenegro as the country neared accession to NATO and unleashed ever more malignant cyberattacks on Western governments. And, for all the effort to make Russia part of the solution in Syria, it had backed the regime of Bashar al-Assad with increasingly ferocious military assaults on the Western-backed rebels as the dictator gassed hundreds of his own people with internationally outlawed chemical weapons.

The leaders of the United States and Europe had covered their eyes to the Kremlin's crimes for so long that the man inside had crept right up on them, and now Putin's actions amounted to an asymmetric war on the West. There had been such bright hopes behind that collective blindness: hopes of coaxing Russia into the warmth of the postwar liberal world order, of sharing in the bounteous riches of its vast oil and gas fields, of reviving recession-stricken Western economies with a steady flow of Russian money. Hopes, too, that Putin might represent a solution to some of the world's most intractable problems: the scourge of Islamic terror, the nuclear ambitions of Iran and North Korea, the crisis in Syria. But now, and not for the first time in history, the West was opening its eyes to the realization that the price of appeasement was too steep.

After hundreds of British citizens were exposed to a deadly nerve agent and the Kremlin responded to Western rebukes with blistering defiance, there was no denying that Russia's killing campaign had spun out of control. Sanctions hadn't stemmed the bloodshed, and waves of diplomatic expulsions only seemed to draw more fire. How, short of all-out war, could Putin be stopped?

That was the question ringing out in the corridors of Westminster in the wake of the attack on the Skripals, but no one had offered a convincing solution. And the government was now facing a growing list of queries to which it could find no good response. In the weeks after the attempted assassination in Salisbury, calls for answers about the untimely deaths of other exiles and their associates in Britain were getting louder by the day.

The previous year, investigative journalists working at BuzzFeed News on both sides of the Atlantic had published a series of stories laying bare Russia's campaign of assassination in the West. The series had mapped a web of fourteen suspected hits in the UK, including the deaths of Boris Berezovsky, his fellow exiles, and their British fixers, as well as the death of Mikhail Lesin in America. It revealed that US intelligence agencies had passed their UK counterparts information linking all the British deaths to Moscow, but in every last case, the authorities responded by shutting down any investigation and locking away the evidence.

In the hawkish atmosphere that gripped Westminster following the attack on the Skripals, a growing chorus of politicians called on the authorities to take action over the spate of suspicious deaths the journalists had uncovered. Bowing to pressure, the home secretary finally announced that the government would reinvestigate all fourteen cases with help from the police and MI5.

The case files locked away inside Scotland Yard and rural police stations across the home counties were decidedly dusty. Some, like the files on the deaths of Berezovsky's lawyers Stephen Moss and Stephen Curtis, in 2003 and 2004 respectively, had lain unread for more than a decade. In many instances, including the death of Scot Young, little or no evidence had been gathered. No witnesses had been sought; no CCTV had been captured; no forensic work had been carried out at the scene. For the officers drafted in to carry out the review, reviving cases that had been left to go so cold for so long was a nearly impossible task—and it must have seemed like a pointless one. What good could come of raking over secrets and skeletons so long buried when any suspects would be thousands of miles out of reach?

Six months after announcing the review, the government quietly closed down all fourteen reinvestigations without explanation. In a short letter to Parliament's Home Affairs Committee, the home secretary confirmed that Scotland Yard had completed its review and decided there was "no basis" on which to investigate further. No reasons were given.

The letter acknowledged that the government had secretly briefed two senior MPs—the chair of the Home Affairs Committee and the head of Parliament's security and intelligence watchdog—on its reasons for refusing to comment publicly on the decision to close the fourteen cases. The briefings were given under special rules, meaning they could be conducted in secret and contain classified intelligence. Meanwhile, the home secretary had obtained a secrecy order to ban the results of the review from being disclosed to the inquest into the death of Alexander Perepilichnyy, which was still snarled up in red tape nearly six years after the event. Three months later, in the absence of any "direct evidence of murder," the coroner ruled that the financier had died of natural causes.

One thing the British government was, at last, prepared to do publicly was talk tough. After it emerged that the attack on the Skripals had been conducted by two serving members of Russia's military in-telligence agency, Theresa May vowed to use the "full range of tools from across our national security apparatus" to hit back, and she lam-basted Russia for its "obfuscation and lies" in connection with the events in Salisbury.

"Their attempts to hide the truth," the prime minister thundered on the floor of the House of Commons, "simply reinforce their cul-pability."

But that kind of talk came easy—now that the British government had hidden the truth about its own quiet complicity in the killing campaign for which it was, at last, prepared to denounce the Kremlin. That would stay safely buried in the secret files it had taken such pains to lock away.

ACKNOWLEDGMENTS

This story would not have come to light without the phenomenal work of my colleagues at BuzzFeed News. Tom Warren, Richard Holmes, Jane Bradley, Alex Campbell, and Jason Leopold: working with you heroes has been the biggest adventure of my professional life, and I thank you for every second. Mark Schoofs led us with his alchemical blend of vision and rigor, daring us to aim higher at every turn, and our work would have been a shadow of itself without his inspirational stewardship. Special thanks are also due to Alex and Mark for their sparkling edits to this manuscript, and to Tom for his meticulous fact-checking. I owe many things to the genius of Ariel Kaminer, including the title of this book. Eliot Stempf kept us all safe as we reported our way through treacherous territory, for which we can never thank him enough. And I'm endlessly grateful to Ben Smith for making BuzzFeed News the sort of bold and brilliant place where the thorniest investigations can flourish.

Thanks to my agent, Bridget Matzie, for seeing the potential to turn our investigation into a book, and for backing the project with such skill and vim; to my editor at Little, Brown, Phil Marino, for his inspired thoughts on framing this narrative; and to Barbara Clark for the sharpest copyediting I've ever seen.

The many sources who took risks to speak out and supply the evidence that underpins this story will always have my gratitude and admiration.

ACKNOWLEDGMENTS

Love and appreciation to my incredible mum, Libby Blake, for her eagle-eyed reading of this manuscript as it flew off the keyboard—and for being a constant beacon of courage, strength, and integrity in my life.

Finally, all the love and thanks in my heart to Duncan Piper-Blake—my first and last reader—for the gift of your garden room, and all the magic you bring, and the endless adventures ahead.

BIBLIOGRAPHY

Dawisha, Karen. *Putin's Kleptocracy*. New York: Simon & Schuster, 2014.

Gessen, Masha. *The Man Without a Face*. London: Granta Books, 2012.

Goldfarb, Alex, and Marina Litvinenko. *Death of a Dissident*. London: Simon & Schuster, 2007.

Harding, Luke. *A Very Expensive Poison*. London: Guardian Books, 2016.

Hayman, Andy, and Margaret Gilmore. *The Terrorist Hunters*. London: Corgi Books, 2009.

Hollingsworth, Mark, and Stewart Lansley. *Londongrad*. London: Fourth Estate, 2009.

Knight, Amy. *Orders to Kill*. New York: St. Martin's Press, 2017.

Litvinenko, Alexander, and Yuri Felshtinsky. *Blowing Up Russia*. London: Gibson Square Books, 2007.

Lucas, Edward. *Deception*. London: Bloomsbury, 2012.

Myers, Steven Lee. *The New Tsar*. London: Simon & Schuster, 2015.

Ostrovsky, Arkady. *The Invention of Russia*. London: Atlantic Books, 2015.

INDEX

313